Lloyd John Ogilvie

God's Best

for My Life

HARVEST HOUSE PUBLISHERS
EUGENE, OREGON

Cover Design by Koechel Peterson and Associates, Inc., Minneapolis, Minnesota

GOD'S BEST FOR MY LIFE

Eugene, Oregon 97402
www.harvesthousepublishers.com
Library of Congress Cataloging-in-Publication Data
Ogilvie, Lloyd John.
God's best for my life / Lloyd John Ogilive.
p. cm.
ISBN 0-7369-1512-5
1. Devotional calendars—Presbyterian Church. I. Title.
BV 4811.035 1997
242.'2—dc21 97-7438
CIP

Printed in the United States of America

05 06 07 08 09 10 11 12 / RDS-GL / 10 9 8 7 6 5 4 3 2 1

Dedication

To my beloved people of the First Presbyterian Church of Hollywood, who shared with me the high adventure of discovering God's best for our lives. Their enthusiasm for daily Bible study and prayer, along with the encouragement to write this book, made the challenge a joy.

—Lloyd John Ogilvie

Preface

It will come to pass that before they call, I will answer; and while they are yet speaking I will hear (Isaiah 65:24 KJV).

This awesome promise is the motivation for writing this daily devotional guide. We all want God's best for our lives. That desire is a gift from Him! He wants to be our Friend, to tell us about Himself, to communicate His unlimited love, to give us His wisdom for our decisions, and to help us live the adventure of the abundant life. He creates in us the desire to know Him and to talk with Him in prayer. The longing in so many Christians today to discover a consistent, daily pattern for Bible reading and prayer is from the Lord Himself. He has given me the vision of how to maximize a quiet time with Him each day. The desire to share the thoughts and insights from the Scriptures for a whole year was clearly guided by Him, and was done in response to the thousands of requests I have received from my own congregation and television viewers across the nation for a practical, applicable way to find God's best for their lives each day and to receive His power for daily needs.

The result is a daily guide which is intended to be revelational and relational. God reveals Himself in the Scriptures and inspires us in our relationship with Him, ourselves, others, and the world. We all need fresh grace each day. All the Scriptures selected for the days of a full year will enable a renewal of our relationship with the Lord, a deeper acceptance of ourselves, and a contagious joy for our relationships and responsibilities.

The distinctly different quality of this particular guide is that it is rooted both in Scripture and in our deepest needs. Each day's meditation on the Word of God is meant to be profoundly personal. I have tried to listen to our urgent questions and deepest longings. Truth becomes real as we live it. The great need today is for Christians to rediscover a daily companionship with the Lord and to enjoy Him throughout the challenges and opportunities that each day brings. When J.B. Phillips translated the Book of Acts into contemporary English, he said it was like rewiring a house with the current turned on! I hope for nothing less each day as we take the great texts of the Bible and spell out the implications for living the promises God gives us.

I have tried to be sensitive to the frustrations and feelings of failure that so many people have expressed about finding a workable plan for daily devotions. Many have told me of grand commitments to get up early or stay up late to spend a prolonged period with the Lord. Guilt and self-incrimination set in when the promise is broken or the length of the devotions shortens.

What most of us need is a daily time which is penetrating and personal, which has residual impact throughout the day. Each of these devotionals is meant to be like a capsule with time-release potency. My hope is that the truths we consider and the aching needs we confront will have a constant explosion of engendering, enabling power throughout the day.

I suggest at least 15 minutes each day. Take 15 minutes when you're freshest and most alert. It will give you freedom from uncertainty, frustration, and anxiety all through the day. Here are three five-minute steps:

1. Take five minutes for praise and thanksgiving. Praise God for who He is and thank Him for what He has done for you. Praise is the antidote to pride. Adoration opens our minds and hearts to receive. Review what has been happening to you—both the delights and the difficulties. Get in touch with your real feelings. Only the real you can meet the reality of God. He loves you and wants to use what's happening to and around you for His glory and your growth. Review your life, relationships, challenges, and concerns. Then ask the Lord to use this quiet time alone with Him as a deeply personal time of discovery and new direction.

2. Next take five minutes to read the Scripture text indicated at the top of each day's devotional, plus the exposition I've written. When you've finished, ask yourself these questions:

A. What does this passage and message mean to me personally?
B. What has the Lord said to me in it about my life?
C. What can I do or say today to live the truth I've considered?
D. With whom am I called to implement what I've learned?

3. Last, take five minutes for supplication and intercession.
    A. Write out or think through the needs, problems, and concerns you are facing this day. Spread them out before the Lord. Ask for His perspective and guidance. Then surrender them to Him. And leave them in His gracious and powerful care.
    B. Pray for specific people—loved ones, friends, people you love or need to learn to love, those for whom you are thankful, and those who frustrate you. Prayer for people in Jesus' name is a sure way to discover a creative attitude toward them!

Many of you will find these 15 minutes each day so exciting and satisfying that it will be the most creative, liberating part of your day. Some of you will find your 15 minutes extended because there is so much more to say to the Lord and receive from Him. The amazing thing you will discover is the miraculous way the Lord will speak to you through His word. I have asked Him to guide every word I've written. I know that He has had you in mind and knew ahead of time what you would need. The Lord's timing is perfect: never ahead of time, never behind, but always exactly on time.

Begin using this guide on the page of today's date. There's a progression which will catch you up in its flow. I am very thankful for the time, effort, and enthusiasm Kathy Guzman contributed in typing this manuscript for the publication.

My prayer is that this will be one of the most exciting years of your life. Gathering these Scriptures and reflecting on them with our needs in mind has been exactly that for me. Power to you as you experience God's best for your life!

—Lloyd John Ogilvie

January 1

The Best Year of Your Life!

Jeremiah 29:11-13

For I know the plans I have for you, says the LORD, plans for good and not for evil, to give you a future and a hope (Jeremiah 29:11 RSV).

THE SURE SIGN THAT WE HAVE an authentic relationship with God is that we believe more in the future than in the past. The past can be neither a source of confidence nor a condemnation. God graciously divided our life into days and years so that we could let go of our yesterdays and anticipate our tomorrows. For the past mistakes, He offers forgiveness and an ability to forget. For our tomorrows, He gives us the gift of expectation and excitement.

What the Lord said to the people of Israel languishing in the Babylonian exile is for any of us who are exiled from Him and hope for the future. He has plans for each of us—good plans for our growth in His grace—so that we can have a future with hope. Emil Brunner said, "What oxygen is for the lungs, hope is for the soul." Hope enables a vital quality of life; it sets us free to dare, gives up confidence for daily frustrations, and the courage to live adventuresomely. The gift of hope for the future is the key entrusted to us which opens the floodgates of the Lord's power and unlocks the flow of His amazing, unlimited possibilities.

So often people say, "You've got to have hope!" as if it were something we could muster out of ourselves. Hope is advertent. It comes from something or someone else. Authentic hope comes from Christ, who He is, and what He is able to do. His resurrection is the ultimate source of hope. Nothing can defeat Him! The worst that man did on Calvary was followed by the best hope for all time. He is with us now today to give us courage for the future. He is in charge of this new year. He has a plan! Surrender the year ahead, thanking the Lord that everything that will happen to us is for what He has planned to help us become like Him. Joyous New Year!

God's best for my life begins with a vibrant hope for the future.

January 2

A Year of Jubilee

Luke 4:16-21

To set at liberty those who are oppressed, to preach the acceptable year of the L*ORD (Luke 4:18-19).*

THE SHADOW OF THE CROSS was over Jesus' heart as He read these words from Isaiah in His own synagogue in Nazareth. He knew that He was to fulfill that prophecy in His own suffering and death.

The last sentence of the prophecy is easily misunderstood. "The acceptable year of the Lord" also meant the Year of Jubilee. Every 50 years, according to the ancient Hebrew custom, the debts were canceled, prison terms were terminated, land holdings went back to the original owners, and people forgave the resentments held through the years.

The cross makes every year the Jubilee Year. Jesus' death cancels our sin and gives us the freedom to be forgiving. This is the acceptable year of the Lord for us. What if we committed this whole year to be one in which we set people free by loving them unconditionally and forgiving them unreservedly? That can happen *through* us only if it happens *to* us. Is there any memory, unforgiven hurt, or unrelinquished hostility still keeping you in a prison of incrimination?

There are three steps to a Jubilee Year: 1) accept forgiveness; 2) ask for forgiveness from any person you've hurt or harmed; 3) offer forgiveness to those who have misused or misunderstood you. Forgiveness is the one gift our Lord offers that we can't have unless we give it away.

Make a list of people who need your forgiveness. What is the Lord telling you to *say* and then *be* to them to assure them that they are forgiven? But don't wait. Your Jubilee Year starts today. Tomorrow may be too late!

Today I will live as a forgiven, forgiving person.

January 3

A Nook with the Book

Psalm 1:1-6

But his delight is in the law of the LORD, and in His law he meditates day and night (Psalm 1:2 NKJV).

THOMAS À KEMPIS SAID, "I have no rest but in a nook with the Book." Communion with the Lord through meditation on the Scriptures provided profound rest and refreshment in the midst of the demands of life. The same theme song is sung by the Psalmist. Meditation on God's law made him like a tree firmly planted by the streams of water; there was an unlimited source of sustenance.

Psalm 1 is an autobiographical witness of what the Lord had done for the Psalmist and a prophetic statement to the wicked who scoff and take their place among those who oppose God's ways. But not the positive affirmation of what is available to us: the Psalmist meditated on God's law. We have the flowing streams of the whole Bible as the water of life to feed the tree of our life.

Each day's reading of a portion of Scripture gives us water for the roots. The residual resource moves through the trunk up into the branches, out into the leafage of a beautiful life, and into the fruit of character. A quiet time in our "nook with the Book" enables quietness of soul in the din of life's demands. Jesus said, "Take care to live in Me, and let Me live in you. For a branch can't produce fruit when severed from the vine. Nor can you be fruitful apart from Me."

The metaphor shifts, but the Psalmist's meaning is the same. Each day we put our roots down in the streams of the Living Water, Christ Himself. Then all through the day we are refreshed by what we took from the artesian brook in our nook. We all need a quiet place for our 15 minutes to freedom each day. Out of His Word Christ will give us a thought which will reorient our day and flower in inspiration all through the day. Expect nothing less today!

My tree of life is planted in Christ.
He will give me all I need to live abundantly today.

January 4

Through the Valley of Fear

Psalm 23:1-6

Though I walk through the valley...Thou art with me (Psalm 23:4 KJV).

ALEXANDER MACLAREN, A GREAT PREACHER of another generation, tells the story of his conquest of fear. As a young boy he took a job in Glasgow, some miles away from his own village. He stayed in the city during the week and returned home on Saturday evenings. There was a ravine on the way to his home that superstition supposed was filled with evil spirits. All during the first week at work, the lad feared most that his long walk home would have to include passing through this ravine. The anticipation blighted every waking moment of that week.

Saturday night came and there was nothing to do but muster up his courage and start home. His heart pounded as he reached the ravine. He paused in panic. His feet were like lead. Then suddenly he heard a voice calling out of the night, "Alex, it's your dad. I came to walk through the ravine with ye."

All through his later life as one of Scotland's greatest preachers, Maclaren never forgot the courage and strength he felt that night when his father graciously walked through the frightful glen with him.

David felt that way about God. The valley of the shadow had been extricated of fear because the Shepherd would walk through it with him. David knew about the comfort the Shepherd could be to the sheep. The Lord was his Shepherd all through his life. Evil and evil people were a threat all through his life from the time he was a shepherd boy to when he became Israel's greatest king.

What are the glens of fearful worry for you? What is the valley of the threat of death or deadly anxiety? The Lord does not ridicule our fears. He understands. Like Maclaren's dad, He comes out to walk us home. He knows what's in the glen or valley and wants us to know that if we place our hand in His, we can make it through.

The Lord does not ridicule our fears;
He comes to walk through them with us.

January 5

A Full Life with Purpose

Psalm 146:1-10

Praise the LORD! Praise the LORD, O my soul! (Psalm 146:1 NKJV).

A FRIEND OF MINE CELEBRATED HIS retirement by having new calling cards printed. On the card is his name and this declaration of new freedom: "No phone, no address, no business, no worries, no appointments, no prospects, no job."

The man gave me the card at a time of intense busyness in my own life. "Wouldn't that be wonderful!" I thought to myself. Then I reflected on what life would be like without all the challenges and opportunities. How would I handle life without a full schedule and more to do in any day than is humanly possible? But that led me to a time of deep gratitude for strength beyond my own to meet the demands. Actually the man whose card gave me a good laugh and a pause to reflect is as busy in retirement as he was in his profession. He spends his days in creative work with people and benevolent organizations.

Many of us complain about busy schedules, but it is good to live a full life. The important thing to consider is what are we accomplishing in all the activities. Justus Schifferes in *How to Live Longer* said, "Live longer so you can love longer, and conversely, the longer you love the longer you live." Can a Christian ever put "no prospects" on his calling card? We always have prospects for love and understanding and the chance to share our faith.

John Wesley, just before he died, wrote a hymn based on Psalm 146: "I'll praise my Maker while I have breath. And when my voice is lost in death, praise shall employ my nobler powers." The abundant life in Christ is life all the way up! At the conclusion of his embattled life, John Knox said something which was not representative of his courageous life as a reformer: "The world is tired of me and I of it." That need not be true. We are never finished!

There's nothing wrong with being busy if we are doing God's work in His way and by His power.

January 6

Stop Complaining; Start Confessing!

Psalm 39:1-13

I said to myself, "I'm going to quit complaining!" (Psalm 39:1 TLB).

I HAVE A SOUTHERN FRIEND WHO has a way of saying things in a pithy, poignant way. One of his favorite responses to critical people is, "When you're complainin', you ain't got no time for confessin'!" His statement is not very grammatical, but his prognosis of a deep human problem is very pointed.

Some years ago I invited a famous Christian psychiatrist to sit in on a retreat. After several days of listening to what people said about their needs, he was convinced that the people had fallen into the syndrome of talking about their problems without any intention of finding or applying a remedial solution. His comment about the retreat was as penetrating as my Southern friend's. "These people are just complaining, not confessing."

That reminded me of a statement on an evaluation form about a young clergyman I was thinking about hiring. "He is a brilliant, talented man, but he's a complainer. If he could only confess as eloquently as he complains about people and their inadequacies, he could find the love to help them."

Complaining and confessing are two alternatives to the things that trouble us about ourselves and other people. Greatness in the Christian life is dependent on knowing one from the other.

The Scriptures are very honest about human nature. There is not a problem we face which is not dealt with in a vulnerable exposure. Psalm 39 helps us identify with the Psalmist. The progression of his thought gives us a plan for dealing with frustration. He expresses his consternation and then goes on to authentic confession. God is ready to hear honest feelings *if* they lead us to confess our need for His power, forgiveness, and a new beginning.

When we confess our faults we link ourselves to the power of God, and our complaints are purified. Today is a day to stop complaining and start confessing!

January 7

The Help of His Presence

Psalm 42:1-11

As the deer pants for the water brooks,
so pants my soul for You, O God (Psalm 42:1 NKJV*).*

THE PSALMIST GIVES US AN EXAMPLE of the difference between praying our prayers and truly praying. He really wanted a relationship with God more than anything else in the world. Many people pray without earnestly wanting intimacy with God. Note Psalm 42:2. Do you want God that much? Also consider the honesty of the Psalmist. He talked to God about what he was feeling—really! That kind of honesty in prayer made way for God to heal the real needs and not just the surface whims. Let's use this psalm as a model to talk to God and let Him talk to us.

Again, the Psalmist leads us into deeper levels of prayer. It was the experience of the steadfast love of God that drew him back into close union with the Father. What God *has done* heightens our expectation of what He *will do*. Praise opens the heart. The more we praise God, the more ready we are to accept the next steps of His strategy for us. Let's make today a day in which we bless God all through the day for His goodness to us in all the problems and perplexities of life.

We need not be anxious when we can turn everything over to the Lord of the universe. Our prayers are to be an honest statement of our need and then thanksgiving for the fact that the Lord has heard us and will act for our ultimate good. Peace beyond our understanding will flood our hearts. Christ will guard our hearts from anything which could distress us. Prayer is a time to meditate on creative, positive thoughts about Christ and what He is able to do with our problems.

Prayer is meditating in a way that our minds and hearts become focused around the positive power of the Lord and not just our perplexities. Then peace replaces problematical living.

January 8

The Answer Is the Asking

Isaiah 65:24-25

It will also come to pass that before they call, I will answer; and while they are still speaking, I will hear (Isaiah 65:24).

THIS IS ONE OF THE MOST EXCITING VERSES about praise in the Old Testament. It reminds us that prayer begins with God, seeps into our heart, and gives us the courage to ask for what God is more ready to give than we are to ask. God has more prepared for us than we are prepared to ask. We need to spend as much time seeking what God wants us to ask for as we do asking. Then our asking will be in keeping with His will. The desire to pray is God's gift. Memorize this verse. Praying is not to get God's attention but focusing our attention on Him and what He has to say to us. Don't make prayer a one-way telephone conversation in which we hang up before we listen to what He has to say!

Prayer is seeking God with all our hearts. God can use our imaginations to give us a picture of His future for us, but with one qualification: that we seek Him with all our hearts. Many of us aim at nothing and hit it because we have not taken God at His Word. We all become what we envision. Prayer is the time to let God paint the mind picture of what we are to be and do.

O blessed life!—the heart at rest,
When all without tumultuous seems,
That trusts a higher will, and dreams
That higher will, not mine, the best.

O life, how blessed, how divine!
High life, the earnest of a higher!
Savior, fulfill my deep desire,
And let this blessed life be mine.

—W.T. Matson

January 9

Who Is Your Burden?

Psalm 55:1-23; Matthew 11:30; Galatians 6:2

Cast your burden on the LORD, and
He shall sustain you (Psalm 55:22 NKJV).

SOME TIME AGO I PREACHED a children's sermon about a Boy Scout I had picked up along the road on his way to camp. He was loaded down with a heavily packed knapsack on his back. He got in the car and rode with his pack still on his back. I thought this was absurd and said, "Young man, wouldn't you like to take your pack off while you ride?" "No, Sir," he said, "it was so hard to get on and would be difficult to take off, so I'll just ride with my load on my back."

I quickly made the point in the children's homily that this was like most of us who ride in God's grace with the load still on our backs because we find it difficult to take our troubles off and entrust them to God. I suggested that to forgive meant to forget, and yet many of us carry the memory of past failures of ourselves and others on our backs.

As is often the case, some adults got more out of the children's sermon than the children. One couple came up to me in the coffee hour. "Meet my load!" the woman said, pointing to her husband. She laughed, and he tried to see the humor of it. But the point was made: he was a burden to her, and she had never unloaded him to God while she rode in grace.

Who's your burden? Whom do you carry emotionally, in memory, or in conscience? Who causes you difficult reactions of guilt, fear, frustration, or anger? That person belongs to God. He's carrying him or her too, you know! Isn't it about time to take the load off, face the unresolved dynamics of the relationship, and forgive and forget?

Who is your knapsack?

January 10

If God Knows, Why Pray?

John 14:1-14

And whatever you ask in My name, that I will do, that the Father may be glorified in the Son. If you ask anything in My name, I will do it (John 14:13-14).

If God knows not only the past, but also the future, how dare we tell Him what is best for the future? This is a knotty question. The answer we give to it determines to a great degree how we will pray and what we will expect from our prayers.

There are four parts to the answer given to us in the Bible. First, we pray because we have been motivated to prayer by the very God to whom we pray.

Most of us believe that prayer is initiated by us when we blunder into God's presence with our requests and concerns. Not at all. Long before we thought of praying, the God to whom we pray was preparing us to pray. Our prayer is response. When a need comes to our mind and we pray, it is because God has an answer to give us for that concern. The answer may not always be "Yes"; it may be "No" or "Later." But the answer is ready when we are moved to pray.

Secondly, we pray not so much to *change* but to *receive* the mind of God. As we pray our prayers and listen to God, He is able and willing to impress His mind upon us. Too often we think of prayer as changing God's mind on a subject. This is not the purpose of prayer.

Thirdly, we pray because God has ordained that there are resources of His power and love which will not be released until we pray. He has called us to be His partners in the world. He often withholds His blessings until we pray. He desires that we come to Him as children to share our needs with Him.

Lastly, we pray because we are most nearly the brotherhood of man when we pray to our Father God. God seeks to bring us closer to one another through prayer. It is His will to withhold much of what we seek for others until we pray for one another.

How exciting it is to realize that through prayer we participate with God in what He desires to do in our lives today!

Prayer is not to change, but to receive,
the mind and will of God.

January 11

Ask and Abide

John 14:1-31; 15:7

And where I go you know, and the way you know (John 14:4).

PRAYER IS CUMULATIVE FRIENDSHIP with God. It is communion and conversation. He is the initiator of the dialogue. He creates in us the desire, not just to tell Him about our needs, but to be with Him. So many questions people ask about prayer expose a false assumption—that prayer is our overture to God. The desire to pray is God's gift. Think of it! The Creator and Sovereign of the universe has created us for communion with Him. Jesus taught us that prayer is not a device for marshaling the resources of Omnipotence to fulfill our desires, but a means by which these desires may be redirected according to the mind of God and made channels for the direction of His will. What does that say about the proportion of time spent talking and listening in our prayers?

Our two biggest problems in life are solved by the two crucial prerequisites of powerful prayer given us by Christ. He taught us that God is omniscient. He has infinite knowledge, awareness, and concern about our needs. When we pray about our problems, we solve the first great need, which is the source of all our lesser problems—our need for communion with the Lord. Jesus gives us two big "if's" for dynamic praying. If we abide—that's the essence of prayer. And then, if we ask in His name—that's the efficacy of prayer. When we abide, we are given life's greatest treasure—intimacy with our Creator. The name of Jesus means His authority, power, and purpose. Our second greatest need is to discover what our Lord wants us to do in keeping with His name. Abiding gives us the mind of the Lord for our problems and perplexities.

He who has learned to pray has learned the greatest secret of a holy and happy life.
—William Law

January 12

Laying Hold of God's Willingness

1 John 3:1-24; 5:14-15

Beloved, if our heart does not condemn us,
we have confidence toward God (1 John 3:21).

And if we know that He hears us, whatever we ask, we know that
we have the petitions that we have asked of Him (1 John 5:15).

THE APOSTLE JOHN ADDS TWO "if's" about prayer to those we considered yesterday. *If* our hearts do not condemn us, and *if* we know that He hears us. The Lord must first deal with our self-condemnation before we can enjoy prayer. Like an erring child who resists his parent when he needs him most, often we refuse the power of prayer because of what we've done or been that makes us feel we have no right to be in God's presence.

But the Lord is not outdone, even by our failures. He says, "Come to me just as you are!" The assurance of the cross gives us boldness and confidence. Note the lengths the Lord goes to to get us to pray. He removes the barriers, creates the desire, gives us Himself, reveals His will, and then gives us the courage to ask for what He is more ready to give than we are to ask.

"Why then do I pray so seldom, and only when I'm in trouble?" That question articulates the feelings of many of us. Nothing indicates our imperious self-will any more than our fleeting or inconsistent prayers. Our reluctance to pray is our resistance to God. But eventually life caves in, and we face problems too great for us. God rushes in to help us in the hope that we will be so amazed at what He can do with problems that we will begin to trust Him with our potentials. The question is: How great do we want our life to be? It is brash nonsense for us to imagine that we can develop a dynamic spiritual life without being willing to set aside time for it. Prayer is waiting on God.

Prayer is not overcoming God's reluctance;
it is laying hold of his highest willingness.
—Richard Chenevix Trench

January 13

What Do You Expect?

John 5:1-15

When Jesus saw him lying there, and knew that he already had been in that condition a long time, He said to him, "Do you want to be made well?" (John 5:6).

"WELL, WHAT DID YOU EXPECT?" is a question we ask when someone has faced a disappointment which we feel he or she should have anticipated. We should also ask it when people are surprised by a gracious intervention of the Lord. Most of all, we should ask it of ourselves. What do we expect? Expectation, multiplied by a Holy Spirit guided imagination, can equal dynamic prayer.

The account of the healing of the man by the pool of Bethesda has a very crucial twist. Jesus asks the man if he wants to be healed. Strange. The man had been ill for 38 years waiting for the waters of the pool to be troubled by the angel's wings. Someone always got in before him. Jesus discovered that the man may no longer have expected a miracle. Thus the question, "Do you want to be healed?" Other translations render this crucial question, "Do you want to be made whole?" It might also be rendered, "Do you want to be saved?"

Christ is able! But do we believe it? Our lack of expectation can stand in the way of the miracles of God in all phases of our lives and relationships. Unbelief, discouragement, and disillusionment can stifle our expectation. We expect little and are not surprised when little happens to us and others. God has made us cooperators in His intervention into the lower law of nature with the higher law of love. We are staggered by Jesus' statement to the man after his healing: "See, you are well! Sin no more, that nothing worse befalls you." Why was it necessary to convince the man that he was well? Could it be that he had become so negative that he did not expect a miracle, and when it happened, was vulnerable to the sin of doubting that it did happen?

I will expect great things from God and live expectantly.

January 14

Expecting Too Little

Acts 12:1-25

And they said to her, "You are beside yourself!" But she kept insisting that it was so. Then they said, "It is his angel." But Peter continued knocking; and when they opened the door and saw him, they were astonished (Acts 12:15-16).

THE MAN WAS AT THE end of his rope!

He had tried everything to find an answer to a difficult personal problem. He had spent hours reviewing what he should do. All the alternatives seemed to have real disadvantages. There was nothing left to do but to turn the whole complicated, confusing situation over to God in a prayer of surrender, asking for His guidance and direction.

"All right!" the man said finally, "I'll turn the whole situation over to God...but tell me...how will I know when He answers me? How do you recognize answers to prayer, anyway?" How would you have answered the man?

If you are like many people, you would have had some difficulty. Many of us not only have a problem with prayer as a natural, spontaneous conversation with the Lord, but we also have confusion recognizing the answers to prayer once we have prayed. But don't be too hard on yourself. We are in the good company of the early church. These outstanding saints also had difficulties in recognizing God's answers to their prayers. The humorous passage of Scripture in Acts 12 of how the church prayed for Peter and then did not (or would not) recognize God's answer gives us some comfort that these great athletes of the Spirit also had sagging prayer muscles, shortness of vision, and dimness of hope. This incident crystallizes a general prayer problem they continually faced in entrusting to the Lord the difficulties they found and expectantly waiting for His answer.

Once we really want God's answer, our eyes will be open to His answers, and we will become coparticipants with Him in the implication of the answer.

Our problem is not to get God to answer our prayers, but to recognize the answers already given.

January 15

The Problem of Seemingly Unanswered Prayer

2 Corinthians 12:7-10

And He said to me, "My grace is sufficient for you, for My strength is made perfect in weakness." Therefore most gladly I will rather boast in my infirmities, that the power of Christ may rest upon me (2 Corinthians 12:9).

WHAT ABOUT UNANSWERED PRAYER? The question exposes a deep fallacy. It may seem that our prayers are unanswered, but what if the lack of an answer is really an answer? Prayer is much more than giving God our list of needs with an "Amen" at the end. It is not a magical way of getting what we want. Prayer is to get us into the position of willingness to receive what God wants. Some prayers are unanswered because we don't really ask in faith. We don't believe that God can answer. Often, prayers seem unanswered because we didn't get what we wanted. We can see so little of reality. Could it be that we are unwilling to accept the answer already given?

We suffer from impatience. Why do my prayers take so long to be answered? Have you ever asked that one? We all have. We want everything yesterday. Waiting is not a part of our speed-oriented society. Prayer is not a computer: put in the question and out pops an answer! The Lord has all things ordered for our good. The Apostle Paul prayed and found the only satisfactory solution to what seems to be unanswered prayer: the Lord is sufficient! Any answer without the Lord is no answer at all. His strength is made perfect in our weakness. We have two choices: frustration or freedom. We can run ahead of God or run with Him. Settle the issue today. Give Him control of life and the timing of answers to prayer. Our peace of mind, health, and relationships are at stake. There is no panic in heaven. Why should there be any in us?

The Lord Himself is the answer to all prayer.

January 16

God's Best Answer

1 Thessalonians 5:16-21

Rejoice always; pray without ceasing; in everything give thanks; for this is the will of God in Christ Jesus for you (1 Thessalonians 5:16-18).

"IF I THOUGHT," said John Baillie, "that God were going to grant me all my prayers simply for the asking, without even passing them under His own gracious review, without even bringing to bear upon them His own greater wisdom, I think there would be very few prayers that I would dare to pray."

All prayers are answered, but not always the way we had hoped or in the time we anticipated. We often judge the efficacy of prayer by how much it produces the results we prayed for. We make God our celestial errand-boy.

Because God can see what we cannot see, and knows dimensions which we can never understand, He works out our answers according to a higher plan than we can conceive. We are to tell Him our needs and then leave them with Him. It's only in retrospect that we can see the narrowness of our vision and can see that His answer was far better than what we could ever have anticipated.

Prayer is not just the place and time we tell God what to do, but the experience in which He molds our lives. In the quiet of meditative prayer, we begin to see things from a different point of view and are given the power to wait for the unfolding of God's plan.

Elton Trueblood was right: "Prayer is not some slick device according to which, when we say the right words, we are sure of the outcome. The promise, fundamentally, is not that the Father always does precisely as we ask, but rather that He always *hears*." James Denney said, "A refusal is the answer if it is so given that God and the soul henceforth understand one another."

God made us in His own image.
We should not return the compliment!

January 17

Wandering Attention

Psalm 139:1-24

Where can I go from Thy Spirit? Or where can I flee from Thy presence? (Psalm 139:7).

"WHAT DO I DO ABOUT WANDERING thoughts when I pray?" I've been asked that question repeatedly. A wandering attention simply tells us that our minds are on other things. Why not talk to God about what's really commanding our attention? Whatever our minds drift off to is an indication of what we really need to ask for help to solve or conquer.

But what about abhorrent thoughts or fantasies? They indicate a deeper need beneath the surface. Allow God to gently probe the cause. We are like a ball of yarn with one strand protruding. The Lord gets hold of that and begins to unravel us. Since He knows all about us, He's never surprised. Why do we think we can hide anything from Him? There is no place we can go, even into the depths of ourselves, where He's not there waiting for us.

How many times should I ask God for something in my prayers? Here is a formula that works for me: ask God once, and thank Him a thousand times. God is not hard of hearing, nor does He forget the requests we've made of Him. Thanks that He has heard is an effective method of recommitting the need to Him. The Lord knows what we need and will act when it is according to His plan and timing for us. Remember that prayer is not an argument with God to persuade Him to move things our way, but an exercise by which we are enabled by His Spirit to move ourselves His way.

O to grace how great a debtor
Daily I'm constrained to be!
Let that grace, Lord, like a fetter,
Bind my wandering heart to Thee.
Prone to wander, Lord, I feel it;
Prone to leave the God I love;
Take my heart, O take and seal it,
Seal it for Thy courts above.

—Robert Robinson

January 18

The Eyes of the Heart

Psalm 32:1-11

*I will instruct you and teach you in the way which you should go;
I will counsel you with My eye upon you (Psalm 32:8).*

HAVE YOU EVER HAD SOMEONE guide you with his or her eyes? The eyes can give approval, express alarm, or communicate love. We've all read how a person feels about us because of what's written in his or her eyes. Think of a time when someone has guided you to move to another part of a room or alerted you to another person who needs your attention simply by darting his or her eyes in that direction. In social gatherings, my wife can move me to a person who needs me just by the way she moves her eyes.

The Psalmist tells us that God guides in the same way. Intimate encounter with the face of God in prayer is like being guided by His eyes. He gives us His reaction to what we have done or are planning. Also, He directs our attention to people and situations where He wants us to move. The Lord will guide us.

Freedom from worry is to be found in the sure knowledge that God is at work in the people and circumstances of life. When we lose that firm conviction, we become grim. If we live with the feeling that everything depends on us, that if we don't do everything it won't get done, or that the only things that are happening are what we can see and account for ourselves, we will be defeated by life's pressures.

The life Christ lived He now seeks to live in us. This is what we need to know. The Lord is at work in the people we love (and some we need to learn to love); He is working His purposes out in the tangled mess of human problems. It is in prayer that the eyes of our heart meet the guiding eye of the Lord.

That the God of our Lord Jesus Christ, the Father of glory, may give you the spirit of wisdom and revelation in the knowledge of Him, the eyes of your understanding being enlightened; that you may know what is the hope of His calling, what are the riches of the glory of His inheritance in the saints.

—Ephesians 2:17-18

January 19

The High Way and the Low

Romans 5:3-5

And not only that, but we also glory in tribulations, knowing that tribulation produces perseverance; and perseverance, character; and character, hope (Romans 5:3-4).

PAUL DELINEATES THE PROGRESSION OF growth in greatness: suffering, endurance, character, hope, love. Actually, you have to read the list backward to know what really happened to Paul. It was the love of God communicated to him through Christ that gave him hope. Paul's experience of the love of God had so deeply touched the insecurity and loneliness of his militant life that he became healed at the core. He discovered a truth so profound that his conception of God had been shattered by the truth of God's uncalculated, undeserved love freely given in Jesus Christ. Paul learned that he could never be good enough to deserve it. In the place of his Pharisaic piety and persistent perfectionism, he now based his life on the absolute power, boundless love, and utter reliability of God.

Because of this he was able to face the disappointments, the physical difficulties, and the rejections he endured. Suffering produced endurance, and endurance produced character because of the foundation God had built in him. The things he suffered did not break him because he knew that he belonged to God. Life in all of its cruel realities made him a better man because he was God's man.

To every man there openeth
A way and ways and a way;
And the high soul treads the high way,
And the low soul gropes the low;
And in between on the misty flats
The rest drift to and fro
...every man decideth
The way his soul shall go.
—John Oxenham

More important than what life does to us is what we do with life!

January 20

God Can Change Our Moods

2 Corinthians 7:1-16

Nevertheless God, who comforts the downcast, comforted us (2 Corinthians 7:6).

WHAT WORD WOULD EXPRESS HOW you feel today? When people ask us how we are feeling today, we will probably answer glibly, "Oh, fine!" But if you were to answer honestly, what one word would capture how you feel? If you had to draw a picture of yourself, not how you look after a good cosmetic job or the assumption of your "happy mask," how would you draw yourself as you feel?

Does God care about how we feel? Does He understand our moods? Can He change them?

The answer to these questions is found in a deeper insight into how God deals with us. The cross proclaims that He loves us as we are. We cannot earn or deserve His love. He loves us utterly. If that's really the case, His love does not change with our moods. But it is also true that He can help us with them. Moods are the outer wrapping of our inner feelings. All moods have their roots in our reaction to what has happened, or we fear may happen, or we urgently hope will happen.

God helps us with our moods by penetrating into the inner reason for our feelings. He forces us to see our resentment, self-pity, defensiveness, fear, anxiety, or insecurity for what they are in the light of His love revealed on the cross. Let us tell Him about our mood right now, and ask Him to help us penetrate to the real reasons we feel the way we do.

The soul that on Jesus hath leaned for repose
He will not, He will not desert to its foes;
That soul, though all hell should endeavor to shake,
He'll never, no never, no never forsake.

—Rippon's Selection of Hymns

January 21

Something More Than Happiness

John 15:11; James 1:2; Hebrews 12:2;
1 Thessalonians 1:6; Romans 15:13

Now may the God of hope fill you with all joy and peace in believing (Romans 15:13).

THERE IS A REAL DIFFERENCE between happiness and joy. Happiness is that condition which is dependent upon the circumstances of our life; joy exists in spite of the circumstances around us.

Ask almost anyone what his main purpose in life is, and almost invariably the answer is "happiness." Most of us, however, are not sure what we mean by happiness. Usually it is related to the conditions in which we are living.

Joy is very different. It can exist when all else seems wrong and disturbed. "Joy" is closely related in its root to the word "grace." Grace is defined as the unearnable, unmerited, unqualified love of God. When a person knows that God loves him just as he is, and accepts His grace in Jesus Christ, then he knows the precious experience of joy.

Most of us fluctuate and are cast to and fro within by our changing emotions. What a volatile, unsteady picture of life we often present! We need a deep experience of joy which does not change as our emotional condition changes.

The New Testament opens with joyous exultation over the birth of Christ and ends with joyous hallelujah choruses over the love, forgiveness, and power of God which have been released through Christ. Open the New Testament anywhere and you hear a note of joy struck in the midst of unfortunate and discouraging circumstances. One could trace our Lord's progress through the countryside by the joy He left behind in the lives of people who dared to accept His unchanging love for them. How about you? Are you a joyous person? Or have you lost yourself in the frantic search for happiness that does not last?

Christ does more than make us happy; He gives us joy!

January 22

Back to Grace and On to Joy

Philippians 2:1-30

Let this mind be in you which was also in Christ Jesus, who, being in the form of God, did not consider equality with God something to be grasped, but emptied Himself by taking the form of a servant and coming in the likeness of men (Philippians 2:5-7).

RECENTLY A FRIEND OF MINE WAS described in a very disturbing way: "He's got a rotten disposition! I wish his conversion had included his disposition!" The man had missed the secret of a joyous disposition. The word for "mind" in today's Scripture can also be translated "disposition." "Have in you this disposition which was also in Christ" is a challenging rendering of the meaning. Think what that could do for us today if we believed it and claimed it! Our dispositions are the outward impact of what's going on in our minds and emotions. We become what we are thinking and feeling. Moods are directly related to our mental condition, our emotional health, and our physical fitness. Often the expression of our disposition is a mood of gloom, apprehension, or discouragement. We can get mentally exhausted, emotionally depleted, and physically run down. Then we begin to take our signals from the world around us rather than from the Presence within.

How's your disposition today? What's your mood? If it's anything but joy, we have the responsibility to sort out what in our minds, feelings, or body is causing this bad mood. Joy is no option. Christ does not change, and therefore we can change our disposition and mood by getting at its root and experiencing His love, forgiveness, and strength. We are responsible. No one or no thing can depress our disposition without our permission. Christ can change us!

Remember, joy is an outward expression of grace. What does Christ's grace need to transform in you today?

Don't wait one minute more:
Get back to grace and give out joy!

January 23

Brooders

Nehemiah 9:17; Mark 11:25-26

As they refused to listen, and did not remember Thy wondrous deeds which Thou hadst performed among them; so they became stubborn and appointed a leader to return to their slavery in Egypt. But Thou art a God of forgiveness, gracious and compassionate, slow to anger and abounding in loving kindness; and Thou didst not forsake them (Nehemiah 9:17).

"CAN GOD HELP A BROODER?" "If God's love is unconditional and His forgiveness unreserved, why does Jesus say that God won't forgive us unless we forgive others?" These questions indicate that the old problem of forgiveness is still lurking in our hearts. So many people express the problem of being unable to feel forgiven even after they have been told about God's forgiveness. A deep problem of pride is exposed. We play God when we refuse to forgive ourselves or others. We really lose control of our lives when we have to admit our helpless need for God's forgiveness or are challenged to forgive someone else. We hold life in control when we withhold forgiveness from another person. The result, however, is that we become brooders, and eventually our lives become cold and cautious.

God forgives and forgets. He can enable us to do the same. If we don't, there is a fracture in our relationship with Him which deepens until our prayers are ineffective, the joy of life drains away, and we become negative, critical people. It is then that we need to recover the basic truth in our two Scriptures for today. Think deeply about that. Are you willing to surrender your brooding to God and let go of the slights and oversights, the hurts and harm that people have done?

Brooding is missing the blessing!

January 24

A Joy-Infused Temperament

Philippians 3:1-21; Nehemiah 8:10

The joy of the LORD is your strength (Nehemiah 8:10).

CAN OUR TEMPERAMENT BE CHANGED, altered, or transformed? Our temperament is the composite characteristics of our mental and emotional peculiarities as manifested in our reactions. It is our makeup, our personality constitution. Our temperament is the result of conditioning, experience; and the influence of people in our growing years. The Latin noun for temperament means a proper mixture, and the verb means to mix in proper proportions.

Conversion to Christ—being born again—and then being filled with His Spirit changes the proportions. He remixes and transforms the things which make us what we are in our temperament. Paul could say, "For me to live is Christ." His "self" became the riverbed for the flow of the Spirit of Christ. The more he thought, prayed, studied, and lived Christ, the more his temperament was changed from harshness to hopefulness, from judgmentalism to joyousness, from legalism to liberation. But he did not follow Christ to get a new temperament; that became the inadvertent gift of attentiveness to the indwelling Christ.

How would you describe your temperament? What difference has Christ made in your peculiarities manifested in your reactions? Now look again at Nehemiah 8:10. That's today's refrain for our new temperament: "The joy of the LORD is your (my!) strength."

When I came to believe in Christ's teaching,
I ceased desiring what I had wished for before.
The direction of my life, my desires, became different.
What was good and bad changed places.

—Leo Tolstoy

January 25

A Mood Modifier

Philippians 4:10-20

And my God shall supply all your need according to His riches in glory by Christ Jesus (Philippians 4:19).

PAUL WAS IN PRISON WHEN HE wrote these mood-modifying words. He was honest about the difficulties facing him but confident in the Lord's power to bring good out of painful circumstances. He was lifted out of the possibility of a down mood by remembering the faithfulness of God in times past.

To see our mood from God's point of view and to experience healing, it is helpful to get out of ourselves and look at our mood from His perspective. What would you say to you if you were God? The formula is eternally true: impression without expression equals depression. We are depressed in a mood until we are released to say, "Lord, this is how I feel right now. Do You care, really? How did I get this way? What do You want me to do with the person, situation, or frustrating circumstance causing my mood?"

Now listen quietly for His answer, and along with the insight of the cause of the mood will come an inrush of His spirit with amazing love and acceptance. Listen to His words, "I love you and will not let you go. Your mood is caused by your self-condemnation for what you have or have not done or been. I am greater than that mood. Give it to Me! Your joyous mood will be maximized, and your bad moods transformed by My grace. Believe My promise and live today in full assurance!"

St. Richard of Chichester, a saint of the thirteenth century, penned a prayer which gives us a key to unlock the Lord's mood-changing power.

Day by day, dear Lord,
Of Thee three things I pray:
To see Thee more clearly,
Love Thee more dearly,
Follow Thee more nearly,
Day by day.

A change in my moods is but a prayer away.

January 26

When We Don't Feel Like It

John 5:17; Luke 2:20; 2 Thessalonians 3:10-12

Jesus' answer to them was this: "My Father is still at work and therefore I work as well" (John 5:17 PHILLIPS).

"WELL, HOW DO YOU FEEL TODAY, Jumbo?" is the question a New York cab driver asks as he begins the day, looking into the mirror while shaving. "If I feel good, I go to work; if I don't, I know that I'd better not go to work! I'd only spread my bad mood to dozens of riders all through the day."

This was the response I got to a simple "How's it going?" question I asked. Quite a philosophy...that! But quite a luxury...at that! Most of us can't plan our life around our moods. We have to go to work, pick up responsibilities, and share people's burdens...sometimes when we don't feel like it. If we waited to feel right, we would get little done.

The secret of life in Christ is challenging: do the thing that love demands and you will feel the love that the thing requires. Glib formula? No, it works! When we get bogged down in our feelings, action is required to change our mood. When we are frustrated about some person, there is something we must do to break the tension. Act—don't react.

Feelings are like clouds which hide the sunshine. The day can seem dark and bleak. But the clouds cannot change the fact that the sun is still there. So too with our life. We can be fogged in by bad feelings, but Christ has not changed! His love and power are just as available as when things were sunny and bright. But is our life orbiting around Him? Or have we tried to be the center of our universe? Doing the thing that love demands will send us jetting through the clouds of feeling, up to a level of life where the *Son* is visible again. We can fly above the clouds. The feelings may still be there, but the strong winds of the Spirit will begin to blow again, and the horizon will be clear.

Go to work anyway!

January 27

What Is Your Body Saying?

Matthew 11:28-29; Mark 6:31

And He said to them, "Come aside by yourselves to a deserted place and rest a while." For there were many coming and going, and they did not even have time to eat (Mark 6:31).

WHAT HAS YOUR BODY SAID to you lately? Have you been listening? It has its own language, you know! Often it warns us when we are overtaxing its strength. It cries out for rest and relaxation, just as it signals when it is hungry or sleepy. In this day of pills and nifty nostrums, we can manipulate the body to pep it up and slow it down, go without sleep or force sleep. But the body does not lie...it tells the truth...now and later.

Many of our difficult moods are physically induced. We feel badly in our emotions because of physical disorders. There are times that we analyze our emotions with little release from a mood because the cause is in our bodies. Introspection does not help; we probably need rest, a break from routine, a vacation, or a chance to rebuild our strength.

Jesus honored the need for rest. He actually left the needs of people to be quiet in prayer. What the Son of God found necessary should not be neglected by us. Often our most creative times come after a time of resting our minds and bodies. There is an ebb-and-flow rhythm to life in Christ. We should not feel guilty for loving ourselves as loved by Him and enjoying the pleasure of being in good physical shape. A manifestation of our self-hate is the way we drive ourselves beyond our energies. Christ gives us strength for the impossible if we have taken time to get the strength from Him. We destroy ourselves when we try it alone.

Are your moods related to your body?
If so, what is your body saying lately?

January 28

A Luxury We Cannot Afford

Romans 8:26-39

Likewise the spirit also helps in our weaknesses (Romans 8:26).

ADMIT, SUBMIT, COMMIT—THESE ARE three steps which can change our mood. Most of our moods trouble us because we do not admit to someone else how we really feel. We keep the mood hidden and it festers and grows. When we admit that we are feeling blue or bland, frustrated or fearful, down or discouraged, impatient or insecure, we have taken the first step to getting free. The next step is to submit our mood to God. When we tell Him how we feel and ask for the power to be different, we experience the internal ministry of the Spirit. We are promised that when we don't know how to pray about our feelings, His Spirit enters in and helps us in our praying. The Spirit interprets our deeper trouble and sorts out the real cause of our mood. He prays on our behalf, giving us the courage to actually commit how we feel to God and leave it with Him. He knows what we need to break the bind and get on with more creative living.

We should hang onto a mood only so long as it takes us to get quiet and ask for God's healing within us. Then He takes us at our word and moves deeply into our psyches to the inner dynamics of distorted motives, confused values, self-centered hurts, and unresolved memories. In meditation and dialogue with Him, we see things as they are and what we must do. Bad moods are a luxury no one can afford; life is too short, and people need our support too much for us to be out of commission. Think of the time we waste nursing our moods! We enjoy them too much and too long.

We have been given the gift of life to live for others. Does our mood stand in the way of that?

January 29

The Decision to Love—Anyhow!

1 John 4:7-12

Beloved, let us love one another, for love is of God; and everyone who loves is born of God and knows God (1 John 4:7).

WE TALKED ABOUT THE MAN'S wife all afternoon. He tried to analyze the broken relationship which had grown between them during the weeks before our visit. The man wanted to understand the trouble, get to the bottom of whatever the misunderstanding was, and work it out. He was persistent in his analysis of the situation, as if insight would immediately release him to do whatever would be necessary for a reconciliation. He wanted to find the key which would unlock the frustration. His wife was acting coldly and angrily, but he could not locate how it had begun or what the contributing factors had been.

I felt guided to ask a question. "What would you do if you could never find the cause?" "Well," he said, "I suppose I would have to love her and affirm her anyway." "Exactly!" I said. "Then why not love her in spite of your lack of insight over what has gone wrong? Is your love conditioned on insight? Do you love her only when you have things straightened out and everything analyzed carefully? Could it be that you are deadlocked in the necessity of talking things out in order to love rather than loving in order to be able to talk freely again?"

Have you ever had that problem? We all have! Each of us can picture some person from whom we are estranged and communication is broken. Do we dare to set our own feelings aside to affirm the other person?

That night the man went home and acted as he would if he had clearly understood the situation. His wife responded. Communication was reestablished. To this day he does not know what was wrong. He doesn't need to know now! Not even his demand to understand broke his desire to love unconditionally. Often people react because of physical and psychological frustrations which they don't understand. Our insistence on insight often cripples the healing process.

Love is not always conditioned on insight or analysis!

January 30

Failure to Allow God to Use Failures

Acts 12:25; 13:13; 15:37-39; 1 Peter 5:4-14

She who is in Babylon, elect together with you, greets you; and so does Mark my son (1 Peter 5:13).

CAN GOD USE EVEN OUR FAILURES FOR our ultimate good? Yes! Consider Mark. He became a missionary dropout. He was not able to take the rigors of the missionary journeys with Paul. He was sent home as a failure. Later, when Barnabas wanted to take the young man on the second missionary adventure, Paul refused. A rift between Paul and Barnabas resulted over what to do with Mark. Finally Barnabas took Mark and went to Cyprus.

We wonder what happened to Mark under the careful healing ministry of Barnabas. The name Barnabas means "Son of Encouragement." That's exactly what he was to Mark. He nurtured a failure back to faith. God had not given up on Mark; nor would Barnabas. When the time was right and Mark was ready, the rebuilding ministry was taken over by Peter.

The Big Fisherman knew what it was like to fail the Lord and be given a new beginning. Out of his own experience he was able to give courage and hope to young Mark. God was working out His plans and purposes for Mark. With Peter, Mark learned firsthand about Christ's life, message, and ministry. Later, based on Peter's account, he wrote the first Gospel, recording for the early church about what Christ did and said as Savior. That would not have been possible if he had remained with Paul. The Lord used a deep disappointment to give us the Gospel of Mark. And eventually, Mark and Paul were reconciled.

What does that say to you and me? Can we trust the Lord with our failures? Do we believe that a hurt surrendered led to a hope supplied? The challenge is to trust the Lord with our failures. He may be leading us into a new direction which would never have been possible otherwise. What an amazing Lord! Henrietta Mears once said, "Failure is not sin. Faithlessness is."

It is not a disgrace to fail.
Failing is one of the greatest arts in the world.
—Charles Kettering

January 31

A Bloomin' Fret!

Psalm 37:1-40

Rest in the LORD and wait patiently for Him; do not fret (Psalm 37:7).

I OVERHEARD A COCKNEY IN London describe his boss: " 'E's a bloomin' fret!" Being a student of colloquialisms, I asked the meaning of the expression. "You know what I mean...the gov'ner is a worrying fretter. 'E puts on 'is walking shoes and climbs over molehills as if each one was a mountain."

I know too well what he meant. As a person who has an overabundance of perfectionism and conscientiousness, with high standards thrown in, I checked the molehills I was climbing as if they were mountains. I made a list of all the frets of my life, responsibilities, and relationships. To my amazement, the list filled a whole page of my daily devotional logbook. I decided to ask the Lord to help me declare war on fretting. I committed each one to Him and kept a record of what happened. Some of the frets never happened, many of them were resolved by the Lord's intervention, and others were the source of growing in patient trust. Now, a year later, this week I reviewed the list. "Why in the world did I fret about that?" I asked myself.

Fretting is the misuse of the gift of imagination to picture the worst that could happen. A Christ-captivated imagination enables us to image with greater clarity what He wants to do with those people and situations which make us fret. In James William Johnson's "Listen Lord," his prayer for the preacher is a good one for all fretters: "Lord, turpentine his imagination..."

We can stop fretting and start living!

February 1

Strain and Stress

Psalm 37:10-40

But the salvation of the righteous is from the LORD;
He is their strength in time of trouble (Psalm 37:39).

A SCOTS FRIEND OF MINE HAS A favorite saying, "Dinna fret!" It's often followed by another, "Not to worry!" Sometimes that's easier said than done. I've found the objective power of Scripture much more helpful than being told not to fret or worry. Psalm 37 has been my constant companion in the pressures of life. The Psalmist tells us not to fret but also tells us to trust in the Lord. The psalm gives us the four "P's" which help us stop fretting and start living: God's providence, provision, protection, and promises. Read the psalm again. Make a list of all the admonitions which are the opposite of fretting. The psalm is filled with key words like trust, commit, wait, rest.

Picture the kind of person you would be if you lived this psalm. Actually form the picture of a new you being and doing what the Psalmist challenges. How would today be different? Now thank the Lord that the image you have formed will be true! The only way to stop fretting is to "get the picture" in our minds of what the Lord can and will do and then to use the energy we waste on fretting to pray and act according to the image He has given our imagination. Dare to transfer the image right now. Tell the Lord you're tired of fretting and that you are ready to accept the freedom of faith in Him.

Take from our souls the strain and stress,
And let our ordered lives confess
The beauty of Thy peace.
—John Greenleaf Whittier

February 2

Power for Pressure

2 Corinthians 4:16-18; 11:22-28

Therefore we do not lose heart. But though our outward man is perishing, yet the inward man is being renewed day by day (2 Corinthians 4:16).

WE ALL LIVE UNDER PRESSURE and pass pressure onto each other. How can we live in a pressure-filled world in a relaxed and released way? Our two texts today join together to form a central message for us. They seem contradictory at first. The Apostle Paul, a great master of the released life, describes the difficulties of his ministry. He talks about the pressure of beatings, sleepless nights, and being opposed by his own people and the Gentiles. In summarizing his pressure, he says, "In addition to this is the daily pressure of my anxiety for the churches." That's honest confession!

The inner pressure of God's love is the only equalizer for the pressure of the world. The gospel has creative pressure of its own. When we take Jesus seriously and listen intently to His message, look long and hard at His death, sense His impelling presence, we know a liberating pressure. We feel the pressure to love and forgive, bring our lives and society under His lordship, be the sacrificial "person for others" He calls us to be. This holy pressure presses us on to grow, share, change. Day by day, as we respond to His gentle, persuasive pressure to reform and renew all of life, we feel the pressure of the world less and less. We know what to do and what to forego in life.

Today the inner, creative pressure of Christ's indwelling power will equalize external pressure, and that will free me from being a source of frustrating pressure on others.

February 3

The Pressure Habit

Ecclesiastes 3:1-8

There is an appointed time for everything.
And there is a time for every event under heaven (Ecclesiastes 3:1).

"I DON'T KNOW WHY, BUT I seem to work better under pressure." How often we have heard people and ourselves say this! We seem to need a deadline to press us on to do our responsibilities. We get so used to living that way that we need the feeling of urgency to get us to do what should be done over a period of time. The syndrome of pressure is constantly at work. We take on more than we can do, put too much in one day, make more commitments than we can possibly meet, and try to handle more responsibilities than we can care for effectively. We do it to ourselves, however much we blame other people. We become so accustomed to a frantic life that we are actually ill-at-ease when there is nothing frazzling our nerves. A habit pattern is formed, and we repeat our inadvertent choices again and again.

There are several reasons for this. Some of us need an excuse for doing many things in a mediocre way. We can justify a lack of excellence by protesting that we have too much to do. Others of us are afraid of unpressured, quiet times of reflection. We fear introspection because it forces us to evaluate our goals and performance.

Others of us are troubled by truly deep relationships. If we run hard enough, we don't have to take a lot of time with any one person. Still others need to feel that we have justified our existence by the multiplicity of involvements. We say, "Look, God, how busy I am!" We equate exhaustion with an effective, full life. Having uncertain purposes, we redouble our efforts in an identity crisis of meaning. We stack up performance statistics in the hope that we are counting for something in our generation. But for what or whom?

Many of us become frustrated and beg for time to just be, but do our decisions about our involvements affirm that plea? A Christian is free to stop running away from life in overinvolvement.

Pressure can become a habit!

February 4

Let Go!

Ecclesiastes 3:10-15

I know that there is nothing better for them than to rejoice and to do good in one's lifetime (Ecclesiastes 3:12).

FREEDOM IN PRESSURE IS TO BE FOUND in the sure knowledge that God is at work in the people and circumstances of life. When we lose that firm conviction, we become grim. If we live with the feeling that everything depends on us, that if we don't do everything it won't get done, or that the only things that are happening are what we can see and account for ourselves, we will be defeated by life's pressure.

The life Christ lived He now seeks to live in us. His confidence in pressure was that God was in control. This is what we need to know. The Lord is at work in the people in our lives who are troubled; He is working His purposes out in the tangled mess of human concerns. We cannot always discern how and where, but He is there, be sure of that! This is the reason that we are constantly surprised by what happens in our complexities. Beyond our expectations or fondest hopes, He gives us insight, strength, an answer, a new chance, or power—when we least expect it. He can take our limited human resources and make something creative that we could never devise. His delight is to surprise us with His innovations on human mistakes.

What a relief! The things we want most are gifts. An insight for someone we love, a healing of a relationship, an opportunity to change a difficult problem, an openness to a new direction in a group of people—these are gifts He gives within people.

We can work hard because the results are up to God. We are responsible for the intention; He creates the result to fulfill His plan.

I will let go of my stranglehold on life.

February 5

The Pressure of Religion

Galatians 5:1-15

Stand fast therefore in the liberty with which Christ has made us free, and do not be entangled again with a yoke of bondage (Galatians 5:1).

RELIGION IS ONE OF THE MOST troublesome sources of destructive pressure in our lives. Religion is man's effort to reach, please, earn, and deserve God. Through rites, rituals, rules, and regulations we faithfully seek to be good enough for God. The pressure of religion comes from our training and background.

This is how it works. The spiritual resources of prayer, worship, study, church activity, and customs become goals, and we feel that we *must* do them in order to please God. These things become an end in themselves rather than help to accomplish our true goal of glorifying God and enjoying Him. Jesus came that we might have life—abundant life without reservations. He did not come to tie people down with more religion. Religious men and institutions put Him on the cross. The Romans were as religious about their gods and government as the Jews were about the heritage they tried so desperately to preserve.

We can be as religious about our cherished habits, practices, procedures, and prejudices as we are about the forms of learned, conditioned adjustment to God. Compulsion results: we do the right thing for the wrong reason. We must satisfy our programmed response mechanism.

Jesus sets us free from all this. When our purpose is to know Him, then we no longer *have* to do the "required" thing, but instead we *want* to do the very things which righteousness motivates. Now the disciplines of discipleship become a delight instead of a duty. We desire to do what for most people is a duty. The pressure is off, and the motivation of love is on!

There is no limit to the good things we can do when love is the motivation.

February 6

Under Pressure or a Source of Pressure?

1 John 3:1-3

We shall be like Him (1 John 3:2).

IN WHAT WAYS ARE WE contributing to the unhealthy pressure in other people's lives? Today let's think honestly about what we do to the people in our lives.

Think about our judgments which create the anxiety of never measuring up to what we demand. Consider the subtle pressure of our solicitous compliments by which we communicate standards of what we want people to be, rather than affirmation of what they actually are. Have we taken time to help people discover a motive to do the things we press on them? Are we creating people in our image of them, or are we helping them to discover their true selves and potential? Must they excel for our satisfaction? Do we want people to believe what we believe for *God's* glory or for our own? Is our love quietly conditioned on their performance? Are they free to fail and begin again without incrimination? Have we robbed people of the delight of doing what they should do out of sheer pleasure? Does our competitive drive force others into competition with us rather than doing their best within their individual capacities?

As we allow the people in our lives to march before our eyes, we can see the times that our pressure has been transferred to them. Often our uneasiness with life's demands is contagious, and our whole office, shop, home, or circle of friends internalize our pressure. When we drive ourselves, chances are that our drives are felt by others. Our standards, hopes, images, and compulsions for them are felt, though we may never articulate them. Often our most eloquent statements of releasing people are filled with the tension of our true feelings. Christ's love communicated through us is the only hope for this. His love is unencumbered by adequacy standards, and it liberates a person to do his best with joy and creative motivation.

Are you a source of pressure?

February 7

An Undeniable Purpose

Romans 12:1-2

Don't let the world around you squeeze you into its own mold (Romans 12:2 PHILLIPS*).*

THE UNDENIABLES...WHAT ARE THEY for you? At the core of your being, what are the undeniable values that you can insist on for your life? What do you want? Are you getting out of life what you believe is irrevocably crucial?

J.B. Phillips' translation of our Scripture is particularly vivid: "Don't let the world around you squeeze you into its own mold." Has that ever happened to you? Do you sacrifice what you really want your life to be because of pressure from people and groups? What price have you paid for popularity, power, or approval? Life is very short! The years slip by before we accomplish the things we believe we were born to enjoy.

We all admire people who cut the binding cords of pressure to "do their thing" with freedom and abandonment. But that's not always possible. We must balance the demands of earning a living and caring for our responsibilities in the family or among our friends.

This causes us to ask what our essential goal in living really is. What does God want us to do with our lives? There must be an undergirding purpose which is applicable wherever we are. We often get entangled in wrestling to achieve secondary goals, and thus we miss the real reason we are alive.

Our purpose is to receive and give love. Wherever we are, there are people who desperately need enabling concern and care. When *people* become the focus of our purpose, it is less important where we live, what position we hold, what external circumstances we experience. Often we hope and plan to find life in these things. But we were created in such a way that ultimate joy can never be found until we are involved in a ministry to people. That's the one undeniable which reorients everything else.

What is the undeniable purpose of your life behind all secondary goals?

February 8

Under Direction or Off in All Directions?

Psalm 48:1-14

He will be our guide forever (Psalm 48:14 RSV).

THERE IS ALWAYS ENOUGH TIME in any one day to do the things Christ wants us to do! Many of us are trying to get His power to live out commitments which He may not have guided. If we are about to go under from pressure, it is probably because we are off in all directions without His direction. He has called us to be faithful, not frantic. We play God by trying to handle more than He has willed for us.

We often marvel at what some people can accomplish with their time. They seem to be able to keep a superhuman schedule. Perhaps it is because they are dependent upon the power of Christ to do what they are doing under His guidance. A Christian can have extraordinary power for life's demands if he is open to the peace of Christ in the midst of the demands. He has not expended his energies on anxious fretting about alternatives. He can work with a holy boldness, knowing that he is a channel of strength from Christ, not a reservoir of human adequacy.

This leads to some penetrating questions about our lives:

How much of what we are doing is an extension of God's will for us?

If God would communicate with us about our commitments, what would He say?

If you could tell God about your life, what would you say?

If this were your last year to live, what would you do with it? What would you continue doing? What would you delete?

If you could start all over, what would you do differently?

Christ gives us the strength to do those things He has called us to do.

February 9

Living with Conflict

Philippians 1:27-30

Having the same conflict which you saw in me and now hear is in me (Philippians 1:30).

MOST OF US FIND IT DIFFICULT to live in conflict. It is painful for us to disagree with people whom we love. We have the idea that if we are rightly related to Jesus Christ and are filled with His love, there will be no disagreement. We feel we should have pleasant, peaceful relationships with no heat of conflict. But experience teaches us that this is not true. Even in the church we need to learn to struggle for truth and handle varying points of view. When good people disagree, what should you do?

First, don't be surprised. We stand in a heritage of conflict. In the early church there was conflict within the church and between the church and the world. Jesus brought conflict through His radical message and call to discipleship. In His own band of disciples there was conflict. Later Peter and Paul had their difficulties understanding each other. There have always been differing theologies and church policy through the ages.

Secondly, be thankful. Paul said, "In all things give thanks." In the turbulent seas of conflict, God is teaching us something we need to learn. "Lord, make us teachable." There is more than one side to any truth. Even if we were absolutely right (what a luxury!) we can be deepened in understanding and freed to see new aspects of old truths.

Thirdly, learn to listen in love. When we listen in love we are able to wait long enough for a person to say what he really means. An interrupted man said, "You haven't let me finish." The interrupter said, "I don't want you to finish. I want you to hear what I've got to say because you won't say what you are about to say if you hear what I've got to say."

Lastly, keep a sense of humor.

Conflict is a part of life. How to handle it is an essential part of the Christian life.

February
10

The Peace Which Lasts

Philippians 4-7

Be anxious for nothing, but in everything by prayer and supplication, with thanksgiving, let your requests be made known to God; and the peace of God, which surpasses all understanding, will guard your hearts and minds through Christ Jesus (Philippians 4:6-7).

REPEAT THE ABOVE WORDS EACH morning when you start the day and each evening when you retire. They will change your life. Note the progression. We are to rejoice! Why? The Lord is at hand. That's the reason we can be free from worry. Each problem, challenge, or opportunity should be surrendered to the Lord in prayer, asking for His guidance and power. Then the peace of God comes flooding into our minds and hearts.

Paul tells us that it is a peace which surpasses understanding. This does not mean that it cannot be experienced, but that the total breadth and depth of it is beyond human comprehension. We cannot produce the peace of God. It is impossible to capture it. Nor can we earn or deserve it. Peace is a gift of God. It cost Him Calvary and is synonymous with His indwelling Spirit. Peace is the Spirit of God in Christ reproducing His character in us. Jesus Christ, God with us, exemplified peace. He was in complete harmony with God. His oneness with the Father was the source of the indefatigable peace we see and feel in the Gospels. There was no panic, no rushing, no worried frenzy.

Christ went to the cross to settle the problem which robs us of peace. He suffered to forgive us and reconcile us. How could His death be a cosmic atonement for all time? That's what surpasses our understanding. Only when we recognize that "God was in Christ reconciling the world to Himself" do we begin to understand. When we accept His love through the cross, we begin to experience the immense peace which is offered to us. It takes a lifetime to plumb its depths. The peace *of* God give us peace *with* God and then pervades our minds and emotions until our total life is oriented around Him and we are made like Jesus.

Peace which cannot be contrived or totally comprehended is a gift. I can be at peace when all the world around me is in turmoil.

February 11

Love Lifts the Burdens

Proverbs 12:1-28

Anxiety in the heart of a man weighs it down, but a good word makes it glad (Proverbs 12:25).

ANXIETY IN OUR HEARTS DOES weigh us down. We all know about that. Think of the times that we have been robbed of joy because of worry and anxiety. Most of the things we feared never happened. What is a good word that can make a worrier glad? A word from the Lord. His words to us are always perfectly suited to our need—a word of love, forgiveness, hope, joy. When anxiety weighs us down, we need to tell the Lord how we feel and spread out before Him what is distressing us. Then listen for His special word. What word do you think He wants to say to you today? Listen!

I asked a friend how he was. His response was intriguing: "Well, I'd be all right if it were not for the boulders in my shoe." "What do you mean by that?" I asked laughingly. "Well," he said with a sigh, "I've got some worries that seem big, but when I look at them they are not anything really. They are like little pebbles in my shoes that feel like boulders until I take off my shoe, shake them out, and feel amazed that such a little thing could feel so big!"

Do you have any pebbles in your shoes? Who doesn't? They feel like big problems until we examine them. They are the cause of a common human disability: burdens. Burdens are a low-grade worry. Like a low-grade fever, they are not enough to put us on our back, but they drain our energies and resiliency. A burden may be a person, an unresolved relationship, or an impossible task for which we have inadequate resources. What has the power to do that to you? Who in your life is a source of fretting? What situations or circumstances weigh you down? What has someone said, or failed to say, that chafes inside you? What disappointment with life, people, or yourself is crushing out your peace of mind? God has a good word for you: "I will come under the burden with you and lift it today. Trust Me!"

Love lifted me! When nothing else could help, love lifted me.

—Howard E. Smith

February 12

A Host with Hope

Romans 12:13; Hebrews 13:2; 1 Peter 4:9; 3 John 1-8

Beloved, you do faithfully whatever you do for the brethren and for strangers (3 John 5).

MAX BEERBOHM ONCE SAID, "The world is divided into guests and hosts." The cross can make a host out of a guest.

We all know people who are guests wherever they are. They do not take the responsibility of a host for people's feelings, comfort, hospitality, needs, or concerns. They are in the world to be served, not to serve. Someone else is always responsible to take care of them. When they come into a room they say, "Well, I'm here," instead of saying, "Well, look who's here. I'm glad to see you! How are you?"

When a man experiences the meaning and power of the cross, he is a guest in the universe no longer. He now shares with God the partnership of hosting life for others. The idea of a Christian being a host for others is a liberating focus of what it means to become involved in creative witness. Most of us put off people when we think of our task of sharing the faith as a compulsive pressure to straighten out people's thinking, rearrange their lives, give advice, and clarify theology.

Not so! We are hosts. What does a host do? He welcomes people into his life; he is concerned. His major desire is that his guests enjoy themselves and feel accepted and loved. A guest feels important, welcomed, free to be himself. Remember how you felt when someone was a really excellent host to you?

That's what communicating the faith is all about. When the forgiving love of the cross has healed us at the core, our abiding concern is for the guests that God puts in our lives. If conversation, sharing of experience, inquiring into another person's need, patient listening, and liberating empathy are seen in the context of joyous listening, we will come across as a person whom others cannot resist. They will want to be with us and know our Savior.

We are to be given to hospitality.

February 13

Beyond Glibness to Greatness

Matthew 21:28-32

Which of the two did the will of his father? (Matthew 21:31).

TAKE A PIECE OF PAPER. Fold it in half. On the left side list the priorities of your life in the order of importance. What do you think is most crucial to demand your time, energy, and money? On the right side of the folded paper list these same priorities according to the amount of time, energy, and money you actually spend. Amazing difference?

I participated in this exercise of self-evaluation recently with a group of friends. Some of us were disturbed to see that the order of priorities was reversed! What they believed was most important actually ranked last in practice.

This points up the great distance between what we say and what we do. Words and affirmations of convictions come all too easily for most of us Christians. Our lives are a contradiction to what we say so boldly.

Jesus was more concerned about follow-through than about easy words of promise. His parable of the two sons makes His point. Our trouble is that most of us are a mixture of both sons. We attempt nothing and accomplish it magnificently! Jesus' challenge for us to be perfect as our heavenly Father is perfect is to lift us out of glibness. Who can make easy promises before a challenge like that? It's so impossible that only a confession of our inadequacy will suffice.

That's just where Jesus wanted His proud listeners to end up: "Who then can be saved?" No one...apart from God's love and forgiveness. Once we acknowledge our need for that, we will be on our way to perfection on God's terms.

What have you said that is important—not in words, but by your life?

February 14

Loneliness

Psalm 25:1-22

Turn to me and be gracious to me, for I am lonely and afflicted (Psalm 25:16).

LONELINESS IS THE ANXIETY OF unrelatedness. It is caused by an inability to establish, develop, and nurture deep, lasting, and satisfying relationships with other people. Most of us do not lack for human contact. We usually have more encounters with other people than we can handle effectively. Our problem is not in the lack of opportunity but in our deep sense of unrelatedness with those with whom we do have contact.

A man who had been married for 40 years put it this way: "We have had a good life together. We have worked hard. Now we are ready and capable for retirement. But we have never really gotten to know each other. I have been occupied all my life in my business. I have not been able to develop any deep relationships with people because my business policy was to always keep my personal life out of my business. I have never been unkind or unjust. I just have never been very personal. My wife has been very busy with the children. We have had the normal kinds of contacts socially. But now, when we have all the time, money, and resources we need, we find that we have very little to talk about. We are just now realizing how lonely we have been all along, although activity and pressures kept us from knowing it." The loneliness of unrelatedness!

A person will always be lonely until he or she discovers a deep relationship with God. Augustine prayed, "Lord, Thou has created us for Thyself and made our hearts restless until they rest in Thee." Our loneliness is rooted in the lack of fellowship with God for which we were created. It is in relationship with Him that we learn what it is to be loved and accepted as we are.

We shall be lonely, in spite of the people around us, until we experience friendship with God.

February 15

Who Will Remember?

Ecclesiastes 2:12-17

Then I said to myself, "As is the fate of the fool, it will also befall me. Why then have I been extremely wise?" So I said to myself, "This too is vanity." (Ecclesiastes 2:15).

IT WAS TIME FOR THE funeral to begin, but no one was there except for the lawyer, the funeral director, and me. The lawyer stepped forward and handed me an envelope containing a check for my services. "But this is not necessary," I said. "I didn't even know the man." "What difference does that make?" came the tart reply. "Apparently no one else did either!"

The lawyer was doing his duty. The will called for a Christian burial, and the money had been left to pay the Pastor to contribute to his church.

This man had spent his life on himself. He had never married; he had lived alone. He had saved his money and died a wealthy man. He never knew the joy of sharing what he had earned with others.

A few weeks later I participated in another funeral. Hundreds of people came. The man had been a powerful industrialist. He had contributed to colleges and universities. His name is on costly buildings. But I had the same strange feeling that I had had in the other funeral. Though there were hundreds of people, there was really no one. The auspicious arrangements, the montage of Cadillacs, the expensive casket—all expressed that someone had planned ahead. But no one really knew the man. No one was close to him. No one confided in him, and he allowed no one close to him as a friend.

I see very little difference in those two men. Neither had cared about people, and in the end no one really cared about them.

But that leads us to a deeper question: What makes life significant? What are the things for which we will be remembered? Whose life is different, really enriched, because of you? The final results of our lives will be written in what we did for people.

What are the things for which you will be remembered?

February 16

Life's Awesome Choice

Luke 18:18-23

And a certain ruler asked Him, saying, "Good Teacher, what shall I do to inherit eternal life?" (Luke 18:18).

CHARLES LAMB RELATES A PAINFUL story of Samuel Le Grice. In his younger days they said of him, "He will do something great!" Later, when he grew older, people said, "He could do something if he tried." Samuel is far too much like most of us. Tomorrow is seldom different from today.

An old man was dying. He related his consistent compromise with life. In college he put off a personal decision about the Christian faith because he said he did not have all the facts. After college he became engulfed in personal advancement in business. Then, when he was married and had a family, he attended church because it was good for the family, but Christ meant little to him as a Person. Now his family was raised and he was retired. As he looked back over his life, he realized that he had never done anything which would make the world different because he had lived.

Denney was right in his *Studies in Theology*: "The very conception of human freedom involves the possibility of permanent misuse..."

Jesus loved the rich young ruler enough not to violate his personality. He let him say "No." He did not run after him solicitously, changing His terms to meet his perception. He let him go. The young ruler had said "No" once too often. How about you?

Thomas Chalmers said, "Mathematician that I was, I had forgotten two magnitudes—the shortness of time and the vastness of eternity."

The gift of life and the freedom to live it as we wish is life's awesome responsibility.

February 17

When Our Name Is Legion

Mark 5:1-20

And he answered, saying, "My name is Legion; for we are many" (Mark 5:9).

HOW DID LEGION GET THAT WAY? What did life do to him, and then, because of that, what did he do to himself? What was he afraid he would do to others because of what he was doing to himself? What memories tormented this desperate man? What led him to a self-imposed separation from the people he loved? If the pain and difficulties of encountering and grappling with people in reality are too difficult or painful, or if we find repeated rejection, the game of self-pity and remorse follow quickly. Legion had removed himself from the channel of healing. He was a leaderless legion, marching off in all directions.

Who is the legion of the hurt child, the frustrated, rejected teenager, the aspiring but disappointed young adult, the memory-laden failure, the demanding parent, the accusing judge, the guilt-infusing elder brother, who lives in our skin? Most of us are a bundle of conflicting inner persons jockeying for recognition. We are a bundle of the unresolved. We too are legion...we know it is so by the strange way we react, almost inadvertently, in some situations. Jesus healed Legion, and He can unify our legion of competitive drives and mixed natures and, like Legion, we can go back into life talking openly about what's inside and what Jesus is doing about it.

The harder a man tries to be himself without being right with God, the less like himself he becomes and the more like everyone else he is. Man was made to have fellowship with God, and man is never himself until he submits to this divine rule...The complete "you" is what God requests and requires—not that He might make you into a slave, but that He might emancipate you.

—Richard C. Halverson

February 18

Divine Discontent

Mark 6:1-6

And He could do no mighty work there, except that He laid His hands on a few sick people and healed them (Mark 6:5).

TELL ME WHAT MAKES YOU discontent and I will tell you what drives you. Show me your indignations and I will show you the imperatives by which you live. Tell me what stirs you up enough to want to change things, and I will tell you whether you are living while you are alive. This inventory can show us quickly whether we are dealing with soul-sized issues or piddling about in the eddies of irrelevant self-pity.

Jesus affirms a creative discontent as a major characteristic of discipleship. This is a part of life as it was meant to be. A driving dissatisfaction with ourselves, our relationship with God, and the world in which we live is evidence that we are in touch with the Holy Spirit. If a dominant desire is in us to grow, to live more fully, to heal the wounds of the world, to bring justice to the dispossessed and suffering, then the Lord is at work in us. Too few of us have a fermentive unrest, disturbed with the inconsistency in ourselves and society.

Jesus took His listeners from an abstraction about God and brought them to the concrete evidences in them and society which indicated that they had no right to be satisfied. They were proud of their growth, but He showed them that they had hardly begun; they were proud of their Hebrew heritage, but He showed them the tremendous responsibilities they had in sharing the secret of God's love with the world. When our dissatisfactions are in harmony with Christ's, then we know that we can depend on His power to find an answer.

Our dissatisfactions show what's driving us.
The challenge is to want what our Lord wants for us.

February 19

When We Are Not Able

Mark 10:35-45

Can you drink the cup that I drink? (Mark 10:38).

THERE'S A GOSPEL SONG WHICH ASKS and answers a vital question. I can remember hearing young people sing it at youth camps and conferences: "Are ye able, saith the Master, to be crucified with Me?" The refrain answers, "Lord, we are able!" Compare that with today's Scripture. James and John misunderstood the real meaning of greatness. They wanted to be given places of power and dignity. Jesus responded by asking if they were able to drink the cup that He would drink and be baptized with the baptism with which He would be baptized. He implied His forthcoming cross and suffering. Still the competitive, recognition-hungry disciples did not comprehend. "We are able!" they responded. Then Jesus told them that greatness would mean being a servant. We ponder with awe His challenge: "And whoever of you desires to be first shall be slave of all. For even the Son of Man did not come to be served but to serve and to give His life as a ransom for many."

The secret of the Christian life is not that *we* are able but that *Christ* is able. Paul asserts, "He is able." But before we can comprehend this promise, we must know that we are not able without Him. More important than what we are able to do for Christ is what He is able to do through us. When we get clearly in mind what we are called to be and do as servants, then we know that we can't take it alone. The refrain of the song is not theologically correct. We should not sing "we are able" but "He is able!"

The Lord will release His power to do what He has called us to do. Whenever we think we are adequate to be faithful on our own strength, we are in trouble; whenever we ask for His power to do His will, we find that, indeed, He is able.

Intercessory Involvement

Hebrews 7:25; Romans 7:1–8:39

Therefore He is also able to save to the uttermost those who come to God by Him, seeing He ever lives to make intercession for them (Hebrews 7:25).

CHRIST, OUR HIGH PRIEST, HAS MADE the ultimate, never-to-be repeated sacrifice for our sins. He offers us the gift of salvation, but also daily power to become new creatures in every facet of life. Once we have experienced salvation by faith in Christ's death and resurrection, we become recipients of the implications of that salvation for all of life. To be saved means to be liberated from our sins, freed from fear of death, and then given the gift of sublime companionship with the Savior. Salvation in the Scriptures also means healing, wholeness, health, protection, and providential care. We are not in the battle alone. *He is able* is with us.

The meaning of "save to the uttermost" should be the center of our attention in this message about the victory of the cross in daily living in the battle with ourselves. Romans 7 and 8 form a backdrop for the description of our struggle and how we can receive fresh strength for each new battle. We must call into question the bootstrap psychology by which most of us live which denies us the delight and dynamic of dependence on Christ, the High Priest who ever (constantly and consistently) makes intercession for us.

He is sovereign Lord of all and yet is watching over all of us and yearning with intercessory involvement. Great is the Lord and greatly to be praised!

Among so many, can He care? Can special love be everywhere? A myriad homes, a myriad ways, and God's eyes over every place?... In just that very place of His where God hath put and keepeth you, God hath no other thing to do.

—J. Sidlow Baxter

February 21

He Knows All About It

Hebrews 2:10-18

For in that He Himself has suffered, being tempted,
He is able to aid those who are tempted (Hebrews 2:18).

TODAY WE CONSIDER CHRIST'S POWER to help us when we are tempted. We need to consider primary and secondary temptations. The greatest temptation is to be our own gods and try to run our own lives. We constantly break the First Commandment: there are other gods we are tempted to worship. They are all related to the worship of self. All other temptations flow from that. When we take charge of our own lives and try to be director of the drama of life, we become vulnerable to doing and saying those things which distort our relationship with the Lord and throw our lives into confusion. The Lord does not lead us into temptation. He doesn't have to: there's enough temptation around for all of us.

Our confidence in temptation is that the Lord is with us. His presence not only gives us an *example* but an *encouragement*. There are things we would never consider doing with the Lord there with us. If we could not do or say a thing with Him with us, it is surely wrong. But in addition to that, when we are tempted to weaken under the pressure of temptation, He actually takes charge and gives us the courage to resist. He knows what we are going through: He's faced it all. That's the invigorating promise of this "He is able" assurance. There's nothing we must endure that He has not confronted and conquered during His incarnate ministry. Think of it! He's constantly pulling for us. We can win over temptation—Christ is on our side.

You need never be afraid that Christ will not understand or enter intimately into your problem and your struggle. He knows all about it....He has been there, is in fact there with every struggling soul today.

—James S. Stewart

February 22

Christ Makes Us Stable

Romans 16:25-27

He is able to establish you (Romans 16:25).

A PERSON WAS DESCRIBED AS a yo-yo personality. What was implied was that his moods and disposition were unstable: he was sometimes up and sometimes down. The problem was that the people around him never knew what to expect. The man was unstable. The stresses and pressures of life got to him and sent him spiraling down into discouragement. Other times, when things seemed to go well, he would soar in a great spurt of happiness.

We all long to get off the yin-yang vacillation of ups and downs. Our desire is to be the kind of people who are consistent regardless of what's happening around us. The result of in-depth growth in Christ is stability.

Paul's benediction at the conclusion of Romans provides us with another "He is able" declaration. Christ is able to *establish* us. Note the key words in this dynamic promise: "Now to Him who is able to establish you according to my gospel..." The word for "able" in Greek is *dunamai,* from the word for "power." All power in heaven and earth can be released through Christ for us.

But for what purpose? To establish us. Here the Greek word is *sterixai,* from *sterizo,* "to make stable." Christ is the Stabilizer. Paul uses the personal pronoun when he tells us the foundation of that stability. When he speaks of "my gospel," he is talking about the good news of Jesus Christ—His life, message, death, resurrection, and indwelling power. Paul was a stable person because he believed for himself that nothing could separate him from the love of Christ. Claim this great "He is able" affirmation as your promise today.

Because of "my" gospel, Christ has made me stable even when things fall apart around me.

February 23

Stability in the Storm

James 1:2-8

But let patience have its perfect work, that you may be perfect and complete, lacking nothing (James 1:4).

A STABLE PERSON ESTABLISHED IN the gospel can be distinguished by patience. He or she knows that God is in charge and is working out His purposes. That was James' conviction from years of experience. He wrote to his friends to encourage them. Note that he did not say *if* but *when* we fall into trials we are to count it all joy. The reason is that trials produce patience. In the midst of difficulty we are to ask the Lord for wisdom, asking in faith, knowing that He will give us exactly what we need to stand firm. The strength of a great oak tree is in its roots. The winds that blow against it only strengthen the roots.

James gives us a frightening metaphor for an unstable person: a wave of the sea driven and tossed by the wind. But the One who is able gives us courage to match the wind.

God, teach me to be patient;
Teach me to go slow—
Teach me how to "wait on You"
When my way I do not know...
Teach me how to quiet
My racing, rising heart.
So I may hear the answer
You are trying to impart...
Teach me to let go, dear God,
And pray undisturbed until
My heart is filled with inner peace,
And I learn to know Your will.

—Helen Steiner Rice

February 24

The Stability of Our Times

Isaiah 33:5-6; Colossians 1:21-23

And He shall be the stability of your times (Isaiah 33:6).

HE IS ABLE TO MAKE YOU STABLE! Has that triumphant assurance made any difference in these past three days?

Isaiah gives us our thought for today. Memorize it; repeat it often today: *The Lord shall be the stability of your times.* Our task is not to try to be a stable person for the Lord but to allow Him to be our stability. Our text gives us a reminder of what His stability provides: a wealth of salvation, wisdom, and knowledge—three great resources to draw upon today. The Lord has saved us through the cross. We are loved and forgiven, reconciled and regenerated because of His grace. That gives us a willingness to receive His wisdom for our decisions. The gift of knowledge is His wisdom in application to the challenges of life.

Years ago I traveled to school in Scotland on an ocean liner with no stabilizers. The old ship rolled and rocked through the turbulent Atlantic. Today most passenger ships have gigantic steel shafts which protrude from the hull of the ship to make the sailing more comfortable in a stormy sea. Christ does that to our lives. The waves around us are no different, but we can move through them with an even course. With Him we have "equipoise," an equal distribution of hope, courage, and fortitude.

So, take and use Thy work;
Amend what flaws may lurk,
What strain o' the stuff,
What warpings past the aim!
My times be in Thy hand!
Perfect the cup as planned,
Let age approve of youth,
and death complete the same!

—Robert Browning

February 25

A Vision for the Night

Acts 18:1-28

Then the Lord spoke to Paul in the night by a vision: "Do not be afraid, but speak, and do not keep silent; for I am with you, and no one will attack you to hurt you; for I have many people in this city" (Acts 18:9-10).

PAUL'S VISION WHILE IN CORINTH gives us a formula for stable, confident living. Paul was one of the most stable persons in Christ who ever lived. We are given the source of that stability in this passage. Note the condition of this great man's heart during the turbulent times of rejection and trouble. He was afraid, tempted to be silent, and in constant danger. Balance that with the confidence the Lord gave him. The Lord promised that He would be with him and that He had many people in the city who would help him.

The same vision and constant companionship with the Lord is needed by all of us for courageous Christian living. There are times when we are afraid. We all have fears of something or someone. The Lord's admonition "Do not be afraid" is always coupled with "For I am with you." The presence of the Lord is the only assurance that can dispel our fears.

Daily times of quiet like this are the source of strength that make us stable. Yesterday's confidence will not do for today's challenges. Tell Him about today's hurts and hopes, and ask for His power. I am convinced that He leads us into situations which are impossible to face without Him. And He's always waiting for us when we come to Him for strength to follow His guidance. If we are not facing something which causes us to need His love and courage, we are probably missing the adventure of life.

What are you attempting which could not be accomplished without Christ?

February 26

Fullness to Fill the Emptiness

Ephesians 4:7-16

He who descended is also the One who ascended far above all the heavens, that His might fill all things (Ephesians 4:10).

ATHANASIUS SAID, "CHRIST BECAME what we are that He might make us what He is." An awesome thought! True stability is growth in Christlikeness. That's the startling message of today's Scripture reading. We have been called to "the measure of the stature of the fullness of Christ," Paul goes on to say that we are programmed to grow. All of life is used by the Lord to make us more like Himself. We are no longer like children in the faith, "tossed to and fro and carried about with every wind of doctrine," but we are to "grow into Him who is the head—Christ." We are all in the process of becoming what we dare to envision. What is your image of yourself in the fullness of Christ? What would you be like when filled with His Spirit, transformed by His love, shaped by His will? Picture yourself! Never let go of that compelling vision. The more we get to know Christ, the more we become like Him in attitude and action, thought and character.

Henry Drummond put it this way: "To become Christlike is the only thing in the world worth caring for, the thing before which every ambition of man is folly and all lower achievements vain." We wonder about that when we consider what demands our time, thought, and energy so much of the time. Yeats writes in his autobiography, "Can one reach the Lord by toil? He gave Himself to the pure in heart. He asks nothing but our attention." What a difference it would make if He had our attention and willingness to be recreated in His image!

For to this you were called,
because Christ also suffered for us,
leaving us an example,
that you should follow His steps.

—1 Peter 2:21

February 27

Exceeding Joy

Jude 1-25

Now to Him who is able to keep you from stumbling, and to present you faultless before the presence of His glory with exceeding joy (Jude 24).

THE THEME OF THE LITTLE LETTER of Jude is found in verse 24. The key word is "keep." Two groups of Christians are focused: those who have not kept the faith and those who are being kept by the power of Christ. Notice the relationship between verses 21 and 24. Jude admonishes us to keep ourselves in the love of God, "looking for the mercy of our Lord Jesus Christ to eternal life." The emphasis is on living in Christ now and forever. Christ keeps us from stumbling. He guards us from anything which would separate us from Him in this life, so that we can claim assurance that we shall live with Him forever.

A Christian who is being "kept" in the grace of Christ knows that his or her destination is assured. George MacDonald expressed the essence of this. "I came from God, and I'm going back to God, and I won't have any gaps of death in the middle of life." A friend of mine said, "Lord, help me to live in confident trust in You every day, so that when I die, all I have to do is die." What he meant was that he wanted to live daily, keeping short accounts with the Lord, so that when the end of his physical life came he would have no fear, no regrets, no uncertainty. It's a great way to live—experiencing each day as if it were the last, taking care of anything that would make us uncomfortable in seeing the Lord face to face!

Resolved, never to do anything which I should be afraid to do if it were the last hour of my life.
—Jonathan Edwards

February 28

Life's Most Crucial Decision

Luke 16:19-31

And besides all this, between us and you there is a great gulf fixed, so that those who want to pass from here to you cannot, nor can those who want to come from there pass to us (Luke 16:26).

THE PARABLE OF DIVES AND LAZARUS is a good companion to the study of Jude. Jesus tells us that death is a demarcation, that our decision to live forever must be made in this life. Jude is concerned about those who have chosen to turn away from the Lord and were facing the danger of disqualifying themselves for eternal life. We will all live forever, but the question is, Will we live in heaven with the Lord?

What if we could hear voices from the dead? What would they tell us? What difference would it make to us? Would some of us be assured and others alarmed? There is a growing interest today in accounts of people who have physically died and have come back to life after a while. We wonder if any of the people we have known who have been long dead physically have been wanting to come back across the great divide to tell us what they have experienced in either the joy of heaven or the excruciating separation from the Lord in hell. What would they say? Would we listen?

Dives, as the rich man in Jesus' parable has been called by tradition, wanted to send a message back to his five brothers. Think about what he might have said. What do you think Lazarus would have wanted to say if he had had a chance to share the glory of eternal life with the Lord?

The parable is a shocking reminder that our eternal status will be determined on the basis of our faith in Christ, His death for our sins, and complete trust in His lordship in our lives.

The old hymn expressed the only basis of what we will be able to say when we die: "Nothing in my hand I bring; simply to the cross I cling."

March 1

Hope for the Hassled

Philippians 3:17-21

He is able even to subdue...(Philippians 3:21).

THIS "HE IS ABLE" STATEMENT is like a trumpet blast. "He is able to subdue all things to Himself." Paul had experienced the conquering power of Christ over Satan, death, physical handicaps, and his own human nature. Our devotional today focuses on the powers and forces in life today that we need Christ to subdue. When we consider verse 21 as a whole, we see that the subduing ministry of Christ in and around us is to conform us into His likeness (also note Romans 8:29). Christ is constantly working to conquer anything which will debilitate us in realizing that magnificent purpose. Often, growth in the Christian life seems like a battle. But remember, the battle is the Lord's!

What has the power to hassle you? What makes it difficult for you to be faithful and obedient to Christ? Think of the situations, circumstances, people, and problems through which Satan seeks to frustrate our discipleship. Focus on that and then focus on the "He is able" power of Christ. Be specific, and then surrender the problem to Him. Make this a day in which you trust Christ's subduing power. Often He waits for our relinquishment of a need before He acts. He wants us to be amazed by what He can do with a problem submitted to His subduing.

One of the complexities of our willful nature is that we wait so long to ask for help. Perhaps the greatest thing in us that Christ needs to subdue is our pride. It is difficult for many of us to admit that we are not able. But whenever we do, the One who is able to subdue all things is ready to help us.

And this is the victory that
has overcome the world—our faith.
—1 John 5:4

March 2

Once and for All and Daily in All

2 Timothy 1:1-12

For this reason I also suffer these things; nevertheless I am not ashamed, for I know whom I have believed and am persuaded that He is able to keep what I have committed to Him until that Day (2 Timothy 1:12).

PAUL GIVES US A GOOD DESCRIPTION of what a committed Christian is in his grand "He is able" assurance to Timothy. He knew in whom he believed. He was sure of Christ. If you can say what Paul said in verse 12, you're a committed Christian indeed!

There are two ways in which the Greek of Paul's statement can be read. Both are correct. One is, "What I have committed to Him;" the other is, "What He has committed to me." The Lord is wholly committed to us, so we can be unreservedly committed to Him. He commits a will and way to us. Our commitment is to accept His love, forgiveness, and guidance, and then surrender our will to Him. He will "keep" what we commit. The word "keep" in Greek means "guard." "Committed" is an ancient banking term implying a deposit. Literally, Paul means that our deposit of ourselves and our needs is secure in the bank of heaven. When we commit our lives to Christ, our eternal status is set. When we commit our daily lives and relationships, our present and future, we become committed to what He commits to us.

Commitment is an act of will. It is taking our entrusted free will and using it to solidify thought and emotion. An unreserved commitment is staking our lives—on Christ. When He says "Follow Me!" we must decide once and for all and then moment by moment in all of the new challenges that each day brings. The Lord stands by to help with each task or problem. When we have committed our lives to Him, we renew that basic commitment in each new possibility that each new day or situation presents.

I dare not go any further in this day without renewing my initial commitment to Christ with a special commitment of all I will face today. There is no limit to the resources of the Lord if I will open the channel by committing today to Him.

March 3

Supernatural Power

Ephesians 3:14-21

Now to Him who is able to do exceedingly abundantly above all that we ask or think, according to the power that works in us (Ephesians 3:20).

"HE IS ABLE…according to the power that works in us." This final "He is able!" assertion is a triumphant crescendo of all the previous ones we have considered in the past few days. Christ is able to do exceedingly abundantly by His power at work in us. What is this power? His own Spirit. Within us He releases the same power that raised Him from the dead. This "He is able!" statement is a promise of our resurrection now. By His power, He raises us from our old life to a new one. Resurrection and regeneration must be kept together. "The old has passed away—behold, the new has come!"

The greatest historical act of God was Christ's resurrection. Now that is recapitulated in us, not just when we expire physically, but now—spiritually, psychologically, and morally. The Lord who has made us in His own image now releases power for us to be recreated in His image.

We all need power. We need an inner energizing of our minds and wills. We were meant to be recreated to be like Jesus. We cannot do it on our own, but He is able! The indwelling Christ, the power at work in us, infuses the tissues of our brains with a vivid picture of the person we can become. Then He guides each decision and discernment of our wills. He shows us how we are to act and react as new creatures. Our depleted energies are engendered with strength. We actually have supernatural power to think, act, and respond with infused capacities.

The resurrection power transforms our natures. Our abilities are an outer expression of the One who is able. Power to you!

March 4

Missing the Mark

Romans 3:1-31

For all have sinned and fall short of the glory of God (Romans 3:23).

WHAT IS SIN REALLY? Sin is separation from God. Sins are what we do because of that separation. The human condition of estrangement, rebellion, and obsession with self is the essence of what the Bible calls sin. It is seeking to be our own gods and running our own lives. All the sins of pride, jealousy, anger, hatred, self-centeredness, and willfulness are caused by the fracture of the relationship with God for which we were created. The root of the Greek word for sin is "to miss the mark" as a misaimed arrow hits wide of the target. A sinner is one who has not fulfilled the reason that he or she was born. God is more concerned about our sin than our sins. That's why He came in Jesus Christ to love and reconcile us. Spend today praising God that He did not leave us in our estrangement but took our sin upon Himself on the cross.

Why was the shedding of blood necessary? What does the new covenant in Christ's blood mean? The sacrificial system of ancient Israel provided specific sacrifices to atone for sin. The most crucial was the sacrifice of an unblemished lamb. The lamb became the substitute for a person's sins. Blood was the life of the lamb. Therefore, the shedding of blood was the giving of the life for the sin of the person or the nation as a whole. The sin was blotted out by the sacrifice.

In that light, glory in the awesome name given Jesus. John called Him "the Lamb of God who takes away the sin of the world." Christ accomplished His atonement for the world in words and actions that the people could understand. On the cross He became our substitutionary sacrifice. We have been forgiven; we are reconciled; we are loved! The word "covenant" means "relationship." We have a new relationship, now and forever.

The measure of God's anger against sin is
the measure of the love that is prepared to forgive
the sinner and to love him in spite of his sin.

—David Martyn Lloyd-Jones

March 5

Creative Pride

Romans 11:20; 15:17; 1 Corinthians 1:14; 5:12; Philippians 1:26

That your rejoicing for me may be more abundant in Jesus Christ by my coming to you again (Philippians 1:26).

IS IT WRONG TO BE PROUD? We talk so much about the evil of pride. How can we be proud, in the sense of being satisfied, without the sin of pride? We can get to the answer of that question by a clearer translation of the Greek meaning of our text for today. What is suggested is, "In order that your pride in me may abound in Christ Jesus."

The Philippians were proud of Paul, and he made no effort to conceal his pride for them. Yet, with a gentle reminder, he brings them back to the source of their relationship in the Master and not each other. If he is able to come to them, it will be because the Lord has made it possible.

Elsewhere, in Romans 11:20, Paul gives the formula for creative pride—"So do not become proud, but stand in awe" (RSV). There is a kind of pride which comes from thinking that what we have or are is our own accomplishment, and a kind of pride which comes from an awesome realization that God alone is the source of our strength. In Romans 15:17 Paul says, "In Christ Jesus, then, I have reason to be proud of my work for God" (RSV). Take the first half of the sentence out, and it would be all wrong. Without Christ he could do nothing of any value.

He speaks of the same quality of pride in his letter to the Corinthians, and yet at the same time he exposes the wrong kind of pride. Pride is a sin whenever it prompts us to play God over ourselves or anyone else. We can afford to play God only if we are willing to assume the responsibilities of God, and that's frightening indeed!

When we recognize God's gifts in us or the people we love or the things we do, then there is a deep sense of gratitude which issues in creative pride.

The Mighty Mite

Mark 12:41-44

And He called His disciples to Him and said to them, "Assuredly I say to you that this poor widow has put in more than all those who have given into the treasure; for they put in out of their abundance, but she out of her poverty put in all that she had, her whole livelihood" (Mark 12:43-44).

JESUS SAT AMONG THE ALMS BOXES and watched people making their contributions. Then a slight, little widow moved Him to exclamation. What He saw was authentic. Out of love and gratitude the widow gave what she had, probably the money which would have been used for her next meal. The 13 big receptacles looked like ear trumpets. They made loud noises when large coins were pretentiously hurled in by contributors who desired recognition.

Not for the widow. Her coins made little or no sound. She gave two of the smallest coins of all, about two cents in our money. But the slight sound drew Jesus' attention. He was profoundly moved.

He knew that God was more concerned about the inner motive of giving. This woman gave the gift that counted because it was a gift that cost. How easily she could have said, "Others have so much more than I. What difference does it make if I withhold my two copper coins?" Jesus has memorialized the widow's mite for eternity. No longer can we escape by saying our little gift of self or our possessions will not matter to God. The size of the gift matters not; the size of the gratitude means everything. When is the last time we gave of our money, time, or privacy to help someone else at the cost of our own convenience? The Lord knows our hearts. Here is a prayer for today:

> Lord Christ, I can see how my own estimates of what is important are very different from Yours. Help me to give of myself today, even to the point of sacrifice, knowing that only the gifts that cost really count. Amen.

The gift that costs is the gift that counts.

March 7

Criticism of Greatness

Isaiah 29:17-24

And those who criticize will accept instruction (Isaiah 29:24).

THE STORY IS TOLD THAT WHEN Michelangelo had completed his sculpture of David, the governor of Florence came to look at the finished work. He was pleased with what he observed, but as he looked at it he dared to offer a criticism. "The nose...the nose is too large, is it not?" Michelangelo looked carefully at David and quietly answered, "Yes, I think it is a little too large." He picked up a chisel and mallet, and also a handful of marble dust, and mounted the scaffolding. Carefully he hammered, permitting small amounts of dust to fall to the ground with each blow. He finally stopped and asked, "Now look at the nose. Is it correct?" "Ah," responded the governor, "I like it...I like it much better. You have given it life."

Michelangelo descended, according to the old chronicle, "with great compassion for those who desire to appear to be good judges of matters whereof they know nothing." What maturity the great artist displayed in being able to take criticism! But we wonder about the right of that governor to criticize in an area where he was not an expert.

There are some of us who have criticism about everything. We consider ourselves as experts with the assignment of putting everyone straight on every subject. The danger is that we also have criticism for God about the way He's running the universe. "Couldn't You do things a little better?" we ask. We come to the Almighty with a lengthy list of criticisms and complaints instead of humbly accepting that He sees so much more than we do and works all things together for good.

I am filled with praise for what God is able to do in spite of mankind's rebellion and willfulness.

March 8

The Ultimate Miracle

Colossians 1:1-29

For it pleased the Father that in Him all fullness should dwell (Colossians 1:19).

CHRIST HIMSELF IS THE GREATEST miracle of history. The incarnation, as the central miracle, helps us interpret the miracles done by the "I Am," Yahweh with us. These special acts of the power of God present with us in Immanuel were signs, wonders, and works of the Almighty Lord of all creation. They are not infractions of natural law, but the intervention of a higher law of love for human need. All of Jesus' miracles were part of the "people business" He came to do as God incarnate. Each mighty work was done so that some person, His followers, and all of Israel might know, "I am He!" Someone has said that the miracles of Jesus were and are the dinner bell ringing, calling us to the banquet prepared for us to enjoy with Him.

The question is, Do miracles still happen? Yes! The miracle of life, our salvation, the transformation of personality, and specific interventions of healing and blessing. A study of the miracles leads us to an "all things are possible" kind of faith for daily living and our needs. Physical, emotional, and spiritual healings are still being done daily by the Great Physician through the Holy Spirit.

Focus on the needs of people in the context of the miraculous power available to us. Fyodor Dostoevsky was right: "Faith does not, in the realist, spring from miracles, but miracles from faith." We believe that faith comes from the Holy Spirit focusing us on the love and forgiveness of the cross; that faith then dares to believe that as God's miracles we can expect and take special delight in the miracles He will do all around us.

Jesus was Himself
the one convincing and permanent miracle.
—Ian Maclaren

March 9

The Miracle Is You!

Luke 6:17-19

And the whole multitude sought to touch Him,
for power went out from Him and healed them all (Luke 6:19).

THE SECOND GREATEST MIRACLE, next to Christ, is what happens to a person who comes to know Christ personally. When we commit our lives to Him and invite Him to live in us, our days are filled with a constant succession of surprises. He is Lord of all life, has unlimited power, and can arrange events and circumstances to bless us. Our only task is to surrender our needs to Him, and then leave the results to Him.

Christ did not use the word "miracle." He talked about the "works of God." Wherever He went, He did "works" which defied both the expected and the anticipated. The reason was that He was the power of God, the "fullness of the Godhead bodily" (Colossians 2:9). That explains what happened in the Scripture we read for today. "They were all struggling to touch Him; for power kept issuing from Him; and He healed them, every one!" We struggle with our needs, but do we struggle to get those needs to Him? It is not our task to decide what, when, or how He will deal with our need, but only to press through the crowd until we make contact.

Where do you need a miracle—what to you seems impossible? Persist! Don't give up. At all costs make your way to the Master. Tell Him your need, and then leave it with Him. Even greater than the miracle you seek will be the miracle you become by seeking Him, touching Him, and experiencing His matchless love. Anything else you may receive from Him is pale by comparison to what you will become with Him.

Every Christ-filled believer is a miracle.

March 10

The Power of Prayer

Matthew 17:14-21

*Then the disciples came to Jesus privately and said,
"Why could we not cast him out?" (Matthew 17:19).*

ARE YOU EVER TROUBLED by how little impact we Christians in the church have on the world? Do you ever get disturbed by the fact that in our homes, community, and world there are tensions, troubles, and tragedies which we ought to be able to heal, but cannot?

Does it concern you that Christianity has had a relatively insignificant effect on history? We have the answer for the riddle of life, the key to unlock the potentialities of life, and the secret for the discovery of joy, peace, and power. And yet we seem to be ineffective in sharing God's secret and really affecting our society. Why?

After the man had left with his healed son, rejoicing, the disciples were eager to know why they had failed so miserably. "What did we do wrong? Why could we not cast out this demon?"

They asked for it! They left themselves wide open. It was a moment for truth. Jesus was simple and direct: "This kind cannot be driven out by anything but prayer."

What Jesus meant was, "In a life of sustained communion with God lies the power to deal with evil. You have not paid a sufficient price of personal devotion to be able to deal with a problem like this." The reason was in their need for prayer.

Jesus' answer would be no different today. If we were to ask Him why we are so ineffective in healing human needs, affecting our society, and shaping our history, He would tell us that the answer is to be found in prayer. The complex needs of a time like this can be met only with the power of prayer. Then our words will be a clarion call with a ring of reality.

We have only so much spiritual power and insight as we can communicate to another person.

March 11

The Gift of Joy

John 15:1-17

These things I have spoken to you that My joy may remain in you, and that your joy may be full (John 15:11).

THE SECRET SOURCE OF JOY FOR US is the indwelling Spirit of Christ. In today's Scripture there is a powerful progression. Christ tells us that He is the vine and we are the branches. We are to abide in Him and He in us. That means we are to draw on the living power of His Spirit to produce the fruit of joy.

John 15:11 tells us that the reason He teaches us to abide in Him is so that His joy may be in us and that our joy may be full. The joy we can't produce and the world can't take away is the joy He imputes by His Spirit. The word "abide" means "to dwell, inhabit, live, lodge, reside, and rest." It implies continuance, faithfulness, and remaining constantly without limit.

The joy we are to put out, Christ puts in. To abide in Him means that we consistently draw on the resources of His matchless grace. His abiding in us means that His characteristic joy becomes the dominant note of our disposition. We are made like Christ! Would the one word people use to describe you be joy? If not, why not?

First a little spark ignited,
Next a burning coal;
Then like a fire through my being,
Faith has made me whole.
Now I am alive and moving,
Now my thirsty soul He fills.
Joy is being in His presence,
Joy is the center of His will.

—Ralph Carmichael

March 12

The Courage of Commitment

Luke 9:51-53

And it came to pass, when the time had come that He should be received up, He steadfastly set His face to go to Jerusalem (Luke 9:51).

WHAT CHRIST HAS COMMITTED to us, plus our commitment to obey, equals our Jerusalem. There is a Jerusalem for all of us for which we were born and to which our life is leading. Jesus set His face steadfastly to go to Jerusalem, knowing that there He would have to face the cross and die for the sins of the world. There at the crossroads He had to make a commitment. One road led back to Nazareth, the other to the frowning fortress of His enemies who were plotting His demise. He could have returned home and lived a safe, secure life. Instead, He set His face to Jerusalem and the cross for which He had come to earth. What do you imagine His face looked like, set for Jerusalem? Determination, faithfulness, trust, an indefatigable commitment to do the will of God.

We all have a Jerusalem. And then little Jerusalems along the way. Our Jerusalem is whatever prayer has discerned is the Lord's will for us. It is a symbolic city of reality rather than a wish-dream and easy religion. It is commitment instead of comfort. But we can set our faces to our purpose with joy and not grimness. Because Christ has gone before us, and now goes with us, we have His victorious presence to give us raw courage. Once we have committed our lives completely to Him, then we are able because He is able. His strength flows through us as we attempt great things for Him and by His power. After He has control of the nerve center of our wills, He can use us to do the otherwise-impossible. Just as Jesus went to His Jerusalem believing in God's vindication, so too we can live out our commitment knowing that He will have the final word.

What is your Jerusalem?

March 13

The Confirmation of Closed Doors

Luke 9:54-56

And they went to another village (Luke 9:56).

THERE'S A PROFOUND TRUTH IN the Scripture we read yesterday that warrants further thought. Note verse 53: After Jesus set His face like flint to go to Jerusalem, a Samaritan village did not receive Him. God closed other doors in affirmation of the fact that Jesus had committed Himself to go through the door of His ordained destiny. It was as if God ratified the decision to go to Jerusalem. The Master had greater works to do than ministering to one village. His task now was to save the world.

God opens and closes doors. A closed door can affirm another open door. When we commit ourselves to do the will of the Lord, He slams other distracting, lesser doors to assure us that we have made the right decision. If Jesus had been received graciously in the Samaritan village, it would have confused the disciples about His decision to go to Jerusalem. "Why leave all these opportunities?" they could have asked.

The task of a committed Christian is to walk through the open doors and not try to beat down the closed doors. There are times when it is clear that we should move on to the next step of God's strategy. Think about the difference between Jesus' attitude and the disciples' consternation. They wanted to punish the Samaritan village for its rejection of the Master. Jesus, whose mind was on the purpose of God, reminded them that He had come not to destroy but to save. When our eyes are on our Jerusalem, the will of the Lord for us, we can take the closed doors as confirmation and can react with confidence and courage rather than consternation.

Find out what the Lord wants you to do,
make a commitment, and get on with it!

March 14

The Cost of Following Jesus

Luke 9:56-62

Follow Me (Luke 9:59).

TODAY'S SCRIPTURE SHOWS US several responses to the cost of commitment. Jesus' mood is determined and decisive: He is on the way to Jerusalem, and He wants followers who can count the cost. The three different levels of commitment represented in people He met along the way expose the ways many Christians relate to their discipleship today.

The first man made a grand, pious commitment that went no deeper than words. He promised to follow the Master wherever He went. Jesus challenged the man to count the cost. So often we come to Christ to receive what we want to solve problems or gain inspiration for our challenges. He gives both with abundance, but then calls us into a ministry of concern and caring. We are to do for others what He has done for us. Loving and forgiving are not always easy.

The second man had unfinished business from the past. He wanted to follow Christ, but a secondary loyalty kept him tied to the past. In substance, Christ said, "Forget the past; follow Me!" We dare not misinterpret His words to suggest a lack of concern for life's obligations, but rather a call to be concerned about His call to live rather than worry about what is dead and past.

The third person wanted to say goodbye to his family. Jesus' response to him stresses the urgency of our commitment. He was concerned about competing loyalties in the man. Our commitment must be unreserved to seek *first* His kingdom. We are left with a question about ways that we have one hand on the plow of discipleship and the other reaching back to the past or to lesser commitments. In what ways are you looking back?

What entangling loyalties have you brought into the Christian life which make it difficult to give your whole mind and heart and will to Christ?

March 15

The Way of the Cross Leads Home

Matthew 7:13-14; John 14:1-6

Enter in at the narrow gate; for wide is the gate and broad is the way that leads to destruction, and there are many who go in through it. Because narrow is the gate and difficult is the way which leads to life, and there are few who find it (Matthew 7:13-14).

IN A DISCUSSION AFTER A TALK I had made at a college, a young woman asked, "Really, isn't one religion as good as another?"

"Yes," I replied emphatically, causing concern to flood across her face. "Why then are you a Christian?" she asked insistently. "Because Christianity is not a religion," I responded urgently. I went on to explain that religion is man's effort to find God. Christianity is God's search for man. We have tried to organize that into one more religion with customs, rites, rules, and regulations. But the essence of Christianity is Christ—life in Him, and He in us.

The Lord who declares that He is the way, the truth, and the life is the One who points the way to the narrow gate to eternal life. What does He mean? We find the answer in His cross and His challenge that we take up our cross. The cross is the narrow gate. It is the only way to know Him, to live forever, and to live now in profound happiness. In the words of the old hymn, "The way of the cross leads home." Eventually we must face the crisis of our helplessness to save ourselves.

Reflect on the words "I go to prepare a place for you." Where did He go to prepare that place? Golgotha! The cross was where our eternal life was won. And there is no other way for us to go but through Him and what He did for us. No one goes to the Father, to heaven, or to present joy except through Christ. Not good works, moral achievement, or human accomplishment. There are not many roads that lead to God; there is one road with a narrow gate. But it is the way that God comes to us, not just the way we come to God. Christ is God's way to man.

When we water down the cross we drown in our confusion and take others down with us.

March 16

There's No Other Place to Go

John 6:41-71

Then Jesus said to the twelve, "Do you also want to go away?" Then Simon Peter answered Him, "Lord, to whom shall we go?" (John 6:67-68).

JESUS' WORDS ARE FILLED with pathos: "Do you also want to go away?" Many of Jesus' followers had turned away. They could not take the challenge He had given. He had boldly proclaimed that He was the Bread of Life to fill their emptiness. Then He said that His followers must eat His flesh and drink His blood. To the Hebrew person, that meant accepting Him completely and taking His message and life into themselves. The words were symbolic but not simplistic. Bread meant sustenance, and blood meant life. Many people followed Jesus for the signs and wonders He did, and not for the message He proclaimed.

Many of us have the same problem. We want our Lord for answers to our needs, but when it comes to absolute faithfulness and obedience, we too are tempted to turn away. But we all know a hunger that no one else can fill. And so we say with Peter, "Lord, to whom shall we go? You have the words of eternal life." Tell the Lord that today!

The problem of contemporary Christianity is that many of us look like we are still with the Lord while in our inner hearts we have gone away. It is possible to be a church member and be active in Christian causes and activities but have left our Lord because His challenge is too demanding. That produces what I call the dishonesty of duality. We are pretentiously faithful on the outside, but our hearts are not committed to Christ. Today is a day to rejoin Christ with mind, heart, and action.

I laid at Christ's feet a self of which I was ashamed,
couldn't control, and couldn't live either;
and to my amazement He took that self, remade it,
and consecrated it to Kingdom purposes.

—E. Stanley Jones

March 17

Self-Pity

Matthew 20:29-34

And Jesus, deeply moved with pity, touched their eyes (Matthew 20:34 PHILLIPS*).*

MEDIATION: THE CROSS IS an expression of creative pity and a source of healing uncreative self-pity. When Jesus went to the cross, it was out of pity for the world. As an act of gracious self-giving, He was faithful in revealing God's love regardless of the anger and hostility of His enemies. At many stages along the way to Jerusalem, He could have transferred the pity He felt for people to Himself and turned from His mission. Self-pity is inverted self-giving. Jesus believed that God would be with Him and would use His death as a means of loving the world.

That love is the only antidote for self-pity. The cross moves us to love others regardless of what they say or do. Jesus' prayer, "Father, forgive them, for they know not what they do," is the prayer for release of self-pity. Most people do what they do because of what they are. They cannot change what they do until they change what they are. Self-pity is usually related to what people have done or said. It is an alarm signal that there is something wrong in a relationship. Rejection and hostility are caused by something in another person which needs to be healed. The cross liberates us from the necessity of "rising to the bait" and being hooked on a hurt feeling. We are freed to care more for reconciliation than being "right." The love of the cross alerts us to the need in the offender of our pride and focuses a new opportunity for ministry to them. That's the costly love of the cross!

What's troubling you? Tell Christ about it, ask for His perspective on the situation, confess your part of the difficulty, and surrender the hurt to Him.

The cross is the answer to self-pity!

March 18

A Calvary Within Calvary

Galatians 2:1-21

I have been crucified with Christ; it is not I who live, but Christ lives in me; and the life which I now live in the flesh I live by faith in the Son of God, who loved me and gave Himself for me (Galatians 2:20).

SPEAKING OF DYNAMIC CHRISTIAN living, George Buttrick said, "And that is costly business, requiring our tiny calvary within His Calvary." Love means the cross. God's mercy was expressed in the cross. He did not condemn the world, but came in forgiving love. The cross is a historical point of reference to remind us that our God is merciful.

But we too have our cross. How can we carry a cross? What is our cross?

Paul said, "I have been crucified with Christ. It is no longer I who live but Christ who lives in me." The Christian life begins with crucifixion—our own. Becoming a Christian means a deathlike surrender of our life to Christ. We die to our own rights, control of our life, and plans for our future. We will to be willing to receive, do, go, stay, speak, and serve as He wills. Christ then comes to live within us to express His loving mercy for others through us.

The cross becomes the basis of our relationships. Our time, energy, resources, and skill are put at Christ's disposal for others. We forgive because we have been forgiven. People do not need to measure up any more than we had to measure up in order for God to love us. We take on the troubles, frustrations, and problems of others as Christ took the cross. We find our new purpose in discovering ways of relating the problem of people to the power of God. Because we have died to self, we have nothing to lose and everything to give.

Each of us has a tiny calvary today.

March 19

Today's Cross

Luke 9:23-27

For whoever desires to save his life will lose it,
but whoever loses his life for My sake will save it (Luke 9:24).

LET'S RECAP WHAT WE'VE said thus far about the cross. Jesus wanted His disciples to know the cost of discipleship. Remember what this means today: our cross means a death to self and a resurrection to new life. Our commitment to follow the Master is once and for all, but also daily in all. We are challenged to love Christ with obedience. Luther said, "He who believes obeys; he who obeys believes." The Christian life is not conservation of self-interest but abandonment—adventure, not acquisitiveness. That demand is so challenging that it has to be acted on daily in every relationship and responsibility. Then we are free to give ourselves away to our Lord, to people, and to situations of need.

There will be a cross in every relationship and responsibility we encounter today. At the heart of each situation is a point of surrender to seek first the Lord's will. There will be people to be loved and forgiven. Most of all, there will be a constant flow of opportunities to care for people as if caring for our Lord. Samuel Rutherford said, "If you take your cross and carry it lovingly, it will become to you like wings to a bird and sails to a ship."

The question we must ask is, "Lord, what do You want me to do?" When we ask that in the complicated issues and difficult relationships, He will show us the way. Then everything is in balance and our future joy and peace are dependent on the guidance He has given. To make Christ's plans our plans will spell a cross of death to self-will, then resurrection power to follow through with action.

Whatever your hand finds to do, do it with your might.
—Ecclesiastes 9:10 RSV

March 20

A Daily Cross of Forgiveness

Nehemiah 9:17; Matthew 10:38-40; 27:32; Luke 9:23

And He said to them all, "If anyone desires to come after Me, let him deny himself, take up his cross daily, and follow Me" (Luke 9:23).

THE CROSS WAS AN ignominious symbol of punishment and execution. Jesus knew His life would end on a cross. And yet He told His disciples that they also would have to take up their crosses. Often the meaning of the admonition is diluted into general discipleship or into some disability which we must bear or problem we must endure. But remember, the Lord said "daily." We can understand and accept *our* cross only if we accept the essential meaning of *His* cross. In His cross He suffered for the sins of the whole world so that mankind might be forgiven. Our cross, then, is forgiving and forgetting what people have been and done.

Our cross is not simply some physical, emotional, or circumstantial burden we must carry. Our cross is *people*—persons who need our forgiveness. To be a follower of Jesus may mean a martyr's death, but right now it means taking up a cross of forgiveness. That must be spelled out in words and reconciling action, regardless of the cost to our pride or what we think are our rights.

It is a source of comfort for us to remember that Jesus did not carry His cross alone. Simon of Cyrene was pressed into service to carry His cross the final steps to Golgotha. Why was Matthew so careful to include this in his passion account? More than to show the humanity of Jesus, it was to remind us that we cannot carry our cross alone. When we dare to be a forgiving person, we need the Lord's help daily, and many times through the day!

My cross is to forgive as Christ has forgiven me.

March 21

We Can Never Say It All

John 21:24-25

And there are also many other things that Jesus did, which if they were written one by one, I suppose that even the world itself could not contain the books that would be written. Amen (John 21:25).

JOHN MILTON ONCE WROTE an exquisite poem on the birth of Jesus entitled "An Ode on the Morning of Christ's Nativity." A companion poem of the death of Jesus had been planned. Milton tried all through his life to finish it. A few lines were written and then left uncompleted with the telling comment: "This subject the author finding to be above the years he had when he wrote it, and being satisfied with what was begun, left it unfinished."

We often feel that way when we try to understand the cross. Whatever we say, there is still something we have left out. No insight, theory, theological viewpoint, isolated Scripture, or idea captures all the dimensions of the magnificent truth revealed in the cross. It is like a diamond held aloft. As you turn it, light flashes from its many facets. That is what we must do with the cross: turn it over in our minds and hearts and allow the many-sided truth to penetrate our thinking and character. No single doctrine of the cross is sufficient to hold all the truth.

Paul felt the wonder: "God forbid that I should glory, save in the cross." We glory in the cross when we grapple with what it means to us—our needs, our failures, our hopes, our dreams. What difference does it make to you that Christ was crucified?

Think of someone you would like to have realize the meaning of the cross. How would you put it into words for a business associate, a friend, a neighbor, someone in trouble, the closest person to you? Write a brief paragraph saying what you feel is the meaning of the cross for that person.

Whatever we say about the cross, our words can never express all that there is to say.

March 22

Where Are the Figs?

Mark 11:12-14

And Jesus answered and said to it, "Let no one eat fruit from you anymore forever" (Mark 11:14).

A PARABLE IS AN EARTHLY story with a heavenly meaning. Jesus used such stories to drive home eternal truth in unforgettable language. The parable of the fig tree is an enacted parable. It is by far the most difficult one to interpret if we look at the circumstances without asking what Jesus was trying to communicate to His disciples.

It was the Passover season, early in the spring. Fig trees could bear leaves as early as March, but they did not bear fruit until late May or June. How could He expect the tree to achieve something contrary to its nature? Why was He disturbed and condemnatory?

Clearly, the fig tree was parabolic of Israel. Like the tree, Israel gave outward signs of producing fruit of faithfulness to God. God had cultivated and cared for Israel through hundreds of years of checkered history. In each crisis Israel had called on God for help, and He was always just and faithful to respond beyond her expectation. But she did not learn. God's miracles, victories, and material blessings were soon forgotten, and the people lost true fellowship with Him in the formalism of rites and rituals. Outwardly, Israel looked like God's people, but there was no fruit of trust and obedience. God blessed His people so that they would share His love and power with the world. Instead, Israel became inverted, separatistic, and selfish.

How about you? Are you like the fig tree? How about the church? To what extent have we shared the resources of God's gracious love with others?

*God has called us to be His people,
not for our own selfish enjoyment, but that,
through us, the world might know Him.*

March 23

Unbinding People

John 11:28-57

Jesus said to them, "Loose him and let him go" (John 11:44).

THIS PASSAGE IS FILLED WITH liberating truth. Christ raised Lazarus from the dead as His greatest physical miracle. It was a prelude to a new age in which He, as resurrected Lord, would raise the dead among the living—people like you and me, those who are alive but dead to what life was meant to be. Put your name in the verse: "________, come forth." Come alive and live forever! But there is another miracle here in this passage which is a portent of a new age. Jesus commanded the people to unbind Lazarus and let him go. He was out of the tomb but bound by graveclothes. Again, like so many of us and our friends, we are out of the tomb through belief in Christ, but are not yet see free to live. Note that Jesus did not unwind the graveclothes. He commanded the people to do that. The same is true today. We are to be the people who unbind others from the graveclothes of fear, sick memories, caution, and reservation. How can we do that? By showing them what it means to be free ourselves and then enabling them by listening, loving, and praying for and with them.

The raising of Lazarus cost Jesus His life. The miracle precipitated the anger of Israel's leaders and solidified the plot to do away with Him. Yet Jesus did what He did out of love for Lazarus and his family. The cost of loving was never too high for Jesus. Nor should it ever be for you and me. We can call on Him with the assurance that He will hear and act. But a question lingers: What are we reluctant to do for people because of the danger or problems it may cause us? We often end up safe but sorry!

The ministry of every Christian is to unbind people in Christ's name.

March 24

The Password to Power

Mark 11:1-10

And if anyone says to you, "Why are you doing this?" say, "The Lord has need of it," and immediately he will send it here (Mark 11:3).

WHEN THE DISCIPLES WERE SENT into Bethany to get a donkey, the password was, "The Lord has need of it." That's all they needed to say. There obviously had been advance planning. A colt had been arranged for and placed at a strategic spot, and a password had been worked out in case of difficulty. The owners of the colt refused to let it go until the magic words were spoken. The underground network of Jesus' followers knew the password.

What a tremendous password of power this should be for us today! As we prepare for Palm Sunday and Easter, Christians should be ready to release anything they have or are when this password is given. "The Lord has need of it" is all we should need to know as we minister to each other in the church and together in the world.

Note the preparation that Jesus had made. The people whom He had reached and healed were ready to be involved with Him. Now was the time they were to serve Him who had so faithfully served them. The owners of the donkey had been prepared for this strategic moment when Jesus would fulfill the Scripture and ride upon a donkey as Messiah. The way in which He rose into Jerusalem seems rather insignificant to us, but to Jesus it was crucial to declare His Messiahship on His own terms. He was both victor and victim, high and humble, God's anointed and suffering Servant, Prophet of Power, and Prince of Peace.

Now we see what an important part the peasants played who had provided the donkey. It seemed like a little thing, but for Jesus it was dramatically significant.

Listen for the password today, and give Jesus Christ control of everything.

The password for Christians is "The Lord has need of it." That should be all we need to know in our lives and giving.

March 25

Nothing to Lose and Everything to Give

John 13:3-11

After that, He poured water into a basin and began to wash the disciples' feet (John 13:5).

SOMEONE WAS MISSING. The disciples noticed it immediately. When they entered the Upper Room to celebrate the Passover Feast with Jesus, they whispered to each other, "Where is the servant? Who will wash our feet?"

Tradition has it that the Passover meal was observed by Jesus and the disciples in the home of the mother of Mark. Why had he overlooked this expression of hospitality? The disciples felt uncomfortable all through the first portion of the meal. Should one of them offer to wash the others' feet? The thought was dismissed as beneath them.

No wonder they were shocked when the Master got up from the meal, took a towel and wash basin, and began to wash their feet! How can this be? They should be washing His feet!

John's contextual statement puts the significant act into perspective: "Jesus, knowing that the Father had given all things into His hands, and that He had come from God and was going to God, took a towel and girded Himself...." Washing the disciples' feet, like Calvary soon to follow, was done because Jesus knew why He had come to the world and where He was going. He was free to be a servant because He knew that He was the Suffering Servant.

Then He underlined the lesson in an undeniable way: "If I then, your Lord and Teacher, have washed your feet, you also ought to wash one another's feet." That means more than water and a towel. Serving one another means really caring, lifting burdens, standing with each other in difficulties, and doing the forgiving, reconciling things regardless of cost to us.

I will think, act, and react as a servant, doing whatever I can to serve others today. Through Christ, I know where I came from and where I'm going, and therefore I have nothing to lose and everything to give.

March 26

Save Now!

Mark 11:9-10; John 5:1-18

Blessed is the Kingdom of our father David that comes in the name of the Lord! Hosanna in the highest! (Mark 11:10).

HOSANNA! THIS IS A VERY interesting word. It is a word of exclaimed supplication. It really means "Save now!" It was used by Jesus' followers and the crowds of pilgrims as a prayer to God to accomplish the expected salvation through the Messiah. For them this meant release from Rome and power for Israel among the nations. But God had a deeper salvation in mind than the release from political bondage or protection in battle. God would answer their "Hosannas," but in His own way, with the cross.

The salvation that God provided would meet man's deepest need. The death of Jesus on the cross was for the forgiveness of the sins of the whole world. Sin means separation, missing the mark. On the cross, the love which was judgment and forgiveness was exposed. God did not change His mind about man's sin on the cross; He exposed what His mind had been all along. There was a cross in the mind of God long before there was a cross on Calvary.

The knowledge of forgiveness would make way for reconciliation and fellowship with God. With the knowledge of God's love as the basis of life, a person could love and accept himself, and an integration of his personality could result. Salvation means "wholeness." The civil way of the ambivalent forces within us which fragment and frustrate us can be healed by the power of loving self-acceptance. We can accept ourselves as accepted by God even though knowing, by our judgment, that we are unacceptable for love like that.

We often come to God with a crisis: "Lord, get me out of this!" but He is up to more than getting us out of life's scrapes. He is getting us ready for eternity. He often uses the crises of everyday life to help us to see the true crisis: that we have established our lives on values which are ultimately unreliable.

We come to God with our desires, and He answers according to our needs.

March 27

When God Cried

Luke 19:28-44

And when He had come near, He saw the city and wept over it (Luke 19:41).

WHAT A MIXTURE OF EMOTIONS there was on the day of the triumphal entry of Jesus into Jerusalem! The Passover crowds viewed Jesus as a conquering Messiah. They used palms to celebrate. They waved them frantically and placed them before the colt on which Jesus rode. Psalm 118 rang in the air. It was the best they could offer. The psalm had been composed to commemorate the time when Simon Maccabeus purified the Temple in 163 B.C. He had made a triumphal entry into Jerusalem after the defeat of the Syrian invaders commanded by Antiochus Epiphanes. A new Simon? Would He drive the Romans from Palestine? The frustration of the people was mingled with genuine praise and wonder for Jesus' raising of Lazarus from the dead. "Hosanna!" they cried.

No wonder Jesus wept. The people had the wrong idea of the Messiah. Had they not heard all that He had said about who He was and what He had come to do? "Save now!" Yes, He would save, but in a much more ultimate sense. The people misunderstood Him because they had not listened; the leaders of Israel were plotting His demise as the parade passed by because they had heard all too well.

When we empathize with what was going on inside Jesus as He rode in that parade observing the crowd—the mixed motives, the expectations, the hatred—we can understand why His heart broke open with sobs of anguish. But remember who He was...and is! He was none other than God with us. It was God who cried that day. What He said as He sobbed tells us why. The people did not know the things which belonged to their true peace. They were missing the time of God's visitation.

What in my life makes God cry?

March 28

You Bet Your Life

John 12:20-26

Most assuredly, I say to you, unless a grain of wheat falls into the ground and dies, it remains alone; but if it dies, it produces much grain (John 12:24).

IN MY EARLY YEARS AT COLLEGE, I worked as a part-time radio announcer to earn money to stay in school. The engineer, named Lee, who worked with me, was an old radio man who had a saying, which he used in response to most anything you said to him. Regardless of whether it was a statement or a question, his response was, "You bet your life!"

During that time in my life I was seriously considering the Christian faith. A couple of friends who were winsome witnesses to Christ's love and forgiveness really had caught my attention. I began listening to what they had to say. But I wondered how to be sure Christ was who He said He was and could do today what He did so long ago. I studied carefully the response made by the disciples when Jesus said to them, "Come follow me!" What a gamble it was for them! Eventually it was focused as nothing less for me. If I turned my life over to Christ, what would He do with it and my precisely laid plans for my career? One of my new Christian friends said, "Lloyd, you've got to bet your life. It's the only gamble in which you always win." I will never forget the night I did just that when I got down on my knees and surrendered my life to Christ. I have been collecting the abundant life ever since.

One of the first people I wanted to tell was Lee. "You know, Lee, how you always say, 'You bet your life'? I don't know what you mean when you say that, but let me tell you what it now means to me. Last night I bet my life on Christ!" I went on to share my newfound excitement and enthusiasm for the Savior.

He was a gambler, too, my Christ. He took His life and threw it for a world redeemed.

—G.A. Studdert Kennedy

March 29

Rejoice Greatly!

Zechariah 9:1-10; 12:1-10

Rejoice greatly, O daughter of Zion! Shout in triumph, O daughter of Jerusalem! Behold, your king is coming to you; He is just and endowed with salvation, humble and mounted on a donkey, even on a colt, the foal of a donkey (Zechariah 9:9).

NO PROPHET IS MORE SPECIFIC about the coming of the Messiah than Zechariah. His prophecy is filled with vivid sentences and phrases which were fulfilled perfectly in the life and death of Jesus Christ. The two in particular we have read for today show how unified the Bible is in its preparation for consummation in the coming of the Messiah.

While the people were rebuilding Jerusalem, Zechariah had his eyes on a very different City of God which would be built when the Messiah came. We are stunned by the preciseness of his prophetic utterances. Looking back, we can see how carefully God prepared for the Incarnation.

The passages we read capture the meaning of Palm Sunday: joyous celebration of the triumphal entry, but also the shadow of the cross. Jesus entered Jerusalem with the shouts of Zechariah's prediction of a King riding on a donkey's foal, but He knew what was coming. He had also read Zechariah 12:10. We wonder how He felt as He knew He would be the One who would be pierced, and for whom His people would mourn.

Reading Zechariah helps us to grasp what our salvation cost God. There was no other way. His gracious, forgiving love required it. He could not condone sin, and yet He had to break its power over us. That's why Christ came and why the cross was necessary. Only a cosmic atonement would do...for all people of all time.

Christ came, lived, died, was raised up,
and lives in me today. I will rejoice greatly indeed!

March 30

The Scrutiny of Jesus

Mark 11:11

And Jesus entered into Jerusalem and into the temple.
And when He had looked around at all things, as the hour was already late,
He went out to Bethany with the twelve (Mark 11:11).

"AND HE LOOKED AROUND AT everything." Jesus moved about the city observing everything. He saw the temple with its money changers, empty rites, and rituals. He saw the Roman legions tramping through the streets. He saw the placards of Roman emperor worship. But most of all, He saw people: the expectant pilgrims, the needy masses, the faithless multitudes. He cared most about the people.

How would you like to have Jesus look around in the city where you live? What would He see? Would He be pleased? Would He say, "Now there is a city of God!"? What would He think of our life? How would you like to have Him look around your house, listen in on every conversation, be in on decisions of what you do and spend? How would He get along in your church? What would please Him? What would distress Him? There is nothing hidden from those eyes! He sees everything and hears all. Can we stand His scrutiny?

But Jesus' eyes of penetrating exposure are coupled with His heart of forgiving love. We can admit our failures and take the creative steps to excellence by His power and love. His judgment is upon those who have eyes to see and yet will not see what He sees.

Here's a prayer for your day:

> Lord Jesus, we feel exposed and disturbed when we realize again that You see all and know all. We think we can hide. Thank You for Your forgiving love. In its context we will take a new look at everything today and see, not only the depressing reality, but the exciting possibilities of what You can and will do. Amen.

If Jesus looked closely at our life in all its public and personal dimensions, what would He see?

March 31

Paint Yourself into Calvary

Luke 23:44-49

And all His acquaintances, and all the women who followed Him from Galilee, stood at a distance, watching these things (Luke 23:49).

CAREFUL OBSERVATION OF THE CROWD in Rembrandt's painting of the crucifixion reveals a dynamic discovery: the faces of the people are filled with pathos and wonderment. One of them is Rembrandt himself! He painted himself into the crucifixion.

Any meditation on the meaning of the cross requires that we take our place at the foot of the cross. When we get inside the skin of those who stood by watching while Jesus was crucified, we begin to capture what the cross meant. But we look at the cross through the lens of the open tomb and Pentecost. We know so much more than those who saw the anguish on Calvary. Now the living Christ comes to us to help us realize that what He did that day He does today for each of us. The same forgiving, reconciling love revealed on the historic cross is reproduced in each of us. By a special gift of faith given to each of us we know that He died for us, that we are forgiven, that His death defeated our fear of death, and that because He lives we can live—now and forever.

H. Wheeler Robinson tells the story of visiting the Paris Cathedral. He observed a man in one of the pews while the choir sang, "Lamb of God, who takest away the sin of the world, have mercy on us!" The man muttered in response, "Oh, God, what a dream! If only he could, if only he would!" He leaped up and ran out of the sanctuary.

We know that Christ not only *can* but *will* take away the sins of the world—your sins and mine. He washes us clean by the blood of the cross. But do we really believe it? Are there any sins of the past which linger in your memory, causing self-incrimination and guilt? Then paint yourself into Calvary. Stay at the foot of the cross until you know He died for you.

Today I will live as a forgiven and forgiving person.

April 1

Oh God, That Was My Cross

Matthew 27:15-26

Pilate said to them, "What then shall I do with Jesus who is called Christ?" They all said to him, "Let Him be crucified!" (Matthew 27:22).

I HAVE OFTEN WONDERED what happened to Barabbas after his release. What did he do while Jesus was being crucified? How did he feel? As an insurrectionist, he had been condemned to be crucified. Pilate's equivocation, and the manipulation of the crowds by the chief priests and the elders, had won him his freedom. But what kind of freedom is it if you know that someone else is taking your sentence? Imagine what he might have done with that awesome realization. Perhaps he tried to drown the thought in drink, trying to forget.

Did Barabbas ever meet Jesus? We do not know. There are some who suggest that Jesus was incarcerated with him while Pilate pondered what to do to extricate himself from the dilemma which the leaders of Israel had dealt him. What we do know is that Barabbas and Jesus loved Israel and wanted to set the people free. But their patriotism was expressed very differently: Barabbas wanted a kingdom free of Rome; Jesus wanted the kingdom of God free of sin. One called for military might, and the other called for repentance and righteousness.

In my mind's eye I can see the panic on Barabbas' face when the earthquakes shook Jerusalem and rent the veil of the Temple. Did he stagger to Golgotha to see? If he did, he had to look in the Savior's face. I can hear him cry the anguished confession, "Oh, God, that was my cross! And He took it for me!"

The cross a substitutionary sacrifice. Christ died for our sins, in our place, taking our rap upon Himself. But instead of remorse like Barabbas', we are filled with gratitude, praise, and love.

April 2

The Paradox of Power

Mark 15:25-32

Likewise the chief priests also, together with the scribes, mocked and said among themselves, "He saved others; Himself He cannot save" (Mark 15:31).

LITTLE DID THE CHIEF PRIESTS KNOW that they declared the central paradox of spiritual power. They thought they had exposed Jesus. Instead, they expressed Jesus' deepest conviction about life. Of course, Jesus could have saved Himself. But He had come to save the world. He gave His life as a ransom for a sin-captivated, suffering world.

A paradox is two seemingly contradictory facts which must be kept together as inseparable parts of a basic truth. The chief priest's statement of paradox presented two aspects of the life which Christ lived and calls us to live. We are to spend ourselves on others and trust ourselves to Him.

All through this last week of Jesus' life we are startled to note His amazing lack of defensiveness: "He defended not Himself." His concern was for His followers and the fulfillment of God's plan—not for His own safety.

Christians are the nondefensive, vulnerable people of God. They waste no energy saving themselves in useless, time-consuming, energy-expending protectiveness. That is God's business. We believe in God's almighty vindication of the right. Our purpose is simply to care for others regardless of what it costs.

The paradox of power is the secret of freedom. It is because the Lord has saved us that we don't have to try to save ourselves. We can become part of the Lord's strategy of saving others. We are released from the necessity of hoarding ourselves, our time, and our privacy. We have been blessed beyond measure in order to be a blessing. Our purpose is to give ourselves away in gracious caring and sharing.

We do not need to defend ourselves if the Lord is our ultimate security.

April 3

Unqualified Love

Luke 23:32-37

Father, forgive them, for they do not know what they do (Luke 23:34).

FOR WHOM DID JESUS PRAY? Who was on His heart? Surely the soldiers who performed the execution of Christ on the cross did not know what they were doing. This was only one of hundreds of crucifixions that year! They did not understand that they were stretching the body of the Son of God out on that cross. They were participating in the cosmic sacrifice for the sins of the whole world. If they had known who it was on that cross, they would have shuddered and fled in panic!

What of Pilate and the Jewish leaders? Did they know what they were doing? Pilate suspected...his wife seemed to know and was afraid. Could ignorance be an excuse for the leaders of Israel? If they believed that Jesus was truly the Son of God, what would they have done? Ah, there's the rub! They would have had to renounce their pride and follow Him.

Was the prayer for the disciples and His followers? Some of them had fled. Judas betrayed Him; Peter denied Him. The others stood by helplessly in excruciating grief. Had they not heard Him tell them about the purpose of His death? Did they think it was the end for Him?

Jesus' prayer was for all people. We have no excuse. We know who He is and what He has done for us, and yet crucify Him anew many times each day. He prays that prayer for forgiveness anew in each situation, even when we know perfectly well what we are doing. When that tremendous truth gets hold of us, the root cause of doing the things which frustrate His purpose can be healed. The knowledge of His forgiveness before we ask frees us of the necessity of doing the very thing for which we will need forgiveness.

The Lord forgives us even when we know what we do!

April 4

Paradise Is Now!

Luke 23:39-43

And Jesus said to him, "Assuredly I say to you, today you will be with Me in Paradise" (Luke 23:43).

THE SECOND WORD FROM THE CROSS focuses on an old question, "What about deathbed conversion? If we can wait until then, why worry about our relationship with Christ now?"

The thief on the cross saw something in Jesus: the love He had for His executioners; the way He was dying! In the presence of true greatness people are always pressed to look at themselves and wonder. While the other criminal writhed and cursed, this man saw that Jesus was who He said He was. Had he had a previous encounter with Him? We do not know. What we do know is that he did not wait.

It's never too late—neither in a crisis nor at the close of our life. It is not *when* but *whether* we believe that makes all the difference: "Jesus, remember me!"

It is never earned! This conversion account shows us that Dysmus did nothing to deserve or qualify for salvation. Those of us who still cherish the belief that our lives can be good enough to earn God's sanction and salvation need to ponder this event. "The just shall live by faith *alone!*"

It's now! If a person can know God's love at the midnight hour, and if this is the wondrous experience for which we were born, why wait? Why do we put off beginning life as it was meant to be? The other thief had said "No" for so long that he now could not say "Yes."

Paradise is for now! Heaven can begin and physical death can have no power over its reality in relationship to the Living Christ. "Whether we live or die, we are the Lord's."

Is it ever too late to believe and trust in any situation or in life as a whole?

April 5

A Gift to Each Other

John 19:25-27

He said to His mother, "Woman, behold your son!" Then He said to the disciple, "Behold your mother!" (John 19:26-27).

WHEN JESUS LOOKED DOWN FROM the cross, He saw not only the ignorant indifference of His executioners, but the anguish of His followers. The third word from the cross was a request and a promise for which He was dying.

He saw His mother, Mary, and His cherished friend and follower, John. In a gesture of sublime love, He gave them to each other for mutual love and care. The sacrificial death He was dying was to break down the dividing walls between people so that the deep relationship of Christian fellowship could be possible. To Mary He gave His friend, John, and to John He gave His mother. They were to be bound together in the divine bonds of love which would be the essence of the church. They were to care for each other as He had cared for each of them. Eventually they would find Him only in the deep relationship which a sacrificial love expressed for each other. He had to leave them so that they could go on to experience this further stage in the birth of the new creation, in them, and in the church.

Note the differences in age, sex, personality, traits, and focus of interest. They were now superseded in a new quality of relationship. The things which naturally divide people—even culture, education, background, interests—have little effect on Christian friendship.

Today Jesus gives us the people in our lives. Once we give them to Him in a releasing commitment, and let go of our self-willed control, He gives them back to us to be cared for and nurtured in His love. Who's at the foot of the cross with you? They are a gift. If you want to know Christ, you will find Him by serving them in His name.

Christ has given us as a gift to one another to express the love and forgiveness of the cross in our relationships. Today I will "behold" each person in my life as a trust from the crucified Lord.

April 6

The Depth of Love

Matthew 27:45-56

And about the ninth hour Jesus cried out with a loud voice, saying, "Eli, Eli, lama sabachthani?" that is, "My God, My God, why have You forsaken Me?" (Matthew 27:46).

C.S. LEWIS POSES A PERPLEXING dilemma in his book *The World's Last Night:* "Does God forsake just those who serve Him best? When God becomes a Man, of all others, He is least comforted by God, at His greatest need. There is a mystery here, which even if I had the power, I might not have the courage to explore."

But today as we consider this fourth word from the cross we must have the courage to pray that God will give the power to comprehend its meaning.

The word suggests the powerful truth that Jesus really suffered. This was not a sham on the cross. Jesus died there for the sins of the world as Son of Man for mankind. The mystery of the Incarnation can never be oversimplified by rejecting either Christ's divinity or His humanity. This word from the cross stresses that, though divine, He plunged into the depths of human suffering. Like all of us, He knew a time when He too cried out for assurance in the midst of suffering.

At that moment Jesus was praying Psalm 22. He was reliving the feelings of anguish of the Psalmist, and He identified with the pain. But did He not also go on to finish the triumphant note of that psalm? We are sure He did. The subsequent words from the cross indicate that.

What does all this mean to us today? Just this: Jesus knows what we go through in times of despair and loneliness. We can pray to Him knowing that He will empathize and lead us out of the valley to triumph.

Jesus Christ has gone through the valley of death so that He can comfort us in our times of deepest need.

April 7

To Quench Our Deepest Thirst

John 19:28

After this, Jesus, knowing that all things were now accomplished, that the Scripture might be fulfilled, said "I thirst!" (John 19:28).

THIS IS A HUMAN, PHYSICAL CRY. Was Jesus still repeating Psalm 22? Did this bring to mind His own burning thirst? "My tongue cleaves to My jaws." We are not sure. What we do know is that Jesus experienced the spiritual suffering of loneliness on the cross, which we considered yesterday, and we also know that He knew deep physical pain and anguish. His thirst is indicative that the horrid stretching of the tissues of His body under the heat of the merciless Middle East sun was having its full effect. His cry of thirst was a cry for some physical relief in the midst of the suffering. The gnostic generalization that Jesus did not really suffer is exposed for the lie it has always been.

Jesus thirsted physically, not only to share our lot, but so that we might thirst much more profoundly. He had said that true joy would be found only by those who thirsted, expressed a dominant desire, for righteousness. Jesus alone can satisfy the spiritual thirst within us. Only fellowship with Him can quench our deep, inner needs for security, love, and purpose. On the cross Jesus thirsted for our thirst, yearned for our yearnings, and wanted us to want Him more than anything else. As Bernard of Clairvaux wrote:

> Jesus, Thou Joy of loving hearts,
> Thou Fount of Life, Thou Light of men,
> From the best bliss that earth imparts
> We turn unfilled to Thee again.

Jesus thirsted so we may have our spiritual thirst quenched.

April 8

The Finish of the Beginning

John 19:30; 17:4-13; 6:38

So when Jesus had received the sour wine, He said, "It is finished!" And He bowed His head and gave up His spirit (John 19:30).

WHAT IS FINISHED? Jesus did not say "I am finished" but "It is finished." The work He had come to do was now complete, climaxed in the cross. He had come to reveal God's love, to communicate grace, to usher in the reality of the Kingdom, and to set people free from the power of sin and death. His work was done, and yet it had only begun.

Think for a moment what the finished work of Christ would have been without the Resurrection. We would have remembered Him as a great, sacrificial leader, but would His message and acts have lived on? No, we are sure they would have been neatly folded into the pages of history and forgotten.

God had the final word. He took the finished work of Christ and made it the basis of man's salvation forever. When His incarnate work was done, His eternal work continued. The Resurrection was the next episode in the drama of revelation of His purpose and plan.

Christ's work is not finished. It is for you and me today. We are to experience a death of self and a resurrection to a new quality of life today. Jesus Christ is alive, continuing what He began so long ago.

When we finish to the best of our capacities what God has given us to do, the resurrection of our frail efforts is close at hand. He will take our human fumblings and use them for His glory, making something glorious out of what we toiled to make great.

When we are finished, Christ has just begun.

April 9

Unreserved Trust

Luke 23:46; Psalm 31:5; 1 John 3:16; 1 Thessalonians 5:10

And when Jesus had cried out with a loud voice,
He said, "Father, into Your hands I commend My spirit" (Luke 23:46).

THE FINAL WORD FROM the cross is a quotation from Psalm 31:5. It was as familiar to every Hebrew child in Jesus' time as the child's prayer "Now I lay me down to sleep" is in our time. At the final moment, Jesus remembers and prays this prayer of deep trust and relinquishment. His great oblation for the sin of the world was completed in unreserved trust.

However old we grow or wise we become, the heart of the dynamic life is in this prayer. Jesus' life had exemplified it at every turn. His times away for prayer and strength, His trust in God for each moment's decision, and His relinquishment in the Garden of Gethsemane were all projections of the basic essence of this prayer. As He lived, so now He died. Jesus was not afraid; with childlike trust He affirmed the embrace of the everlasting arms.

This final prayer could mean the difference between frustration and victorious living for us today. If we could pray it without reservation, it would take the strain out of the duties, tasks, relationships, and worries we must go through today. God is in control. He is working His purposes out. An excellent barometer of when self-effort has distorted our trust is when we are not able to rest in the midst of tensions. God is able to do impossible things through us if we come back to the orienting center of our power in Him. Do you believe that for today?

Jesus' final prayer gives us an alternative to exhaustion.

April 10

Putting Our Life on the Line

Mark 15:42-47

Joseph of Arimathea, a prominent council member, who himself was waiting for the kingdom of God, coming and taking courage, went in to Pilate and asked for the body of Jesus (Mark 15:43).

WE ADMIRE JOSEPH OF ARIMATHEA'S courage. Where were the disciples? If they loved Jesus deeply, why did they scatter with frightened frenzy? Why didn't they come forward and perform this last act of honor of burying Jesus? They were afraid for their lives! They were not yet transformed into courageous men.

Joseph came forward with costly courage and asked for the body of Jesus. His request of Pilate clearly identified him as a follower and supporter of Rome's executed criminal.

This man of position and power knew how to use influence for the glory of God. Pilate could not take lightly this respected member of the council of Jewish leaders. He had to listen and comply with his request. The lovely thing that Joseph did will be remembered forever, and his name will be spoken with respect because of his love for Jesus.

Joseph challenges us to question how we use for the glory of God the positive influence we have within our circle of friends and the respect and honor that we have developed through the years. These put us in those crucial places where we can influence others for Christ. The world listens and cannot deny our authentic witness.

Joseph is conspicuous on the pages of history for the way in which he used his position. How about you? What influence do you have? How have you used it?

Positions of influence have been entrusted to us to be used for the glory of God in the difficult times of decision.

April 11

A Realistic Easter

1 Corinthians 15:1-19

And if Christ is not risen, your faith is futile; you are still in your sins! Then also those who have fallen asleep in Christ have perished. If in this life only we have hope in Christ, we are of all men the most pitiable (1 Corinthians 15:17-19).

LAST YEAR I TALKED TO two people, one on the day before Easter and the other a few days after. Their comments have lingered on my mind. On Saturday the man said, "I hope you give your people an honest Easter." "A what?!" I responded. "One that doesn't promise more than they can expect in their frustration... When I go to Easter services and hear about the power of the Resurrection, I think we hold out false hopes for people's needs. Just because Jesus was raised from the dead doesn't mean that life is going to be a bed of roses for us."

A woman's comment after Easter impacted the man's caution. She said, "It's been difficult coming down after Easter to the realities of life's frustrations. The promises of Easter were like a dream, a spiritual high, but they are hard to live in a real world!" I was struck by the contrast between the Easter hope and our helplessness. What do you expect?

We all have wants and needs. Easter meets our needs so that we can deal with our wants. Without the Resurrection, faith would be empty, for Christ would have been defeated! The cross would not be our assurance of forgiveness, and our hope of eternal life would be lost. Every need we have is met because Christ rose. A realistic Easter is one in which we not only remember Jesus' resurrection, but one in which we realize our own. Christ lived and died to redeem us. He rose from the dead in defeat of death and to offer us a deathless life. A personal relationship with Him offers us a profound regeneration so that we can live a new life now as well as forever.

A realistic Easter is realizing that the same power which raised Jesus is for our problems.

April 12

Death with Dignity

1 Corinthians 15:21-49

The last enemy that will be destroyed is death (1 Corinthians 15:26).

THE PHRASE "DEATH WITH DIGNITY" is used a lot these days concerning the right which people have to die without prolonged support systems to keep them physically alive long after they lose consciousness and all hope of recovery. The phrase has broader and deeper implications for a Christian. On the cross, Jesus defeated the power of death to separate us from God. Fear of death is past.

Why then is death feared so much by Christians? Death is a transition in eternal life, not a tragedy of termination. How can we look at death as unanswered prayer? When we pray for a person's healing, and he or she dies, we feel that the worst has happened and that God did not hear our prayers.

We can't really live until we have faced our own death. Once that is behind us, we can live triumphantly. To die is gain, because we shall know the wonder of heaven, complete union with our Lord, and the fellowship of the saints. When we have come to grips with our death, then we can say, "Lord, I want to live however long You've planned, and when death comes, I'll not fear it any more than I fear going to sleep. And when I awake! Oh, that will be heaven!"

The resurrection that awaits us beyond physical death will be but the glorious consummation of the risen life which we already have in Christ.

—D.T. Niles

April 13

Our Worst Fear Defeated

1 Corinthians 15:50-58

The sting of death is sin, and the strength of sin is the law. But thanks be to God, who gives us the victory through our Lord Jesus Christ (1 Corinthians 15:56-57).

THE WORDS PRINTED BOLDLY ON a billboard advertising a new movie invaded the privacy of the inner soul of any person whose attention they caught. The words tore the carefully woven fabric of repression separating conscious fears from deeper anxiety. Ingeniously, they cut into a level of self-awareness that most people struggle to avoid. The words were: "Imagine your worst fear a reality."

Into each of our minds marches a fiendish procession of fears. What is it for you—sickness, failure, loneliness, a loss of love or a loved one? Whatever comes to mind, it is a manifestation of a deeper fear, the one great fear—the fear of death and dying. And yet, we can't really live until we face our own death. Mark Twain said, "Don't take life so seriously; you'll never make it out alive." Poor advice. We will make it out alive. We will all live beyond death. The concern is where we will spend eternity.

Paul gives us the basis of the conquest of the fear of death. Our death as Christians is the beginning of the next phase of our eternal life begun there through a personal relationship with Jesus Christ. Multiply the joy of knowing Christ now a billion times, and we have some idea of what is ahead for us. The sting of death has been removed. We are alive forever!

Death is not a final crescendo. It is the last note of the overture to the opera of life to be played out in heaven.

April 14

A Transition in Living

Philippians 1:19-26

For to me, to live is Christ, and to die is gain (Philippians 1:21).

MOST OF US COULD SAY with Paul, "For me to live is Christ," but many of us would find it difficult to say, "To die is gain." The words stick like a bone in our throats. This part of eternity, our life here, has become so important to us that we can't imagine dying being a gain. That's because we clutch living here so tightly and because we don't understand what is promised us in eternity.

I have discovered that people who live the abundant life fully now are those who are sure of heaven. When our destination is set, we are free from worry over the little disturbances of life now. Daily pressures and the frustration over things in this portion of eternal life fade into proper perspective when we know that we are on our way to heaven. God is more concerned about quality than quantity. It is not the length of our days but the depth of our lives that counts. The grave has no power over a Christian!

When an aircraft breaks the sound barrier, it soars with freedom. A Christian must break the death barrier while living, so that he or she can live without the haunting uncertainty and fear of dying. Christ can "keep" a person from falling when that person knows that he or she is "kept" for heaven. Do you have that assurance?

We are told that fear of death is at the root of all our anxieties. Confront that. Tell the Lord that you trust Him and that your walk through the "valley of the shadow of death," whenever it comes, will be a walk with Him, your hand in His, on to the next phase of sublime life with Him. Death is graduation.

When we look forward to heaven,
life now becomes a heaven.

April 15

Between the Lightning and the Thunder

Mark 16:9-13

And they went and told it to the rest;
they did not believe them either (Mark 16:13).

WHAT A DIFFERENT MOOD pervaded the Upper Room! Four nights earlier the disciples had gathered for the Passover Feast with Jesus. The mood then had been one of closeness and love. Even the tragic news which Jesus disclosed that the time of His suffering was at hand drew them closer to one another in dependence and mutual support. As long as He was with them they could take anything. They did not fully understand; their minds were blocked to the terrible truth that their Master would suffer and die. How close they felt to Him that night!

Now they were back in the Upper Room again. But this time they had to face the cruel realities without Him. They had been through the tragedy of the crucifixion, when life had fallen apart for them. They had watched Love Incarnate writhe through the excruciating hours of the cross. Their hearts were ripped open in anguish and pity. Then followed the loneliness of that dark Saturday while Jesus was in the tomb. Easter morning had brought the triumphant good news of the Resurrection. But their emotions were ragged. They did not dare to believe it. Even the witness of some of their members, "We have seen the Lord!" did not heal them. They had to be sure. The reality of the Resurrection was not yet the experience of their lives.

That's how we are until the Resurrection becomes the central fact of life for us. We are afraid of life, what people do and say, and what the future will bring. We close the doors to opportunity for fear of imagined dangers. The period between the Resurrection and Pentecost is marked by fear and unbelief. That's just where many of us find ourselves. Christ is risen and He stands at the door knocking, waiting for us to invite Him into our lives. His victory can be ours!

Fear closes the doors of life. The resurrected Christ gives us the courage to open them.

April 16

Peace Be with You

Luke 24:36-39

And as they said these things, Jesus Himself stood in the midst of them, and said to them "Peace be with you" (Luke 24:36).

THE DISCIPLES HAD HEARD the greeting thousands of times before. They had used it themselves all through their lives. It was a normal, everyday greeting in Palestine. But on that Easter night it was as if they had never heard it before. Now it was like a trumpet blast of hope and victory because of who said it and what it meant because of Him. Jesus entered the Upper Room and invaded the mood of gloom with the traditional, but now triumphant, "Peace be with you."

Jesus offered peace to replace their fear. He alone could bring peace to their troubled hearts. It is interesting to note that these first words spoken to His assembled disciples summarized what He had lived and died to make possible—peace. The peace that Jesus offered was the fulfillment of the longing for peace that Israel had endured for generations. But the peace of the cross was much more profound. Jesus had come to bring the peace of forgiveness: "God was in Christ reconciling the world."

The rebellion and self-centeredness and pride which robs people of peace of mind and soul had been confronted on the cross. If the disciples could catch a view of that fact, the fear which gripped their hearts would be healed. The memories of past failures and the uncertainty of the future would be exorcised by the peace of the cross!

What is the dominant attitude of our feelings—peace or fear? Has the peace of Christ, through forgiveness and love, invaded us to the point that the great fears of our life can be faced and healed? What makes us afraid? Christ stands among us right now as we read this devotional. Do you dare to believe that? Can you hear Him speaking His words of greeting to you? Listen—"Peace be with you!"

Peace is the gift of Christ.

April 17

An Open Door

2 Corinthians 2:12; Colossians 4:3;
Acts 14:21; John 20:26; Revelation 3:7-8

And after eight days His disciples were again inside,
and Thomas with them. Jesus came, the doors being shut,
and stood in the midst, and said, "Peace be with you" (John 20:26).

THE DOORS WERE STILL SHUT. Why does John keep stressing this each time he records a postresurrection encounter of Jesus with the disciples? Each time He comes to them they are behind tightly barred doors, still afraid for their safety.

Their "closed-door" policy was symbolic of the condition of their lives. They were not yet open to the challenges Christ had given them and the power He would provide to help them respond courageously to the opportunity to join Him in changing the world. The One who said "I am the door" had a good deal to do with them before they could see that His resurrection was an open door to eternal life forever and triumphant living in the present.

Paul pressed on into unevangelized regions knowing that it was God's will for all men to hear the gospel. He knew that God would open the doors of opportunities. He had the assurance of a modern man who confidently walks toward the electric door knowing that the electric eye will trigger the opening of the door. Just so, Paul knew that if he forged ahead, God would open the doors.

The Christ who holds the keys has entrusted the keys for the opening of human lives to His people. Just as Christ told Peter that the keys of the kingdom were his, so too He tells us that these keys are ours to open the doors of faith in the lives of unbelievers. The keys of listening in love, sharing with honesty, bearing burdens without reservation, communicating the gospel with clarity, and helping people begin a life of faith—all these are entrusted keys in our hands. An awesome power has been given to us!

Jesus sets before us an open door which no one can shut.

April 18

Power to Match the Potential

John 20:19-23

Then Jesus said to them again, "Peace be with you. As My Father has sent Me, I also send you" (John 20:21).

JESUS DEALS WITH DEPRESSION BY giving a Great Commission. He took the discouraged disciples from frenzied fear to fearless courage. He liberated their thoughts from the prison of their own safety to a vision of the salvation of the world. He lifted them from anxiety to adventure. That's what He does for us. When we are filled with the depression we often feel, resulting from our own judgments on ourselves and others, He comes and shows us that He has a task for us which is a part of His strategy for changing the world.

It is an awesome challenge: "As the Father sent Me, even so send I you." That means that we are to be extensions of the Incarnation, continuing the ministry He began as Jesus of Nazareth. The things He did, we are to do; the power He exposed, we are to experience; the victory He had over evil, we are to witness in our own lives.

This commission gives us a point of reference when we become uncertain about who we are or what we are to do with our lives. He comes to us and says, "Let's get on with it!"

The awesome purpose of the Great Commission was followed by the promise of an amazing power. Jesus said, "Receive the Holy Spirit." That's the answer to the riddle of our inadequacy. The Spirit is the inner driving power of love from within us. Jesus does not give us tasks to do greater than the power to do them which He provides in the Holy Spirit.

This is our source of courage. We do not need to apologize or equivocate. We have a purpose now. He sends us into our homes, places of work, the community, as His people—extensions of His love and power.

Let's get on with it!

April 19

Are You Surprisable?

John 20:19-20

Jesus came and stood in the midst, and said to them, "Peace be with you" (John 20:19).

THE OTHER DAY A LETTER ARRIVED when I needed it most to give new courage and hope. The Lord's timing was perfect for my need. I was surprised and delighted.

Surprisability! That's a great word to describe what life can be for the Christian. We are to be surprised by what God can do in the dark and discouraged times of life. How surprisable are you? Have you gotten to the place in Christian growth where the discouraging moment is seen as a prelude to the "new thing" God is about to do?

Jesus surprised the disciples in the Upper Room. Their conception of the future was locked in the tight compartments of their own preconceptions. They had figured things from a human point of view. They had not imagined that at any moment Christ would invade their gloom with hope. Then He came and the disciples were surprised. Why? He had told them He would come to them. He had promised that He would be with them to show the way. They had not really believed it to be true. The Scripture used for today captures their revived surprisability: "They were glad when they saw the Lord." Indeed! Their joy was almost beyond containing.

To see the Lord! That's our great need, isn't it? Not in visions of grandeur or magnificent manifestations to see or touch, but in the power of His Spirit. He comes to us in people who incarnate His love for us, in amazing, unanticipated circumstances, in answers to questions which haunt us, in resolutions of problems which were declared unsolvable.

He comes! And we are glad!

Lord Jesus, we are on the lookout for You today. We know that You will come in ways we least expect You, in answers we never hoped we could find, in love we do not deserve. Lord, keep us surprisable by Your innovating power. Amen.

April

20

Honest Doubt

John 11:1-16; 20:24-29

Then He said to Thomas, "Reach your finger here, and look at My hands; and reach your hand here, and put it into My side. And do not be unbelieving, but believing." And Thomas answered and said to Him, "My Lord and my God!" (John 20:27-28).

THE THOMAS IN ME REACHES OUT to the Thomas in you. In this passage we see him honestly facing the reality of what will surely happen to Jesus if He goes to Jerusalem. But Thomas was faithful. When he saw that the Master could not be dissuaded, he was ready to go and die with Him. But at the time of the Crucifixion, Thomas was not as courageous as his words had been. He fled for safety. When the news reached him that Jesus had been raised from the dead, the discouraged man would not accept it. Christ had to come to the Upper Room just for Thomas. Then he knew it was true! Discouragement was turned to delight and determination by the power of the resurrected Lord.

There's a great spiritual secret to be learned from Thomas. He was an honest man. He could not pretend. Christ can help that kind of honesty. Whenever we tell Him about what's going on inside us, the answer is perfectly timed. He honors realism and integrity. If we confess however far we've come in our faith, and ask Him to help us grow, He will increase our faith, deepen our wisdom for our intellectual uncertainties, and give us a vision for how He is working out His plan in our lives. All our difficulties expose our need for a closer relationship with the Lord. Whatever it will take to make us sure of Him and His resurrection power, He will provide. He wants us off the dead-center of discouragement and on the move again!

Discouragement is a warning signal that we need a renewed relationship with the Lord. Don't wait for the discouragement to end before you go to Him; go to Him to end the discouragement.

April 21

The Thomas Test

John 20:24-29

And Thomas answered and said to Him,
"My Lord and my God!" (John 20:28).

THOMAS HAD TO SEE FOR HIMSELF. He was not willing to take anyone else's word that Jesus was alive.

That kind of doubt can be creative. All too often we have a second-hand faith based on the experiences of other people. We do not have a dynamic faith because we have never experienced the Living Lord for ourselves. We need to be able to say with the Samaritans to whom the woman by the well witnessed about Christ, "It is no longer because of your words that we believe, for we have heard for ourselves, and we know that this is indeed the Savior of the world."

The story of Thomas reveals more than the struggle of a doubter to believe. It reveals the struggle of the love of Christ to penetrate the resistance barrier of human nature. In the story we are confronted with the amazing love of Christ. It's one thing to accept and love a man on your own standards; it's something altogether different to be willing to love on His standards. Thomas set up the rules. He would believe only if he was satisfied according to his own presuppositions.

Our first reaction would have been to say, "Listen, Thomas, who do you think you are, making a demand like that?" But not Jesus. He leaves Thomas alone for eight days—days of anguished doubt and question. When He returned He loved the depressed disciple enough to offer Himself unreservedly to him so that he might believe. He was deeply concerned about Thomas. If touching His nail-wounded hands and side would help him, He was ready and willing.

Thomas was overcome! He knew how much Jesus loved him. His response was one of overwhelming love and loyalty, and he cried out, "My Lord and my God!"

What would it take to convince you completely?

Not even our doubts can make Christ stop loving us.

April 22

Is it a Sin to Doubt?

James 1:1-8

But let him ask in faith, with no doubting, for he who doubts is like a wave of the sea driven and tossed by the wind (James 1:6).

WHY IS IT SO WRONG TO DOUBT? There are two kinds of doubt—one that is a fixed position, and the other that is a creative sign of growth. An atheist says that there is no God and is closed to any possibility. A deist says that God exists but has no contact with the world He has created. An agnostic says that he simply does not know. In all three there is a solidified stance. That's the kind of person James is talking about. They have refused the gift of faith. His apt description fits millions of people today. God wants to give us the gift of faith to know Him and the gift of wisdom to understand His ways. As we grow in both gifts, there will be constant questions. We can accept those doubts as growing pains and ask God for His wisdom to move beyond our present stage of intellectual growth. He is faithful to answer!

Is it a sin to doubt? Yes, if it is our way of holding God at bay—if we demand that He fit into our presuppositions and our limited experience. Doubt is sin when we refuse to be open to new discoveries. God wants us to be intellectual adventurers. However much we have grown, it's only a beginning. There's so much beyond our own theories and rationality. There's a wonderful line in Christopher Fry's "The First Born." Moses says to Pharaoh, "A man must be more than a Pharaoh; he must dare to outgrow the security of partial blindness." Doubt is partial blindness. But Christ can and will heal the eyes of our minds. The battle with doubt must be waged in a relationship with the Lord. Give Him as much as you know of yourself, and He will become a partner, not an enemy.

When I am sure of Christ, I have power to battle doubt.

April

23

When Doubt Turns to Negativism

Matthew 13:53-58

And they were offended at Him. But Jesus said to them, "A prophet is not without honor except in his own country and in his own house" (Matthew 13:57).

"WHAT YOU ARE SAYING IS THAT there is one person whom God cannot change!" I said to a woman about her estranged husband.

"No, I believe God can change him, but I doubt whether he will let Him," said the woman in her own defense.

"Isn't that doubt about God? Do you really believe that your husband can resist God's love and forgiveness forever? Is your God that limited?" I asked.

This woman had given up. She had given in to despair and was not able to believe that God would find a way to communicate with her husband. She resisted the idea that this was doubting God.

Often our doubts about God's sovereign power are manifested in a despair about people and the human condition. We get listless in our capacity to hope because we wonder about whether God can or will do anything to intervene. We would reject the idea that there is anything lacking in our relationship to God; it's *people* who are wrong.

Doubt can be lack of trust. It can be a protective mechanism to cover our lack of faith. It results in a negativism about ourselves and other people. Often we feel sorry for ourselves and blame God for what has happened to us. Actually, our lives are the result of the values and ideas we have held about life. People have lived up to our worst picture of them. We doubt whether they will ever be different. Actually we are doubting that God will make them different. This destructive doubt debilitates our ability to trust the people and situations of our life to Him, to expect and receive what He is able to do in His timing and according to His plan. Our doubts become a contagious virus of frustration to the people around us. The Lord can and will change that today if we are willing to let Him.

Debilitating doubt results in negativism.

April 24

The Soul's Invincible Surmise

Ephesians 4:17-24

Put on the new man, which was created according to God, in righteousness and true holiness (Ephesians 4:24).

DOES EVERYONE, EVEN a mature Christian, have some doubts? Of course. If we think of doubts as the condition of a mind on the edge of discovery, then who hasn't some doubt? The key word which described the response of the disciples and the crowds to Jesus was astonishment. It means to be driven outside oneself. A mature Christian is constantly astonished by how great the Lord is and how shallow his own understanding and experience.

Our perspective is crucial. If we but dare to believe that the indwelling Christ is pressing us on to new discoveries, then we can befriend that attitude of doubt. We can say, "I am truly alive and on the move!" The test of a mature Christian is that he can look back and see how effectively Christ has moved him from uncertainty to growing assurance and conviction.

Goethe said, "Give me the benefit of your convictions, if you have any, but keep your doubts to yourself, for I have enough of my own." He was right. The world around us does not need us to preach our doubts. Everyone has enough of his own. An honest admission of our intellectual growth on the edge of new discoveries is one thing, but dragging people down to our level of uncertainty is quite another. God says something very different from Goethe: "Give Me your doubts. Be honest to admit them, and I will help you demit from them as a false security." The Christian will always have wonder. Wonder is awe in the face of mystery which we cannot totally explain.

To trust the soul's invincible surmise
was all his science and his only art.
—George Santayana

Welcome To
BACK YARD BURGERS
436 Perkins Extended
Memphis, TN 38117
(901) 763-1833

9

Host:	03/11/2011
9	12:06 PM
	10032
Order Type: Dine In	
1/3 LB Burger	3.79
White Bun	
Snr. Drink	0.00
Subtotal	3.79
Tax	0.35
Dine In Total	**4.14**
Visa #XXXXXXXXXXXX6119	4.14
Auth:111164	

Join our eClub and receive a
Free 1/3lb Back Yard Burger.
Sign up at www.backyardburgers.com

--- Check Closed ---

Welcome To
BACK YARD BURGERS
436 Perkins Extended
Memphis, TN 38117
(901) 763-1833

9

Host: 03/11/2011
12:06 PM
9
10032

Order Type: Dine In

1/3 LB Burger	3.79
White Bun	
Sml. Drink	0.00
Subtotal	3.79
Tax	0.35
Dine In Total	**4.14**
Visa #XXXXXXXXXXXX6119	4.14
Auth:111164	

Join our eClub and receive a
Free 1/3lb Back Yard Burger.
Sign up at www.backyardburgers.com

--- Check Closed ---

How to Handle Failure

Mark 14:66-72

And a second time the rooster crowed. And Peter called to mind the word that Jesus said to him, "Before the rooster crows twice, you will deny Me three times." And when he thought about it, he wept (Mark 14:72).

IT IS INTERESTING TO NOTE the different ways in which Judas and Peter dealt with failure. They both denied their Lord and betrayed Him before others. Judas sold Him to the priests; Peter refused to acknowledge that he knew Him when asked in the courtyard while Jesus was being tried. Defection was in both of them.

But how differently they dealt with it! Judas could not handle his failure and hung himself; Peter broke down and wept. Judas took his punishment into his own hands; Peter eventually trusted Christ to forgive. One man ended his life, the other came to the end of an old life and began anew. Peter was indeed the rock, but a rock that cracked. Later, as we will see in tomorrow's meditation, Christ got to the bottom of Peter. He reinstated the disciple with a new commission. As a broken man, Peter received grace.

How do you deal with failure? Self-condemnation? Many people hang themselves inch by inch with self-remorse which grows into self-hatred. "Why did I do that!" "How could I have ever said that!" We judge ourselves as ineffective and useless. Others, however, are finding what Peter found. Our failures are only a prelude to deeper realization of Christ's love and enabling power. Forgiveness and a new change are but a prayer away from any of us! Christ is listening right now. What do you need to tell Him? How have you denied Him? Life in Christ is a succession of new beginnings. Why not start anew today?

Failure will bring us to either self-condemnation or repentance. Which one will determine our character?

April 26

Meet the Real You

John 21:1-14

This is now the third time Jesus showed Himself to His disciples after He was raised from the dead (John 21:14).

OF ALL THE POSTRESURRECTION appearances, one of the most moving is when Jesus came to His disciples early one morning when they had spent the night fishing on the Sea of Galilee. Recently I was seated on the rock just above the seashore where Jesus came in the early hours of dawn and called to His disciples who were in their fishing boats a short distance from the shore. I had read and reread John 21 to recapture the scene and to think through the implications for our contemporary experience of the Resurrection.

It is fascinating to reflect on why Jesus had instructed His disciples to go back to Galilee where He promised He would meet them. He knew they would have to experience the reality of the Resurrection in familiar surroundings to know that it was true. Just above the place where Jesus met His disciples for breakfast on the seashore is the Mount of Beatitude, where He gave the Sermon on the Mount. What Jesus taught there and lived out with His disciples during His ministry they would now be called to live in the future. They needed to be as sure of His resurrected presence as their Master.

What the risen Lord put Peter through is what we all must go through in order to be the Easter people all through the year. Peter needed forgiveness for betrayal, restitution to the reality of a loving relationship with the risen Lord, and an experience of total dependence on the power of the indwelling Spirit of Christ. For that, Christ had to reintroduce Peter to himself, his loyalty and love, and give him a reorienting commission which he could do only by the power of the resurrection.

Christ has introduced me to my real self!

April 27

A New Beginning

John 21:15-19

He said to him again a second time, "Simon, son of Jonah, do you love Me more than these?" He said to Him, "Yes, Lord, You know that I love You." He said to him, "Tend My sheep" (John 21:16).

PETER WAS AN ACTIVE, aggressive superachiever. Like most of us, he was ambitious. As the leading disciple, he had shifted the focus of his achievement-oriented nature. But he persistently denied his inner person, and eventually denied his Lord. His denial of the Lord was really a denial of the new person who was being formed in him. It was that true inward person whom Christ came back to Galilee to reclaim. He wanted the do-er to become a be-er. His problem was allowing the Lord to love him profoundly so that he could reclaim the essential fact that Christ and His love for him were most important to him.

That is why Christ asked him three times "Do you love Me?"—so that Peter could be sure. He needed to know once and for all that it was not what he did or failed to do that was important, but rather that he was loved, forgiven, and cherished. The experience of Peter's spiritual resurrection took place that morning beside the sea he loved so much. Now he knew he loved Christ most of all and was ready to enact resurrection living by feeding Christ's sheep. We will spell out further tomorrow what this means for our resurrection living.

Christ will not let us go!

April 28

Debilitating Comparisons

John 21:20-23

Peter, seeing Him, said to Jesus, "Lord, and what will this man do?" (John 21:21).

WE BLUSH WITH EMBARRASSMENT over Peter's response. The Lord has just given him an awesome challenge and commission. Instead of responding with gratitude, he wants to know what John was going to do. An old sibling rivalry is showing. The competition and jealousy of the years is creeping up again. Jesus' retort is sharp: "What is that to you? You follow Me!"

But how like most of us Peter was. He wanted to evaluate John's assignment before he accepted his own. Would John be given a higher position, a better title, greater opportunities? How often we miss the sublime, unique calling that Christ gives to each of us by comparisons with others. How often the cultural standards of value in positions, power, salaries, size of office or home, and material possessions beguile us, and we are blinded, unable to see what has been entrusted to us.

Comparisons lead us to competition; competition leads to consternation. We muddle and then meddle with others and their lives. And the Master says, "Claim what I've given to you; assume the calling I've given you, and get moving. Never mind what I'm giving to or doing with others. You follow Me!"

Each of us was called into discipleship for a task and opportunity which is uniquely given to us by our Lord. The question is not how our assignment compares with what is given to anyone else to do. We are to discover and do what the Lord guides. That will keep us so busy that there will be little time for evaluating how other people are following the Lord. Jealousy will be replaced by a joy in how the Lord is working in us and others.

Envy is uneasiness of the mind, caused by consideration of a good we desire, obtained by one we think should not have it before us.

—John Locke

April 29

The Fellowship of the Flaming Heart

Luke 24:13-35

Did not our heart burn within us while He talked with us on the road, and while He opened the Scriptures to us? (Luke 24:32).

THE CROSS IS THE EXPOSURE of the caring heart of God. It was an on-time, in-time, for-all-time revelation of what was and is now in His heart. Right at this moment, the same love exposed on Calvary is available to you and me. When we dare to care for others, a little Calvary is enacted. We die to ourselves and open ourselves to receive the enabling love which throbbed through the cross. We cannot know the depth of that love until we care about people and their needs. When we become involved in costly caring, the love of the cross flames through our words, actions, and concern. We become a part of the fellowship of the flaming heart—of God!

When Jesus came to the men on the road to Emmaus, He taught them from the Scriptures who He was. We can imagine how exciting it must have been to be led in a Bible study by the Lord Himself! He showed the discouraged disciples that He was the sacrificial lamb, the scapegoat, the atonement for sins. Then He guided them through the prophets, underlining for emphasis all the references to Him. It was then that the cross and Christ's resurrection became real. Later, when He broke bread in their home, they knew that it was the Lord. He had set a fire burning in their hearts, God's fire revealed on Calvary.

There is a cross in the heart of God in every moment of time.

April 30

In the Palm of His Power

Revelation 2:1

To the angel of the church of Ephesus write, "These things says He who holds the seven stars in His right hand, who walks in the midst of the seven golden lampstands" (Revelation 2:1).

WE NOW TURN OUR ATTENTION to the messages of the resurrected Christ to the seven churches in Revelation. There is a familiar spiritual of faith and trust which has the refrain, "He's got the whole world in His hand." The spiritual goes on enumerating the situations and people that Christ has in His hand.

This is the picture of the Living Christ which John presents in our Scripture. The seven candlesticks represent the seven churches to which the letters of Revelation are being sent. The Greek verb "to hold" is *kratein,* which is usually followed by a genitive of what is held. It normally means that we take hold of a part of an object. When, however, the verb takes an accusative, it means to hold the whole of an object within one's hand. This is what is meant here. It means that Jesus holds the whole of the church within His hand. He grasps all of the churches within His loving care.

The imagery is extended further when it says that Jesus walks in the midst of the seven candlesticks. He is in the midst of the troubled churches feeling the frustrations and persecutions of Rome. He has been faithful to His promise, "Lo, I am with you always."

These are the simple but powerful images of assurance for us today: Christ will not let us go; He is with us; He holds the situations and problems of today in the palm of His concern. He will give us the power and insight we need for today. If we ask Him, He will give us His *perspective* on our needs and His *partnership* in facing and conquering our problems, however impossible they appear.

Jesus Christ is with us and He will not let us go.

May 1

Christ Sees Beneath the Surface

Revelation 2:2

I know your works, your labor, your patience, and how you cannot bear those who are evil. And you have tested those who say they are apostles and are not, and have found them liars (Revelation 2:2).

JESUS CHRIST KNOWS! That is both a comfort and a challenge. We are comforted that He knows everything beneath the highly polished surface of our lives which we show to others. He understands the true motives and purposes which guide our lives. He sympathizes with the limiting difficulties within us which hinder and debilitate. He knows what we have been through. What others cannot appreciate, He knows and appreciates. This is a comfort when we are misunderstood or unappreciated by those around us.

But this is also a challenge. There is no place to hide! Jesus' X-ray vision of us penetrates and sees beneath our external front. We can fool others, but not Jesus. He knows our works, just as He knew the true work of the Ephesians. He sees not only the positive acts of obedience to Him, but also the inner rebellion and resistance to His will and way for us.

Jesus could see the patient endurance of the Ephesians, their faithful exposure of heresies, and their unwearying work for the cause of right. But He could also see that they had lost the joy of their relationship with Him and were trying to live by their own resources.

We cannot pretend with Jesus, so why try? Let's begin anew with Him today and allow Him to change our inner motives and values, which will produce a fresh and vital exterior for others to see.

Jesus Christ sees beneath the surface of our lives and knows what we are really like.

May 2

The Need to Fall in Love Again

Revelation 2:4-5

Nevertheless I have this against you, that you have left your first love (Revelation 2:4).

DO YOU REMEMBER YOUR first love? Do you remember the joy, the excitement, the thrill, the fulfillment, the sheer fun of being in love? The whole world was alive in a beautiful springtime of new discovery and delight. You had found someone who loved you and whom you loved. Everything was different in the light of that triumphant fact. Emotions ran high, each day was welcomed as an opportunity for further contacts with the one you loved, and all other aspects of life took on a new meaning.

Jesus uses a very common human experience to help the Ephesians remember what it was like when they first knew of His love for them. When they learned of the love and forgiveness, the plan and purpose, the power and strength, the hope and the victory of Jesus Christ, they had come alive with a new joy and excitement.

But something had happened. They had become dutiful and drab as the years had gone by. They had lost the wonder of knowing and loving Jesus. Now they were so busy living out the Christian life that they had lost that personal relationship with Him which makes the life of a Christian warm and exciting. Like so many couples in marriage who take each other for granted, they had taken Christ for granted and had failed to have time with Him; they had worked *for* Him and not *with* Him, and now they were anxious and strained. Jesus asks them to remember and rediscover the joy of when He first loved them and they first responded.

Recently a man in the Middle West told me, "I have lost the adventure and excitement of my relationship with Christ. I guess I want to fall in love again!" We all need that often. Every day. Today!

A new beginning with Christ is even better than our first experience of His love.

May 3

Turn Around!

Revelation 2:5-6

Remember therefore from what you have fallen; repent and do the first works, or else I will come to you quickly and remove your lampstand from its place—unless you repent (Revelation 2:5).

THE CHRISTIAN LIFE IS dynamic, not static. Unless we continue to grow in Christ, we will stagnate in immature piety. The fact of life is undeniable: love must not be cherished as an end in itself; it is the power to drive the machinery of life. The fact that we are Christians means little unless we become Christian in all dimensions of life. The painful truth of our Scripture today is that the privilege can be taken from us if we do not use it for God's glory, concern for people, and service in society. When our Christianity becomes dull and drab—the exercise of a few religious rites or the rehearsal of a few cherished pet ideas—it will putrefy and die.

What can we do? Jesus prescribes repentance. This word conjures up many false images of tears and emotional remorse. For the prophets and for Jesus, it meant turning around and beginning again in a new direction. If the drift of our life has been increasingly away from Him and costly obedience to Him, then today is the day to turn around, and we will find Him there waiting with forgiveness and a new chance. He will refresh us with His love and send us on a new life of faithfulness to Him where we live and work. William Barclay put it this way: "The sorrow of the repentance is not an emotion in which we luxuriate, but an antiseptic which cleanses our lives."

Remember today what it was like when you first knew that Christ loved you and had a plan and purpose for your life! Then turn around and go back to Him. He is waiting with outstretched arms.

May 4

Fruit from the Tree of Life

Genesis 2:16-17; Revelation 2:7; Romans 8:18-24

He who has an ear, let him hear what the Spirit says to the churches. To him who overcomes I will give to eat of the tree of life, which is in the midst of the Paradise of God (Revelation 2:7).

OUR TWO SCRIPTURES PRESENT two different trees of life. One is forbidden, and the other is freely offered to those who endure faithfully. In Genesis we learn of the tree of the knowledge of good and evil. God warned that man should trust in Him for his knowledge. Man wanted to know for himself, without the need for dependence on God. He wanted to be like God, not trust in God. We all know the terrible results. Man ate of the fruit and has not been able to handle the responsibility ever since. The tree of life offered to the Ephesians in our Scripture is quite different. The rabbis taught that in Paradise there would be a tree of life in the middle of heaven. It was a tree which symbolized immortality and all the fruit of eternal life with God. Unencumbered by the limitation of physical life, the joys and delights of fellowship with God would be given without limit.

Jesus tells the Ephesians that this will be their reward if they endure and conquer. All the trial and tragedy of their present life would be rewarded if they remained faithful. This promise is for us too. We are alive in eternity now. Death is not an ending, but a triumphant transition. If we know, love, and serve the Lord now, we will be given a taste of heaven now in friendship and fellowship with the Lord today and forever. Whatever trials we have faced, whatever difficulties we are going through, they are "not worthy to be compared with the glory which shall be revealed to us."

Christ is with me in any trial that may come today.

May 5

All or Not at All

Revelation 2:8-9

And to the angel of the church in Smyrna write, "These things says the First and the Last, who was dead, and came to life" (Revelation 2:8-9).

SMYRNA WAS A CITY of syncretism. Here in this beautiful city of Roman glory a person could exist with whatever private belief he wished, if only he would acknowledge that "Caesar is Lord." All the Christians had to do was to burn a pinch of incense, say "Caesar is Lord," receive their certificate, and go off to worship as they pleased. This was the old problem of syncretism—worshiping more than one God in comfortable coexistence—which the people of God have always faced.

It was no different centuries before, when expedient Jews worshiped Yahweh and Baal at the same time to keep peace and be sure of the best of two worlds. In Smyrna there seemed to be no alternative. In A.D. 26 the Romans erected a temple to Tiberius, but the Christians would not conform. They refused to worship Caesar as lord. Jesus Christ alone was their Lord! They would not give lip service to Caesar, or go through Caesar worship, just to be safe from persecution. And so history records some of the most terrible persecution of the early church at Smyrna. Nowhere was it more dangerous to be a Christian.

How easy it is for us to worship more than one lord! The diminutive gods of materialism, professionalism, popularity, safety, another person, our heritage, or our potential future are some of the gods we call "Lord." The Lord is the One on whom we depend, the One from whom we receive life's purpose and power, the One who is given our ultimate allegiance. Who—or what—is a competing lord of your life? Anyone who says, "Jesus Christ is Lord" must eventually allow Him to be Lord of *all* life.

Christ is all or not at all!

May 6

Beyond the Breaking Point

Revelation 2:9; John 16:33

I know your works, tribulation, and poverty (but you are rich); and I know the blasphemy of those who say they are Jews and are not, but are a synagogue of Satan (Revelation 2:9).

"IN THE WORLD YOU SHALL HAVE tribulation." Jesus never fools us about that. He has told us plainly. The Greek word for "tribulation" is "pressure." We all know pressure. We know the pressure of too much to do and too little time to do it, the pressure to conform to ways of life which are abhorrent to us, the pressure to fulfill other people's images of us, the pressure to give in to life's annoyances, and the pressure to compromise our trust in Christ.

H.G. Wells wrote in his autobiography, "Most individual creatures, since life began, have been up against it... They have had to respond to unresting antagonism of their circumstances." We know what he means. The pressures of material circumstances, opposition, antagonism, and persecution are known by anyone who dares to be sensitive and to stand for anything worthwhile. But sometimes it is too great for us, and we collapse. Life is too much and we cannot stand the strain. But we were never meant to take the pressure alone. When we are under His equalizing pressure of love we can take the pressure of the world.

Note the parenthesis of power in today's Scripture. Jesus tells the troubled, persecuted Christians that He knows their tribulation and poverty. Then in the parentheses are the words which make all the difference. They were indeed rich! They were rich beyond human standards and values. Their riches were in Him, in His love and power, and in their calling, election, and status with God as His beloved people. And so are we!

When Christ lives in us we need not break in anger, hostility, weakness, or health. But remember, the victory will be His own victory in us.

In Christ we can pass the breaking point and not break.

May 7

Praise and Not Presumption

Revelation 2:10

Be faithful until death, and I will give you the crown of life (Revelation 2:10).

THE LIFE, MESSAGE, AND MARTYRDOM of Polycarp, the bishop of Smyrna, helps us to focus the meaning of Jesus' message to the church there. He would not join the Caesar worship, and he instructed the Christians to be faithful to Jesus Christ as Lord. Finally his witness cost him his life. On an excited, festal day the frenzied mobs were in an inflammable state. They gave Polycarp a choice: worship Caesar as a god or die.

Polycarp's answer has become immortal: "Eighty-six years have I served Christ, and He has never done me wrong. How can I blaspheme my King who saved me?" The people were enraged and gathered the fagots for the fire to burn him at the stake. As the flames devoured his body, he prayed a great prayer: "I thank Thee that Thou hast graciously thought me worthy of this day and of this hour, that I may receive a portion in the number of the martyrs, in the cup of Thy Christ." And so Polycarp died. In the light of this, we can understand Revelation's Scripture. Jesus praised the faithfulness of His people at Smyrna.

We are the recipients of a great heritage. The faith we often take for granted has been defended at great cost. We are fortunate to have freedom of worship in which we can openly follow Christ. But we dare not take it for granted. It should spur us on to faithfulness and obedience to Christ today. There are forces which are seeking to negate our freedom and the greatness of America as a nation under God. We should battle that trend with the passion of a Polycarp! Praise is the antidote to presumption.

Jesus Christ is Lord! This is the basic Christian creed. What does it mean to you?

May 8

The Alpha and Omega

Revelation 1:9-20

I am the Alpha and the Omega, the First and the last (Revelation 1:11).

IN THE CONTEXT OF WHAT we have learned about the difficulties of being a Christian at Smyrna, we can see why Jesus used the self-description He did when addressing that church. The words "the first and the last, who died and came to life" could give them courage for the life they faced.

Only One who was Lord of history could help the Christians at Smyrna. The One who was the source and end of all could give perspective to their troubled lives. Jesus was not just a historical figure who had revealed God and given a way of life; Jesus was God in human history. His message and life was not just a thing to be accepted, but a living power for conflict. The One through whom all things were created, the One who was the Word of God, the sustainer and source of life, would sustain them. In Him God had incarnated Himself, and in Him God had approached and saved His people. Jesus was not just a thought about God; He was God in fellowship with man.

The most triumphant, fear-dispelling fact about Him for the Christians at Smyrna was that He was the One who died and came to life. The Resurrection was not just an event in history; it was the answer to the riddle of history: "Because I live you shall live also." This gave them hope for every day, and the last day in death.

Be very clear about who Jesus Christ is for you! Is He the living, resurrected Lord? If so, He is a present Lord who offers us a new dimension of resurrected life for today as well as the hope of eternal life.

The One who created and called us,
who sustains and strengthens us, is the One
who is utterly reliable for life's problems.

May 9

Given Away to Serve

2 Timothy 1:3-7

When I call to remembrance the unfeigned faith that is in you, which dwelt first in your grandmother Lois and your mother Eunice, and I am persuaded is in you also (2 Timothy 1:5).

ABOUT THIS TIME IN MAY each year we celebrate Mother's Day. I want to pause in our consideration of the churches of Revelation to reflect on the meaning of this day. Some years ago I had an experience I will never forget. It was a gala occasion. I had just finished preaching in the church where I began my ministry. It was a time for memories and reflection.

Suddenly I was face to face with a gracious, radiant woman in her early seventies. She had tears of joy in her eyes, and somehow a handshake was not enough for us. She embraced me and drew me close. Then she kissed me and whispered in my ear, "Pay no attention to me. You belong to these people tonight." I kept an eye on her throughout the evening, catching a glimpse every so often through the crowd. She sat alone, greeted every so often by some of the people. She waited until most of the people had left. We looked long and hard at each other…and then laughed with joy. "Mother, how are you?" I said.

She had come to attend the service from a nearby community which had been my hometown, and to have a few hours together before I returned home. The memory of the visit has lingered pleasantly, but her words to me in the crowd have persisted for deep thought and reflection. She did not know all that she had said, but the true meaning of Christian motherhood was affirmed: "Pay no attention to me; tonight you belong to these people…"

In so speaking, she proclaimed the true essence of Jesus' message about the family and the special calling of mothers to prepare their children for service and then give them away to follow Him.

The freedom of true motherhood is to release children to God and service to others.

May 10

Twice Born—Never to Die

Revelation 2:11; Romans 6:1-5; Romans 8:38-39

He who overcomes shall not be hurt by the second death (Revelation 2:11).

A CHRISTIAN IS ONE WHO lives each day with the knowledge that there is nothing which can separate him from the love of God. It is fairly easy to see this in retrospect. We can look back and see God's hand at work in difficult times. We can discern that it was His providential care which brought us through perilous times. But to have this same confidence for the future is not easy.

Jesus told the Christians at Smyrna not to fear what they were to suffer. They could accept this hopeful word of confidence only if they believed that there was no pain or humiliation which could ever destroy their relationship with Him. Jesus wanted to bring them to the brink of realization that He was not an escape from trouble but a companion in the midst of it, and that He would intervene to help them.

Christians are twice-born men and women. They have had both physical and spiritual birth. Fellowship with Christ ushers us into a dimension of life which is life abundant. Nothing can destroy this spiritual vitality which lives within our frail physical bodies. Just as surely as Christ was raised from the dead, so too will we be raised up for eternal fellowship in heaven.

The term "second death" was a rabbinical Hebraism often used at that time. It meant the total extinction of the wicked. Christ turns a negative condemnation into a positive confirmation. His promise is that there is no second death for those who are twice born. We die to ourselves when we turn our lives over to Him and He comes to live in us. Only those who do not know Christ die, never to live again. For a Christian, fear of death is past.

Christians are twice-born and therefore have no fear of death.

May 11

The Four "C's" of Communicating with the Lord

Revelation 2:12-17

These things says he who has the sharp two-edged sword (Revelation 2:12).

THE LETTERS TO THE CHURCHES IN Asia Minor show us the way Christ deals with individuals and churches. There is a confirmation of an aspect of His nature which specifically meets our particular need. This is followed by commendation for our strengths and progress. This gives us an assurance of His love and affirmation of our efforts to be faithful and obedient in our discipleship. With that, we are ready to hear any creative confrontation of things in our lives which need to be changed. After that, we desperately need His comfort. He tells us what He will do to help us change what He has exposed. A decisive encounter with the Lord usually includes all four. What is He saying to you in each?

Look at how this is exemplified in the letter to the church at Pergamos. It was the capital city of the Roman province of Asia. It was the center of emperor worship in that part of the Roman Empire. There were temples to a variety of gods. But for Christ, Pergamos was the throne of Satan focused in imperial worship and Roman might. The aspect of His nature needed most by the Christians was that He had the two-edged sword. The Romans claimed the "right of the sword"; Christ claimed the ultimate sword of authority over history. Persecution of the Christians was severe, and one of their members, Antipas, had been a faithful martyr.

And yet, Christ had to condemn the fact that some in the Church had blended their belief in Him with the sins of idolatry and immorality. Christ calls us to impeccable moral integrity as an outward expression of an inner experience of His love. The comfort He offers us is a "hidden manna" which, as during the exodus of the Israelites in the wilderness, will give us daily strength from His Spirit.

*Whenever the Lord touches a raw nerve in us,
it means that He is ready to heal it.*

May 12

The Dearest Idol

1 John 5:19-21

Little children, keep yourselves from idols. Amen (1 John 5:21).

THIS FINAL SENTENCE IN John's Epistle was written to Christians. The Apostle's admonition carries the same impact as Jesus' word to Pergamos. They were tempted to worship all kinds of idols in Asia Minor of old. How about us today? What are the idols that beguile us in our society? What purpose, passion, person, position, place, or possession could have the power to demand our attention and adoration? Can we sing these words with William Cowper?

The dearest idol I have known, Whate'er that idol be,
Help me to tear it from thy throne, And worship only thee.

Our heart is a throne. Who or what reigns there? It is possible to say we believe in Christ and have something or someone on the throne of our hearts. We can even become active church members and be involved in social concerns, all while our lives remain in our control. We pray our prayers for Christ's help, but it is to get Him to help us accomplish our predetermined goals and plans. Our lives can be moral, honest, industrious, and responsible. What is lacking is commitment to Christ as absolute Lord of our lives.

The most exciting thing I see happening today among Christians is that a growing number are discovering the freedom and joy of committing the throne of their hearts to Christ. Many have been in the church for years but suddenly realize that their purpose and passion has been some idol that they have subtly syncretized with Christ. An unconditional commitment to Christ opens the floodgates for His power and love to flow into the emptiness. What about you? Can you make Andrew Reed's hymn your song for today?

Holy Spirit, all divine, Dwell within this heart of mine.
Cast down every idol throne; Reign supreme, and reign alone.

Christ is all or not at all!

May 13

Follow as They Follow Christ

Revelation 2:18-20

Nevertheless, I have a few things against you (Revelation 2:20).

IN THE LETTER TO THYATIRA the name "Jezebel" stands out. We must remember that in apocalyptic literature (like the Book of Revelation) esoteric terms and titles are used which would be understood by the readers but would be purposely oblique to the uninitiated.

The term "Jezebel" had tragic connotations for God's people. They knew that Jezebel had been the daughter of the King of Sidon and the wife of King Ahab of Israel. Her sin was that she had brought her own gods and goddesses, such as Baal and Astarte, and had introduced them to Israel's worship. Eventually she forced pagan rituals on Ahab's kingdom. Her name was synonymous with an evil which had plagued God's people through the years.

Jesus clearly identified one of the leading women in the church of Thyatira as a Jezebel. She had preached Christ but had led the church into the pagan guilds where idols were worshiped and where despicable, immoral acts were condoned and encouraged. She was a prophetess who had nearly destroyed the church.

How easily the church can drift from its sole purpose and end up resisting Christ rather than preaching Christ! When we read Christian history we can see the Jezebels of both sexes who led the church into compromise with evil. Look at the Middle Ages, or at Hitler's Germany, or at some churches in our own time that resist the dynamic of the Spirit and live on as dull, drab establishments of the status quo. Judgment begins with the household of God.

A Christian must always be free to examine the authenticity of his leaders.

May 14

Creative and Destructive Compromise

Revelation 2:25-27

But hold fast what you have till I come (Revelation 2:25).

ONE OF THE MOST PERSISTENT problems of living the Christian life is compromise. The heart of the problem is to discover the difference between creative and destructive compromise. In one sense, Christian maturity makes us free to compromise. We lose the rigid necessity of always being right and we begin to see the other person's point of view. We are able to enter into dialogue and real agreements which are acceptable to all concerned. With Christ's love in our hearts and with the law of love as the basis of our thinking, we can enter into each situation asking, "What does love demand?"

But the Christian is also freed from destructive compromise. He is able to stand firm when he is tempted to become part of a situation where people will be dehumanized or frustrated. He can seek what Christ's will is and be strong in his convictions.

The Christians at Thyatira had fallen into destructive compromise. In order to exist economically they had to become members of the trade guilds which dealt in the wool and dying industry for which Thyatira was famous. But the guilds required participation in pagan rituals and sacrifices to pagan gods. The meetings of the guilds began and ended in sacrifices, and in between they were filled with sexual immorality. Could a Christian participate? Many of them had done so, and this is the content of the challenge that Jesus addressed to them. The Christians had gone too far. Their compromise was destructive to their relationship with Christ.

Consider your opportunities today: in which does Christ call you to compromise and in which does He offer you power not to compromise?

Today Christ will show me the difference between creative and destructive compromise.

May 15

How Churches Die

Revelation 3:1

You have a name that you are alive, and yet you are dead (Revelation 3:1).

THERE ARE FEW CRITICISMS of a church which would be more cutting than to say that it had the *reputation* for being alive but is actually dead. Yet this is exactly what Christ has to say to the Sardis church. It was known for its life, but Christ said that it was dead. Though it had prosperity, it was dead in what really mattered. Materially there was life, but spiritually it was dead. What did He mean? When is a church dead?

When it worships the past. Memories are comforting and reassuring, but not always stimulating. We can look back only in thanksgiving, never in self-satisfaction. The Sardis church was resting on its reputation.

Also, a church is dead when it loves success more than Christ. The church is to be light, salt, and leaven in the world. It must do what God demands, not what society decides. The church at Sardis tolerated Sardis; it did not transform it.

Further, a church is dead when its members are dead. A church comes alive when its people are filled with the Holy Spirit and when they study, share, and serve. A church is raised from the dead when religious people who do not know Christ trust themselves completely to Him and receive His living Spirit.

Jesus challenged the church at Sardis to wake up and strengthen what was on the point of death. The lethargic church was not acceptable to Him.

Christ wanted faithfulness. The church had drifted from the source of its life in Him. He wanted vitality. The church is to live out a style of life motivated by Christ, lived in freedom, expressed in service, and communicated with joy. He wanted authenticity. The gospel makes Christians relaxed, released, renewed people, able to outlive, outsuffer, and outserve the pagan world. Lastly, He wanted reproductivity. The sign of a living church is that its members are introducing others to Christ.

What would Christ say about your church?

May 16

As Strong as the Weakest Point

Revelation 3:2-3

Be watchful and strengthen the things which remain (Revelation 3:2).

THERE IS A STORY OF the capture of Sardis by King Cyrus which helps us to understand Jesus' word to the church there. He tells them to watch, to be on the lookout, and to wake up to the danger. Just as Sardis was once captured in a memorable way, so too the subtle forces of evil could capture the church.

Sardis had been regarded as impregnable. Behind her was Mount Truolus. There was a narrow ridge of rock that went out from that mountain like a pier, and it was on that ridge that the citadel of Sardis was built. It defied assault. When Cyrus wished to capture Sardis, he offered a special reward to the man who could work out a method of scaling the unscalable cliff so that the fortress could be taken.

A Mardian soldier named Hyeroeades saw a Lydian soldier pick his way down the cliff to recover his helmet which he had dropped and then climb back. Hyeroaedes marked the way the soldier had taken. Later at night, he led a picked band of men up the cliff, and when they reached the top, they found the defenders completely unprepared, and they took the city. A strange twist of history is that Antiochus was able to take the city in the same way some 200 years later. The warning "Watch! Stay awake!" was particularly significant to Sardis.

It is a good word for the church—any church. Churches, like people, have weak points from which the evil powers can divide and conquer. Fear of change, traditionalism, formalism, worship of leaders, indifference, self-satisfying safety, materialism—all these make easy points of entry for the enemy. Watch!

We are most vulnerable for spiritual defeat at our strong points where we become careless.

May 17

The Need of Having No Need

Revelation 3:4-6

He who has an ear, let him hear what the Spirit says to the churches (Revelation 3:6).

THE CHURCH AT SARDIS HAD NO need. It was adequate, successful, and prosperous. The Christians were satisfied and pleased with themselves and their church. They had worked hard to build up the church. There had been little resistance and no conflict. Now they settled back to enjoy being the church with their own select few whom they loved and who loved them. How delightful...and dangerous!

Strange, isn't it: we work hard to plan and provide for a comfortable life. We use our energies and skills to get life to a place where it is controllable and tolerable. We want to be responsible for ourselves and those we love. But in so doing we engineer ourselves out of a place of receiving grace. The result of our own careful management is often that we take control and no longer need Christ!

This happened at Sardis, and it has happened to many of us as individuals. Christ is only an addendum to an already full and carefully planned life. He no longer is Lord of all life. He becomes a pleasant helper to accomplish our purposes and to keep our life running smoothly toward the goals we have established. We want Him to help us when there is sickness or trouble, but we no longer need Him to guide, save, or forgive us.

Thank the Lord for His exposure of a life like that! The good life can keep us from a *great* life of dependence on Him and a costly concern and care for others.

If we arrive at where we are headed, where will we be?
If we achieve our goals, what will we have?
If we accomplish our purpose,
will it be God's best for our lives?

May 18

Opportunities Unlimited

Revelation 3:8

See, I have set before you an open door (Revelation 3:8).

PHILADELPHIA HAD ONE OF the most strategic sites in the world. It stood at the place where the borders of three countries, Mysia, Lydia, and Phrygia, met. The border was the gateway to the East, and commanded one of the greatest highways in the world which led from Europe to the East. The position awarded it the responsibility of becoming a missionary city for the spread of Greek culture, language, and a way of life.

The very crucial site of Philadelphia made the church there strategic. The church had opportunities to spread not Greek culture but the gospel. For this reason Jesus challenged the church with a reminder that He had given them an open door which no man can shut. The self-descriptive words He used reminded the Christians that He had the keys to open these doors for them. As the One who had Himself been the doorway to God, now He opened the doorway to spreading His love. The door of missionary opportunity was there before them.

"Behold, I have set before you an open door!" That's the good news for today's living. What's yours? What door of opportunity has He set before you? Your family, your office, your shop, your friends, your neighbors—all are open doors.

But we all need Christ to help us discern the doors. How often we miss them and fail to go through them in joyous commitment!

A man in a crucial industrial position asked Christ to guide his decisions which affected thousands of others. A young man asked Christ to use him in sharing His love in his living unit at college. A widow found meaning and purpose by giving herself to other widows who needed reassurance of Christ's victory over death. What door has Christ set before you?

Each one of us is strategic in Christ's plan for our time.

May 19

The Command to Persevere

1 Peter 3:20; Colossians 1:11; 1 Timothy 1:16; 2 Timothy 4:2; Revelation 3:9-10

Because you have kept My command to persevere, I also will keep you from the hour of trial which shall come upon all the world, to test those who dwell on the earth (Revelation 3:10).

WILL RIGHT ULTIMATELY TRIUMPH? Will evil always be on the throne? How long must we wait for the vindication of God's people and purposes in human history?

Have you ever asked that question while reading the daily news? Have you ever wondered why God allows wrong and hatred to exist? Of course; we all have. But the question becomes poignant and personal when something that we know is right is being ignored or defamed or when we are being judged and criticized for a stand we know is true and just.

Jesus tells the Philadelphian Christians that He is still in control of history. There will be the constant rise and fall of evil empires and the ebb and flow of the tides of godless people. The very nature of the Christian faith is that it will always be in conflict with powers and causes that are against God.

The Lord praises their patient endurance. That's what we need, isn't it? Christ intercedes for us in the interfaces of transition when the world groans for peace, social justice, honesty, and love. Patience is seeing things from God's point of view and by His timing. Endurance results as the strength of our lives. We can live faithfully at any point of history, knowing that evil cannot prevail forever. The sense that God is still at work gives us courage to get to work wherever He would deploy us in His battle with evil.

Patient endurance is God's gift for living in a sick and evil world.

The Rewards of Faithfulness

Revelation 3:11-13

Behold, I come quickly! Hold fast what you have, that no one take your crown (Revelation 3:11).

THOSE WHO BEAR THE CROSS wear the crown. The Greek word *stephanos* was used for a crown of victory given to an athlete who overcame his competitors and won in a game or race. It was also used as a word for the crown given at festive occasions to guests of honor or someone who had been faithful in municipal service. Both meanings are implied here. The Christian was to run the race of life and he was also to serve faithfully in obedience to Christ. What the Lord meant here was that they had won a crown and no one would take it from them.

Another promise made by Jesus to the Philadelphian Christians who overcame the difficulties of conflict and persecution was that they would be made pillars in the temple of God. This imagery would have great significance to the Philadelphians. It was the custom to honor one who served well with an inscription on a pillar in the temple of some god. When someone had been particularly conspicuous for his performance for the city, a pillar was added to the temple in his honored memory.

God's temple is the kingdom, His rule over all of life. We are to be pillars in God's purposes, and will be pillars in the temple of heaven.

The phrase "never shall he go out of it" also meant something special to the Philadelphians. Their city was beset by frequent earthquakes because it lay on the edge of a great volcanic area. At the time of an earthquake, the people would vacate the entire city, including the temple. But now there was a temple of the Lord, His eternal kingdom, from which they need not flee. The people who conquered over the obstacles would be pillars in the triumphant purpose. How great of God to include us in His plans to make us essential elements of His purposes!

We have been crowned by Christ. We are pillars in His temple established in heaven.

May 21

When Culture Captures the Church

Revelation 3:14-19

Because you say: I am rich, have become wealthy, and have need of nothing—and do not know that you are wretched, miserable, poor, blind, and naked (Revelation 3:17).

LAODICAEA WAS A CITY OF commanding geographical location on the River Lycus. Because of this position, it was a city of commercial prosperity. It became a very wealthy city through the cloth and clothing industry. Added to this, it was a center of healing. A famous ear ointment made of nard and an eye powder were used in Laodicaea. *Men*, the god of healing, had a shrine in the city. The people developed great confidence in material prosperity and physical health. They attempted to establish and build their civilization on material advancement. They believed that, given enough time, they could solve all of life's problems by human skill and ingenuity.

The church had become part of the wealth-oriented city. It said that it was able to cope with the vicissitudes of life by what it could buy and possess. Jesus tried to tell them that in the things that really count, they were poor. They were bankrupt in spiritual power.

The preoccupation with clothing is not new today. This garment center took pride in its products. Jesus was like the wise lad who said, "The emperor is naked." The Scripture speaks of the garments of righteousness. These alone can clothe our spiritual nakedness.

Lastly, Laodicaea was arrogant about its health center. Jesus offered them a spiritual salve to heal the blindness of their souls. They had eyes but they could not see. No amount of Laodicaea's famous salve or healing powders could heal this blindness. He alone could heal their sight spiritually if, unlike the Pharisees, they could admit their blindness and desire to see. What a great communicator Christ was and is!

In what ways are you like the Laodiceans?

May 22

Christ at the Door

Revelation 3:20

Look! I have been standing at the door and I am constantly knocking. If anyone hears me calling him and opens the door, I will come in and fellowship with him and he with me (Revelation 3:20 TLB).

RIGHT AT THIS MOMENT, AS you read this, Christ is at the door knocking. He always makes the first move. He comes to us in a new way each day. Yesterday's experience or fellowship with Him will not do for today's challenges. He seeks entrance into our minds and hearts, as well as all of the aspects of our life today. Sallman's great picture of Christ at the door reminds us that the latchstring to open the door is on the inside. We are given the choice to open the door of our lives or leave it shut in the Master's face.

The invitation to open the door comes to us at the time we are introduced to Christ. We learn of His unconditional love, His unqualified forgiveness, and His willingness to make His home in us. I am constantly amazed at the number of Christians who believe in Christ as Savior but have never surrendered their lives to Him as Lord of all. The power to live the Christian life is Christ Himself. So many Christians are defeated because they are trying to live on their own strength. The secret of victorious living is in Christ's indwelling, impelling power within us.

I lived as a self-propelled and self-justifying Christian for eight years before I discovered what I now call "the second half of the blessing": Christ in us, the hope of glory! William Law, one of John Wesley's teachers, said, "A Christ not in us is a Christ not ours." The abundant life really began for me when I opened the door and invited Christ to live in me. How about you?

Lord, I open the door. Welcome! Come in! Use my mind to think Your thoughts, my emotions to express Your love, my will to discern and do Your will, and my body to radiate Your joy.

May 23

The Victorious Life

Revelation 3:21-22; 1 Corinthians 15:54-57; 1 John 5:4

To him who overcomes I will grant to sit with Me on My throne, as I also overcame and sat down with My Father on His throne (Revelation 3:21).

THE VICTORY THAT JESUS OFFERED the Laodiceans was the victory of coronation. He offered them, and now us, the privilege of sitting with Him on His throne. This is colorful language, but it is also powerful. Jesus is offering us the same victory He knew with the same result in authority and power. But what is Christ's victory? How does He overcome the world? His victory is over the forces of evil. When Christ lives in us, He continues to battle for us and through us the same besetting forces of evil that He met as Jesus of Nazareth. His victory is over death. When we live in Him, we live in a fellowship which death has no power to end. As He lives, we will live also. And His victory is final and ultimate. Though defeat is all around us, we need to remember the cross and acknowledge that God can take over failure and weakness and create His own glory. Christ always has the last word. That's our victory!

True faith is not white-knuckled, teeth-gritting determination to survive in trouble. It is rooted in the confidence that the Lord will invade the trouble at just the right time with His unlimited resources. He knows, cares, and will intervene. Troubles are an opportunity to experience the power of the Lord in a fresh way. Faith-nurtured endurance grows out of the realization that the Lord will come to us in the midnight darkness of trouble. He comes not only to comfort but to perform miracles we could never have imagined. He has resources to unleash we had not counted on. He can untangle knotty problems, change the attitudes of troublesome people, give us wisdom beyond our understanding, and open closed doors.

Christ is our victory!

May 24

Learning to Wait

Acts 1:1-4

Wait for the promise of the Father (Acts 1:4).

IN THE NEXT DAYS WE WILL focus on the meaning of Pentecost. The period between the Resurrection and the outpouring of the Holy Spirit at Pentecost is marked by waiting: expectant, excited, excruciating waiting.

The disciples had to learn to wait. They lived in an impetuous age. Jesus told them again and again that His kingdom was not of the kind that men yearned to establish. They persistently wanted proof, action, of the power of His kingdom. "My kingdom is not of this world," He cautioned, and they had to learn the most difficult lesson of following the Master: they had to wait for His timing. Jesus Himself had displayed the power to wait. In the early morning watches before He healed and preached, He waited for God's direction and blessing. There in the long hours of quiet, He learned from Isaiah and the Psalmist: "They that wait upon the LORD shall renew their strength; they shall mount up with wings as eagles; they shall run and not be weary; they shall walk and not faint" (Isaiah 40:31 KJV). "Wait for the LORD; be strong, and let your heart take courage; yes, wait for the LORD!" (Psalm 27:14).

Repeatedly He considered these words. He knew that, as the Son of God, He could not accomplish the Lord's purposes without His timing and power. Now He had raised up a group of people who were to be the foundation of the church. He could be satisfied only with people who had learned how to wait...on Him. They dared not run ahead of Him. They dared not go in unguided directions. They dared not seek to perform their mission for Him alone. They had to learn to allow Him to accomplish His mission through them.

The power of Pentecost is for those who are patient enough to wait.

May 25

Wait for the Power

Acts 1:4-8

And He said to them, "It is not for you to know times or seasons which the Father has put in His own authority" (Acts 1:7).

WHAT WAS GOD WAITING FOR? Why didn't He give the power of the Holy Spirit to the disciples immediately?

They were not ready! They still had the impatience of human verve. They wanted to do things for Christ in their own strength. They wanted to get going with the mission He had given them. We can empathize with them. We too want to get moving in bringing the kingdom of God into the world. We read our newspapers, we see people in need, we have a sense of the urgency of getting the good news of the gospel to all the areas of suffering in society. Our temptation is to try to straighten people out and set them in order for God.

The amazing thing which is discernible on the pages of every period of Christian history is that there are always those people who are willing to wait for power to do the Lord's will. Most of the great men and women of history have had long periods of excruciating preparation for participation in Christ's mission. It is during these periods that the Lord who does His work *in* us before He does His work *through* us, gets us ready to do His "new thing" in each age.

When we are quiet we realize our impotency to follow Christ. We feel the inadequacy of our love at the very time we catch a vision of the world's need for His love. It is at that moment that preparation for Pentecost is taking place. The tremendous infilling of power to love which the disciples received at Pentecost is exactly the same power we are being prepared to receive today.

Pentecost is God's gift for those who see the need for love in the world but do not have the power to love.

May 26

The Baptism of the Holy Spirit

Acts 1:5

For John truly baptized with water, but you will be baptized with the Holy Spirit not many days from now (Acts 1:5).

WHAT IS THE BAPTISM OF the Holy Spirit that Jesus promised His disciples? Can it be experienced today? What does it mean?

Jesus took a known to teach and prepare for an unknown. He reminded them of the baptism by John. This had been a baptism of repentance. People were baptized by immersion into the water. This was an outward sign of God's cleansing of the failures and sins which a person confessed. This baptism gave tangible assurance of God's forgiveness and acceptance. The practice of baptism by immersion was carried on by Jesus' disciples. Jesus Himself was baptized by His cousin, John the Baptist. Now He led their thinking to another, greater baptism, a baptism by the Holy Spirit.

Some of the same elements would be present. A sense of need, a willingness to be totally committed to God's plan and purpose, and a realization of sin and inadequacy were necessary preparation. The baptism of the Spirit would also be an assuring outward sign of the work of the Lord within a person's mind and heart. But the great difference was that the person would be immersed not in water but in the power of the Spirit of God. He would come within a person as a new driving power to participate in the continuing ministry of love begun in Jesus of Nazareth.

The baptism of John was a baptism of repentance; the baptism of the Holy Spirit would be the baptism of regeneration, of new life, new power, new gifts for ministry beyond human talent. The promise was that the Spirit of the living God would infuse, indwell, and inspire the disciples from within. The same is available to us.

I need the Holy Spirit; I want the Holy Spirit;
I am open to be baptized by the Holy Spirit.

The Threefold Test

Matthew 3:11-12

I indeed baptize you with water to repentance, but He who is coming after me is mightier than I, whose sandals I am not worthy to carry. He will baptize you with the Holy Spirit and fire (Matthew 3:11).

JOHN THE BAPTIST PREDICTED THAT those who believed in Jesus would be baptized with the Holy Spirit and fire. There is an identifiable fire burning in people who have received the Holy Spirit. The image is an exciting one. What does it mean to you? The answer is both challenging and disturbing.

Fire means illumination. In John's day, fire was the chief source of light in darkness. When we receive the Holy Spirit there is the light of truth about God, life, and ourselves. Jesus said that the Holy Spirit would bring to our remembrance the things He had said. The Holy Spirit interprets the deep things of God to the believer. We have insight and discernment. We see both what is and what can be. There is a new power to understand God's love and His ways with us. But that ability to see is often disturbing, for we can also see ourselves.

The second aspect of the fire of the Holy Spirit is purification. He burns out the false and leaves us pure. To receive the Holy Spirit means a purging of old ways of thinking and feeling. The smoldering fires are blown into red-hot flames, burning off the evil dross of confused self-centeredness.

Thirdly, the Holy Spirit's fire brings the warmth of love. He kindles the emotions with love for God and other people. There is a warmth about a Holy Spirit-filled person. He has new affection and tenderness toward people of all kinds and conditions.

There is nothing our cold world needs more than the fire of the Holy Spirit! God's frozen people in the church need to be melted and poured out in service.

A Christian man is the most free lord of all, and subject to none; a Christian man is the most dutiful servant of all, subject to everyone.

—Martin Luther

May 28

Come, Holy Spirit—We Need You!

John 17:1-26; 14:18-24

I in them, and You in Me; that they may be made perfect in one (John 17:23).

WHO IS THE HOLY SPIRIT? Is He someone or something separate or different from Jesus Christ? Do we believe in three Gods—Father, Son, and Holy Spirit?

These are questions which immediately arise whenever an emphasis on the Holy Spirit is proclaimed. It is important that we do some clear thinking. We believe in one God. He is our Creator, Savior in Christ, and resident power in the Holy Spirit. The Eternal Spirit who created the world and revealed Himself in Jesus Christ is now present in the world, continuing the ministry of reconciliation.

When we speak of the Holy Spirit we are talking about God, whose nature is focused in His self-impartation in the life, message, death, and resurrection of Jesus. He is the Creator God who acts! He has been at work since creation, seeking to call, transform, and empower His people to participate with Him in human history. The Persons of the Trinity are not to be considered separately as if independent from one another, but as affirmation of the ways that God has of being God.

The names for God help us to consider how He works in our lives. The ancient benediction helps: "The grace of the Lord Jesus, the love of God, and the fellowship of the Holy Spirit be with you all." That proclaims the sweep of God's historic movement, but also the ways He works in our lives. Out of love He created us for Himself; in grace He came in Jesus Christ to suffer and die that we might be forgiven and healed; through fellowship in the Holy Spirit He is with us now to guide and strengthen us. We dare not miss all that God has to give us. The Holy Spirit is not an addendum. He is the Holy God of all creation who wants to transform us and give us power to live the abundant life revealed in Jesus and available to us now.

Lord of all creation, who came in Jesus Christ, come now to live in me.

May 29

The Inner Special

Acts 2:1-4

And they were all filled with the Holy Spirit (Acts 2:4).

ONE OF THE LETTERS ON a marquee outside a fast-food restaurant had blown off. What resulted was quite an offer. With the "D" missing, the sign read, "Complete Inner Specials $2.95."

Pentecost is the celebration of the inner special. But it is not a special in the sense of an extra; Pentecost was the purpose of the Lord's passion. The Incarnation was to prepare the way for the infilling of a new breed of humanity to be the new creation.

If you had to choose between Christmas, Good Friday, Easter, Ascension Sunday, and Pentecost, which would you say is most important? Few of us would say Pentecost. We think of it as a mysterious addendum to the gospel. And yet we would not celebrate the crucial events of the Incarnation of Christ if it had not been culminated in Pentecost.

The reason Christ came, lived, taught, suffered, was resurrected, and ascended was so that He could prepare a people in whom He could live. Calvary's atonement and Easter's victory are penultimate to the ultimate gift of Christ making His home in His reconciled and expectant people. Now the Holy Spirit came within His willing disciples to give them the power to live the life He had exemplified and called them to live.

The outward manifestations of Pentecost were signs of the inner special. Wind represented the Breath and Spirit of God. Fire meant both purging and purification. It also signified a dynamic inclusive warmth in Jesus' followers. John had predicted that Jesus would baptize with the Holy Spirit and fire. The result was unfettered praise. Don't miss Pentecost!

The abundant life is life as Christ lived it, life as we live it in Him, and life as He lives it in us.

May 30

Pentecost Is Every Day

Acts 2:5-13

And they were all amazed and perplexed, saying to one another, "What does this mean?" (Acts 2:12).

SOMETHING VERY SPECIAL happened at Pentecost. It ought to be everyday Christianity for us today. Here was a fellowship of people utterly open and ready for the Gift that God had been yearning to give His people through history. Now these men and women who had learned to know Him in His love and forgiveness in the cross, who had been given the grace to believe in Christ as Savior and Lord, were like dry kindling ready to be set afire. The Spirit who had spoken to His people in every generation through patriarch, psalmist, prophet, and spiritual pioneer now gave impetus to a new and fresh movement of His people.

But Pentecost must reoccur every day. Can Pentecost be our experience today? I believe it can. How can we be prepared? There are two questions to be answered: 1) Have we responded to the gospel of Jesus Christ, turned our life completely over to Him, and responded to His call to be totally His person? 2) Has life, in all its problems and potentials, brought us to the realization of our own inadequacy to live the Christian life on our own strength? If we can answer both of these questions with a "Yes!", Pentecost can happen to us today. It can be our personal baptism into power as the Spirit indwells our whole nature, and it can be the church's corporate rebirth to a new stage of effectiveness in our communities and our world. Here is a prayer for power.

> Holy Spirit of God, we pray for Pentecost to happen to us and to our local churches today. We long for an outpouring of Your power to enable us in Christ's ministry of love and suffering for the world. We cannot do or be what You have called us to perform in the world or exemplify to others without Your life within us. Amen.

Pentecost can and will happen in us today!

May 31

A Spirit-Filled Life

Acts 2:14-39

Repent, and let every one of you be baptized in the name of Jesus Christ for the remission of sins; and you will receive the gift of the Holy Spirit (Acts 2:38).

YESTERDAY'S MEDITATION WAS meant to be like a time-release capsule. It had residual impact as the conviction explodes within us. Peter's sermon on Pentecost gives us an intellectual framework for realizing the total sweep of God's action to prepare a people to receive and communicate His power. It outlines what God has done in the Incarnation, what His people did in refusing the gift of His love in Christ, and then what He did in spite of that rejection. The sermon ends with a challenge of what we can do because of what He has done.

Christ revealed the abundant life that God intends for all. He went to the cross so that we could be forgiven, reconciled, and fully prepared to experience the indwelling of the Spirit. When the first phase of Jesus' work was completed, He ascended into heaven. From there He returned to continue what He had begun. At Pentecost, the reason He had come was accomplished. He indwelt those who had been His followers in the earthly phase of His Incarnation. Now the indwelt disciples became extensions of the Incarnation.

What does this mean to us today? We say with the crowd that heard Peter's sermon, "What shall we do?" The three steps are undeniably given: repent, believe, receive. To repent means to acknowledge what we have been and done; to believe means to trust Christ completely for forgiveness and acceptance; to receive means to invite Him to live in us as absolute Lord and motivating power. The result will be that we are Spirit-filled Christians living with unlimited resources.

Beginning today I will be a riverbed for the flow of the Spirit.

June 1

Occupied by a Through Passenger

Acts 2:1-4; 4:8; 13:9; 1 Corinthians 3:16-17; 6:19; 2 Corinthians 6:16

For you are the temple of the living God (2 Corinthians 6:16).

I HAVE A FRIEND WHO HAS a fascinating sign on his desk. The bold letters spell "Occupied By a Through Passenger." He told me that it was a duplicate of an occupied-seat sign he had seen on a commercial airplane flight. He used it for a conversation starter to talk about his faith: "That's what I am—an occupied, through passenger. I'm only passing through. Heaven's my destination!"

A Christian is occupied territory on his way to a sublime destination. But when Christ makes His home in us the joy of the destination has begun already. Christ occupies our minds to think His thoughts, our emotions to express His love, and our bodies to radiate His power. We are the temple of the living Christ! Like an occupied territory after a war, we have a new authority and direction.

We often speak as a person being "filled" with an emotion. We say he is filled with self-pity, anger, concern, or anxiety; or we say that he is filled with life, joy, peace, or excitement. What we mean is the self as a container is filled or occupied by a dominant emotion or conviction which is expressed in our countenance, attitudes, words, and actions. Whether we are a delight or a drag to those around us depends on what is filling our thoughts and emotions.

At Pentecost, the disciples were described as being "full of the Holy Spirit." That means that they were occupied by the Living Christ. This alone can release us from preoccupation with self and our feelings and needs. When we look closely at what made that possible, we see that they were completely open to each other and God. They wanted to be possessed by a power greater than self-effort. They asked simply for power and were filled with Christ Himself. That's the occupied life!

All the way to heaven is heaven.

June 2

A Benchmark for a Great Church

Acts 2:40-47

Then those who gladly received His word were baptized; and the same day about three thousand souls were added to them (Acts 2:41).

HERE IS A PICTURE OF THE church as it was meant to be. It provides a benchmark for any church in every age.

It was Christ-centered. The people who joined the church had responded to the straightforward preaching of Christ—crucified, resurrected, indwelling. The living Christ was their Savior, Lord, and intimate Friend. Churches become ineffective, impotent religious institutions when they drift away from Christ. The preaching and teaching of life in Christ and Christ in us is the source of vitality and power of a dynamic church.

It was a praying church. Prayer was the channel for the flow of the Lord's Spirit in the believers and through them to one another. A praying church becomes a supernatural church. It dares to attempt the impossible, knowing that what the Lord guides He provides. So many churches today are attempting only those things they could do on human strength. What is your church daring in Christ's name which only His Spirit could accomplish?

It was a caring and sharing church. They were not only committed to Christ, but also to one another and their life together in the church. Spiritual and material needs were shared with the realization that what each had been given was for the mutual benefit of all.

It was a healing church. The same power to heal the psychological, physical, and spiritual needs of people which had been revealed in Jesus of Nazareth was now unloosed in the church. He gave the gift of healing through prayer to meet the hurts of people.

It was a growing church. But note that it was the Lord who added to the church daily. He had created a magnetic church where people loved Him and one another.

No commitment to Christ is complete without a commitment to the renewal of the church.

June 3

The Most Joyful People Alive

John 13:1-35

If you know these things, happy are you if you do them (John 13:17).

THE CHURCH IS THE SERVANT society. Christians are called to be servants. The Greek word for "servant" is also used for "minister." All Christians are called into ministry. To be in Christ is to be in the ministry. Once we turn our lives over to Christ, then people and their needs become our agenda. Our calling is to care about people—helping them to know the Savior, grow in grace, and face life's challenges. Our happiness is inseparably related to pouring ourselves out for people. That means giving up our privacy, schedules, and judgments. The Lord puts people in our lives so that we can be to them what He has been to us. In every situation, our only question should be, "Lord, what am I to do to be Your servant?"

People who become servants are the most joyful people alive. They become channels of the Lord's love and forgiveness, strength and compassion. And we can't care for others by the Lord's power without having some of the blessing spill over on us. Our attitudes will change when our perception of ourselves is of being a servant. The drudgery of life leaves and is replaced by an abiding delight. Often our service must be done in the little things before we can earn the right to help people in the big problems of life. A man said, "Until I changed my self-image to that of being a servant, I always felt put upon, drained dry by people's demands. Then I realized Christ's calling to be a servant. Now I look for opportunities to serve in Christ's name. Now I want to be a boost and not a burden, a lift and not a load. It has changed my life!"

Could you say what this man said? Can you say it just for today? Try it—it could change all the days of your future.

June 4

Look at Us!

Acts 3:1-10

And fixing his eyes on him, with John, Peter said, "Look at us" (Acts 3:4).

WE LIVE IN A CRIPPLED world. Daily the crippled world cries out as surely as the lame man on the step of the Temple Beautiful. We are crippled not only in body, but also in spirit. We come to the Temple steps unable to love, unable to forgive, unable to relate deeply, unable to face our insecurities, unable to live out our deepest convictions in life, unable to bring peace to our strife-filled, war-saturated world. The sickness of our world is only an outer reflection of our inner condition. It's the big picture of what is inside us all. The residue of the sickness of the ages is in all of us. We all need healing and release far more than the beggar on the steps needed to walk.

What can we say to a sick and troubled world? Can we say, "Look at us"? "Look at the quality of new life in our faith we have discovered"? Can we say that we have the answer? Peter and John unashamedly asked the lame beggar to look at them. They did have an answer.

The man fixed his gaze on them, expecting to receive *something* from them. This is the story of a man wanting *something* when what he needed was *someone*. He was the eloquent spokesman of materialism for all ages. He expected something. The disciples had nothing to offer, but they had Someone. Yes, they had a Someone who had changed their lives and had given them purpose and power, healing and holiness, wisdom and will. They had no answer; they had *the* answer. H. Wheeler Robinson expressed it when he said, "The discovery of God is not, then, the discovery of something in a corner of our experience. It is the discovery of Someone whose presence gathers the whole of our experience into the comprehensiveness of His being, and gives it a new unity."

The world yearns for something;
we offer Someone—Christ Himself.

June 5

What Do You Know for Sure?

Romans 15:22-33

And I am sure that when I come to you, I shall come in the fullness of the blessing of the gospel of Christ (Romans 15:29).

WHEN I WAS A BOY, my father would often ask, "Well, Lad, what do you know for sure?" I would search for some new thing that I had learned about which I was absolutely sure. I was not too sure of anything in those days. My answer now would be very different. If my father were alive today, I would answer him with one word: "Christ!" I may have questions about myself, but I am absolutely sure of Christ.

I am thankful that I can say with Paul what he said to the Christians at Rome: "And I am sure that when I come to you, I shall come in the fullness of the blessings of the gospel of Christ." Now there is a daring, dynamic promise! It's one we can all make with assurance.

Paul wrote from Corinth. He eagerly anticipated his visit to Rome, the strategic center of political and military might. The conviction began to grow: What if this earthly power could be won by the power of Christ? "I must see Rome!" Paul asserted.

He would come to the struggling church there with an overflowing cornucopia of superabundant power. He would come with Christ, the gospel, the blessing, and the fullness. Christ was everything to Paul. He was the Author, Mediator, Redeemer, Victor, Essence of Indwelling Power, and Crown of Life for the Apostle. When he arrived in Rome he taught, preached, lived, and shared Christ. While there, he wrote the Philippians "For to me, to live is Christ." Paul's gospel was Christ. In Him all the blessings of God had been lavishly poured out in fullness. Nothing was left out. Christ's fullness alone can fill our emptiness.

Christ is the end, for Christ was the beginning; Christ is the beginning, for the end is Christ.

June 6

Yes!

Matthew 12:31-32

Therefore I say to you, every sin and blasphemy will be forgiven men, but the blasphemy against the Holy Spirit will not be forgiven men (Matthew 12:31).

IS THERE ANY SIN WHICH cannot be forgiven? Yes. The sin against the Holy Spirit. We can understand what that is if we consider who the Holy Spirit is and what He does in us. The Holy Spirit is God working in our minds and hearts. He creates a sense of need, assures us that we are beloved, convinces us of the gospel, gives us the gift of faith to accept forgiveness and new life, and seeks to empower us to live abundantly.

The sin against the Holy Spirit is to say "No!" to His overtures of grace. That sin is unforgivable in that we can say "No" so long and often that we no longer can say "Yes." That tells us a frightening thing about human nature. God is always ready to forgive, but has given us free wills to choose to let Him love us. And if we say "No"? The unforgivable sin is to refuse to be forgiven...to resist the ministry of the Holy Spirit! Bishop Fulton J. Sheen said, "The really unforgivable sin is the denial of sin, because, by its nature, there is now nothing to be forgiven."

The Pharisees and scribes in today's passage refused to believe that it was God's Spirit who was at work in Jesus. But the real problem was that to accept Christ as the Messiah would have meant listening to what He said and responding to His diagnosis of their sin and need for forgiveness. They had stonewalled the impact of the Spirit. The same can happen in religious people today. The danger is saying "No!" once too often.

Yes! Yes! Yes!

June 7

The Crucial Question

Acts 8:1-40

For as yet He had fallen upon none of them.
They had only been baptized in the name of the Lord Jesus (Acts 8:16).

NOTICE THAT THERE WERE TWO steps in the Samaritans' experience of the gospel. Philip preached the good news of Christ's death and resurrection. The people believed, and there was great joy in the city. Then Peter and John came and prayed that they might receive the Holy Spirit. Why was it necessary for the two apostles to follow up on Philip's preaching? Perhaps it was because the Samaritans needed power to live their new life. They needed the indwelling power of the same Holy Spirit who had given them the gift of faith to believe.

After we accept Christ as our Savior, we quickly realize that life in Christ must be coupled with Christ in us. The great need in the lives of most of us contemporary Christians is for the Holy Spirit to infuse our human impotence with power to live the adventure of the Christian life. Would you say that your life is most like the Samaritans' before Philip preached, after they believed but had no power, or after Peter and John prayed for the gift of the indwelling Spirit? That's probably one of the most important questions you will ever answer! How you answer determines the difference between living for Christ on your power or fulfilling Christ's plans by His power.

I want and need the fullness
of Christ's indwelling power.

June 8

An Engine Without Fuel

Acts 19:1-7

He [Paul] said to them, "Did you receive the Holy Spirit when you believed?" And they said to him, "We have not so much as heard whether there is a Holy Spirit" (Acts 19:2).

CHRISTIANS ARE TWICE-BORN people. We have been born into physical life in our natural birth, but we have also been born again. There are words which were used to describe to Nicodemus the nature of beginning the new life in Christ. We are people who have died to ourselves, our will for our circumstances, and our hopes for the future. When we committed our mind, emotions, will, and body to Christ, we began a new level or quality of life and friendship and fellowship with Him. We sought to follow Christ and be obedient to His will, plan, and purpose. We started life all over...we were born again. Some of us reclaimed the baptism which had been done years before, accepting the fact that we belonged to Christ through the years. Others were baptized as an adult as a sign and seal of their new birth.

This first baptism prepares us for the baptism of the Holy Spirit. The great need today is for traditional, believing, struggling Christians in the church to receive this baptism of power. In Acts, Luke uses a vivid phrase to describe this: "They were *filled* with the Holy Spirit." We were created to contain and transmit the Holy Spirit. Our Christian life is not fulfilled until we have had an infilling of power. All the things we try to be and do as faithful believers in Christ are impossible until we receive the Holy Spirit's power.

We are like the men along the road whom Paul met. They knew about Jesus and about what God had done for the salvation of the world in Him. But they lacked power. When Paul prayed for them they received the Holy Spirit. That's the question for all of us: "Did you receive the Holy Spirit when you believed?"

We were meant to be twice-born and twice-baptized.

June 9

Put It in His Hands!

John 4:43-54; Matthew 17:20

Jesus said to him, "Go your way; your son lives." And the man believed the word that Jesus spoke to him, and he went his way (John 4:50).

DISTANCE IS NO DETRIMENT in the power of prayer. Jesus did not have to travel the distance to physically touch the fevered son to heal him. This is a magnificent promise of what we can know today. We do not have to be physically present with the person for whom we pray. The same Lord who motivates our prayer is also there with the person for whom we pray. Geography makes no difference for the prayer of faith, nor is psychological distance of any consequence. Often we are separated in various ways from people for whom we pray; some live far away from us, and others with whom we are present can be so distant in their defensiveness that it is difficult to break through their barriers. But we can pray and know that God is at work. We can participate with Him in the release of His amazing resources in their lives if we pray.

Incisive intercession is rewarded by the "Go your way, your son lives" kind of assurance that Jesus gave to the courtier. He gives us the freedom to let go of our worry over a person. When we pray in faith, we can thank God repeatedly that He has heard, and be assured that He will answer according to His will and in a way that brings the *ultimate* good for the person for whom we've prayed. It is a gift of release to "go our way," leaving in God's hands the matter we've brought to Him earnestly in prayer. Worry after we've relinquished a person or situation is a sure sign that we have not let go of the need and are still holding onto the burden ourselves. The Lord has heard! His power is being released. Our job is to pray in faith; God's job is to intervene. If we do our job, He will do His!

I will live today in the liberating assurance that God has heard my prayers and is active in answering in a way that is best. I will not compete with Him in trying to do His job by continuing to worry. I will "go my way," leaving the matter in His hands.

June 10

A Recognition of Need

Matthew 5:3; Luke 6:20,24; Ephesians 3:7-13

Blessed are the poor in spirit, for theirs is the kingdom of heaven (Matthew 5:3).

HOW CAN A PERSON WHO IS poor in spirit be blessed—that is, joyous? The Greek word used to translate Jesus' Aramaic word is a severe word. It is *ptochos,* which means absolute and complete poverty. What did Jesus mean?

The answer is found in an observable spiritual law: the closer you grow to Jesus Christ, the greater your sense of need for Him. We know that we are distant when we begin to feel self-sufficient. Self-complacency is a sure sign of spiritual paralysis. To know one's absolute dependence on Christ for life, love, hope, power, insight, discernment, wisdom, courage, and strategy is to know creative spiritual poverty. This is poverty of spirit.

The keynote of this first beatitude is realization. Joyous are those who realize their need. Moffatt translates: "Blessed are those who feel poor in spirit!" Goodspeed suggests: "Blessed are those who feel their spiritual need." Canon Wade: "Happy are those who are feeling spiritual need." J.B. Phillips: "How happy are the humble-minded, for the kingdom of heaven is theirs."

It is difficult for most of us to recognize our poverty of spirit. We have learned to be independent and resourceful. Given time and opportunity, there is no limit to what we think we can do. To depend on God in a world which has taught us self-reliance is difficult. Often we must be taught by painful experience. We discover in sickness, loss of a loved one, circumstantial failure, or interpersonal conflict that we are not as capable as we thought. The joyous are those who recognize their helplessness apart from God and quickly put their trust in Him.

Joyous is the man who has realized his absolute helplessness and has put his whole trust in God.

June 11

The Poverty That Leads to Richness

Luke 18:9-14

God be merciful to me a sinner! (Luke 18:13).

THE POOR IN SPIRIT KNOW their need and can cry out, "God be merciful to me, a poor sinner." Jesus exalts the tax collector in the parable because he could accept his need for God's mercy. The Pharisee, comparing himself with others and not with God's standard of righteousness, was thankful that he was not as other people. He was filled with pride, self-satisfaction, and self-assurance. He could not receive what Jesus offered.

We must come to grips with the fact that the gospel of love means little to most of us because we are like the Pharisee. We compare our lives with others, thinking little of Christ because we have learned to manipulate life around to an acceptable pattern which we can control.

Many of us do not realize our poverty of spirit because we are not living an adventurous enough life. We aren't living courageously enough to have any other invisible means of support than Christ. Once we get involved with people and their needs, and really care about them, we will soon find that we do not have adequate patience or persistence. People try, test, and trouble us if we dare to care. Whenever we try to change social conditions, we meet obstacles of closed minds and resistant wills. Then we realize how poor in wisdom we are. We do not realize our poverty of spirit until we accept the potential challenge in which we are to live out our faith.

*We cannot realize our poverty in spirit
until we recognize our potentiality.*

June 12

To Be Truly Sorry

2 Corinthians 1:3-11; Matthew 5:4

Blessed are those who mourn, for they shall be comforted (Matthew 5:4).

Blessed be the God and Father of our Lord Jesus Christ, the Father of mercies and God of all comfort (2 Corinthians 1:3).

HOW COULD IT BE BLESSED to mourn? The two realities seem antithetical. "Blessed" in Jesus' use of the word means to be truly happy—not the fleeting happiness of having everything go our way, but the happiness of being God's person and doing things His way. It is the sublime happiness of being in fellowship with Him, and being filled with His Spirit. True blessedness is being in touch with the heart of God, to feel what He feels, to delight in what He delights, and also to be disturbed by what disturbs Him. He loves us so much that anything which separates us from Him or others is of grave concern to Him. He mourns when we hurt ourselves or others. The cross is a constant reminder of how deeply He loves us and how profoundly He cares. Golgotha is the mourning of God. Our sin breaks God's heart.

When we mourn, we feel the pulsebeat of that loving, forgiving heart. Jesus' meaning of mourning is more than grief at the loss of a loved one. It encompasses deep sorrow for our sins. Jesus knew that if we ever caught a glimpse of what our sin does to God, we would mourn with Him. That would lead to confession, forgiveness, and the joy of reconciliation. There is no happiness, no joyous blessedness, quite like knowing that we are accepted and loved. When we know that, we want everyone else to experience it.

Mourning in this profound sense also means feeling God's heart of forgiving love for others. The joy of the forgiven is the delight in being forgiving. We mourn over what people do to us and themselves and then become channels of the flow of God's heart.

True happiness is so crucial to me that I will seek forgiveness and become forgiving.

June 13

Grief That Leads to Grace

2 Corinthians 1:3-7

Blessed be the God and Father of our Lord Jesus Christ, the Father of mercies and God of all comfort (2 Corinthians 1:3).

THERE IS A JOY TO BE experienced when we care deeply about people and their needs. This joy comes when we let our hearts mourn over the things which bring grief to the heart of God. When we are involved with God in caring for people, we are also recipients of God's comfort.

The more we know of the person's potential, the more we mourn over his failure in squandering life. When we know what life was meant to be, we ache for people to see it and experience it to the hilt. The mess people make of life is a source of mourning for us. What peace and power they could know!

We also mourn over what people do to one another. Our hearts ache when we read the daily newspaper and observe the grotesque ways people hurt and destroy one another. We dare to get involved with the people in our lives and feel with them the pain of what other people have done. Discernment is a powerful gift to receive from the Holy Spirit. It enables us to see what is going on in our world and to feel the anguish of it. Comfort is God's gift to those who share life this deeply with Him. Joy grows out of the realization that God is at work in people's lives and calls us to communicate His love to them in spite of everything.

Those who truly care know the comfort of God.

June 14

Under the Reins

Ephesians 4:1-25; Matthew 5:5

With all lowliness and gentleness, with longsuffering, bearing with one another in love (Ephesians 4:2).

Blessed are the gentle [meek], for they shall inherit the earth (Matthew 5:5).

ANOTHER USE OF THE GREEK word for meekness, *praus*, is "domesticated." It is the word which describes a wild animal which has been brought under control. The animal now has been trained and can follow commands in accomplishing tasks of labor. It has learned to respond to reins. Picture a wild horse which has been broken and trained and now can respond to the direction of its master.

A meek man is a God-controlled man. He is a man who can respond to the reins of God's direction, and he is free within the guidance of God's command.

Make me a captive, Lord,
And then I shall be free;
Force me to render up my sword
And I shall conqueror be.
My heart is weak and poor
Until it master finds;
It has no spring of action sure;
It varies with the wind.

Paul speaks of himself as a prisoner of the Lord. He had a turbulent, unruly spirit until captured and guided by the love of Christ. He speaks of Jesus leading a host of captives. That has always been the vivid image of the church: a fellowship of men and women under the control and power of Jesus Christ. The meek people of the Master are sensitive to listen and obediently follow the commands of their Lord.

Meekness is life under God's control.

June 15

True Comfort

Luke 6:21; Isaiah 61:1-2; 2 Thessalonians 2:16; Acts 9:31

Blessed are you who hunger now, for you shall be satisfied. Blessed are you who weep now, for you shall laugh (Luke 6:21).

THE MOTTO OF FAMOUS newspaperman Joseph Pulitzer owes much to Jesus: "Comfort the afflicted and afflict the comfortable." Jesus does just that! He comforts those who mourn over their own, others', and the world's separation, suffering, and selfishness. The Greek word means "to call to the side of." Christ stands by our side when we become sensitive to the need of the world and our part in it. When we become comfortable in any other security than Him, He unsettles us with His disturbing exposure of what life was meant to be.

Only Christ knows when we need to be comforted and when we need to be afflicted. He knows when to assure and when to alarm. Our own judgment of our needs is often wrong. When we think we need comforting, He often comes with a disturbing challenge which gets us on our feet. Then too, when we do not know our need for fortification, He builds us up in love to face some imminent difficulty we must go through.

The wonderful good news is that He stands beside us. The Messiah was called the Comforter. Jesus Himself said the Holy Spirit would be the Comforter. He comforts us by helping us to get perspective on what we face, to see what He is teaching us in it, to learn what He can do with a life surrendered to Him, and to experience the power of His sustaining power. That's comfort!

True comfort assures and challenges, each at the right time.

June 16

Flexibility

Isaiah 45:9-10; Romans 9:19-33

Will the clay say to the potter, "What are you doing?" (Isaiah 45:9).

WE ARE TO BE LIKE CLAY in the potter's hand. The clay does not determine the shape of the object fashioned, nor does it argue with the wisdom or skill of the potter. The image is vivid and a bit humorous. We laugh at the idea of clay rolling off the potter's wheel and saying, "Now look here, Potter, I have an idea or two about how I want to be shaped and how I want to end up when you're finished. I have my rights too, you know!" How absurd! But how like our relationship with God, our Potter!

We are to be soft and adjustable. Clay responds to the potter's hand when it is warm and supple. We are to be this way in God's hand. He knows best about what we are to do and become. We are to trust Him. Meekness is the willingness to trust God with the molding of our lives.

Have Thine own way, Lord!
Have Thine own way!
Thou art the Potter;
I am the clay.
Mold me and make me
After Thy will
While I am waiting,
Yielded and still.

God can mold us beyond our fondest expectation. He is able to shape our lives in magnificent dimensions which we could never imagine. We are to be willing, open, free. God does the rest. The meek are moldable.

Meekness is flexibility.

June 17

Moldable Meekness

1 Corinthians 2:1-16; James 3:13-18

But the wisdom from above is first pure, then peaceable, gentle, open to reason, full of mercy and good fruits, without uncertainty or insincerity (James 3:17 RSV).

WISDOM IS THE SPECIAL GIFT of the Holy Spirit. Note how wisdom, the Holy Spirit, and the mind of Christ are used almost synonymously in this passage. They are all part of one experience. We can be empowered to comprehend the deep things of God's nature, purpose, and plan. Guidance, insight, and discernment are ours because the Holy Spirit dwells in us. We are not alone. Human understanding is maximized by the Spirit. He infuses the tissues of our brains to think His thoughts, fills our emotions with His love, and frees our wills to know and do His will. Spirit-filled Christians are free to be channels of the living God!

Meekness is moldability. It is a dynamic freedom rooted in God's graciousness which overflows in love for one's self in spite of our shortcomings and then love for others just as they are. Meekness is a kind of abandonment to God as the Potter of life, asking for His guiding, shaping hand to develop our life.

In this light, a meek man is the only kind who can experience wisdom. He alone is open, flexible, free enough to receive what God has to give. Most of us are so filled with our own ideas of what is best for us and the people we love that it is difficult for God to get through to us. We are darting off in all directions trying out alternative solutions. God has so much more to give than we will accept. We limp on with half-answers, distorted insight, and the bland boredom of little adventure in life because we do not have the meekness of moldability. The Lord of all creation stands by to guide in wisdom, but we cannot sit still long enough to listen! Is that true of you?

There is a quality which is absolutely necessary to find wisdom: it is the meekness of moldability.

June 18

Hunger and Thirst

Matthew 5:6

Blessed are those who hunger and thirst for righteousness, for they shall be filled (Matthew 5:6).

THIS IS THE MOST DIFFICULT beatitude for us to understand, not because it is complex, but because there is so little in our experience which would give us a sense of the meaning. Few of us have ever hungered or thirsted. Food is plentiful and a turn of the water tap brings water without limit. The hunger of which Jesus speaks is not famishment before mealtime; the thirst is more than a parched need for a refreshing drink. It is the hunger of a person who is starving and thirst of a person who will die without a drink. We have experienced nothing like that!

What are the dominant desires of our life? What do we truly long for? What demands our loyalty and allegiance? Most of us would have to be honest to say that we do not long for righteousness! Robert Louis Stevenson spoke of "the malady of not wanting." This is our malady. We do not want God enough to pray, study, worship, or serve. We retreat when following becomes difficult.

Organized religion has played a terrible trick on most of us. We have drifted into Christianity through religious activities. We have been ushered into the faith by a series of steps which have not exposed us to the real thing. We have a watered-down, undemanding form of Christianity. We do not hunger and thirst for God because we have been given a substitute in a labyrinth of religious activities and formalities. We are starving through malnutrition, but we do now know it because we keep eating something which looks and smells like food.

We are to hunger and thirst for righteousness as a starving person for food and a perishing person for water.

June 19

A Family Likeness

John 17:20-26

That they all may be one, as You, Father, are in Me, and I in You; that they also may be one in Us, that the world may believe that You have sent Me. And the glory which You gave Me I have given them, that they may be one just as We are one (John 17:21-22).

I WAS IN A WORLD OF MY OWN as I flew home. I had just finished a very emotional talk with my sisters and brother. We had prepared the old family home in Kenosha, Wisconsin, for sale. All the furnishings had to be cleared out and keepsakes divided among us. My sister, Elaine, had put in a box all the personal things left to me by my father: pictures, his diary of the First World War, some Ogilvie tartans, and his pocket watch. I had rushed to meet my flight, and then, in the anonymity of 3½ hours to myself, I opened the box and sorted through the precious gifts of memory. The pictures of my father, taken through the years, made me laugh and cry—the family portraits, the pictures of fishing trips and never-to-be-forgotten times together. I relived a portion of my life and was thankful for a father who had loved me and believed in me.

About this time in June each year, we set aside a day to honor our father. It's a time for memories and gratitude, a time to say to our fathers still with us, or those with the Lord, "Dad, I love you!" But it's also a special day to claim one of Jesus' most awesome promises. We can be like our heavenly Father. He came in Jesus Christ so that we could reclaim our family likeness. In a way, He gave us a photograph of Himself so that we could never forget our divine destiny to be children of the Father, and a part of His forever family.

Our heavenly Father wants us to be like Him in a full family likeness through Jesus Christ, our Brother and Lord.

June 20

Truly Satisfied

Psalm 17:1-15

As for me, I shall behold Thy face in righteousness; I will be satisfied with Thy likeness when I awake (Psalm 17:15).

SATISFIED! WHEN ARE WE ever satisfied? When can we say in honesty that we are satisfied with what we have done or given or finished? We deal constantly with the incomplete, imperfect, and fragmented. How shall we be satisfied?

The fourth beatitude promises that those who seek righteousness will be filled. Some translations say "be satisfied." Our emptiness can be filled. The deepest longing of our minds and hearts can be met. What does this mean?

Just this: Our created purpose to know God, love Him, and do His will can be fulfilled. All other hungers will reoccur and persist. Only our hunger for God can be satisfied. This is a tremendous promise. We can experience the love and power of God! We shall be satisfied!

There is an assurance that comes to a Christian which drives out fear and frustration. He knows that he still needs to grow and that there is much that he still must discover, but he knows that he is called, appointed, set apart, loved, forgiven, and elected by God to be His person. This is not arrogance; it is joyous realization of God's gift. He does not spend his life checking up on his spiritual status, taking his spiritual pulse, constantly asking how he is doing. He belongs to God, and he knows it. This fact liberates him to love and serve. He has been filled with God's own Spirit, because his deepest desire is for righteousness.

*Become what you are; live in the status already given.
Use the resources already released;
claim the gifts already appropriated.*

June 21

How to Be "Right" All the Time!

Romans 3:21; 4:5; 5:17; 6:13

But now the righteousness of God apart from the law is revealed, being witnessed by the Law and the Prophets (Romans 3:21).

WE ALL WANT TO BE RIGHT. No one likes being wrong. But more than our desire to have our facts right is the desire to "be right," to be in harmony with other people. We desire open, loving relationships with everyone and are disturbed when misunderstandings, hostilities, or resentments occur. There is something within us which abhors a broken relationship as nature abhors a vacuum. We are propelled to justify ourselves to be sure we were right and not the cause of the separation.

The same thing is more profoundly true of man's relationship with God. Because of rebellion and the desire to run our own lives, we are separated from fellowship with God. Sin is separation. But there is also the desire to be right with God. We try to make ourselves right by being good enough to desire His love. We never can be, because there is in us the ambivalence of desiring and rejecting God at the same time.

God knew man's inability to be right with Him. Therefore He came in Jesus to reveal a righteousness which would be given as a gift. The cross was the tangible, historical event in which God reconciled—that is, forgave and accepted—man to Himself. That's righteousness which is "right-ness." This is the righteousness which Jesus anticipated in the beatitude. We are to yearn with hunger and thirst to possess this right relationship with God. We are told by Paul that it is a free gift appropriated by faith.

Righteousness is "right-ness" with God.

June 22

Steadfast Love

Matthew 5:7; Psalm 103:1-22; Lamentations 3:19-26

Blessed are the merciful, for they shall obtain mercy (Matthew 5:7).

THIS BEATITUDE GIVES US another quality of family likeness we can have with God. He is merciful and wants to reproduce that crucial aspect of His nature in us. We are truly happy—blessed—when we are receiving His mercy and are communicating it to others. When we have felt God's mercy in our failures and needs, we become merciful to others in their inadequacies and mistakes. Christ is God's mercy incarnate. As He lives His life in us, our minds are captured by His amazing grace, our emotions are infused by tender love, and our wills are liberated to do whatever people need to feel loved and forgiven by us.

Mercy is profound identification. The Hebrew word implies living in another person's skin, to feel, know, and experience what he or she is going through: empathy; sensitivity. The outer manifestation of our inner experience of God's mercy is a graciousness which offers understanding, gives others another chance, and freely forgives. The qualification for receiving the continuous flow of God's mercy is to give out what He has put in.

Psalm 103 has been a charge and charter for me in attempts to live this beatitude. The steadfast love of the Lord endures forever. Nothing can change it. Note all the things that quality of mercy overcomes. That gives us assurance and courage, strength and endurance. Reread the psalm as a prayer from your own heart as your expression of gratitude for mercy and as a commitment to be merciful. Now turn to Lamentations 3:19-26 and read again the good news that the mercy of the Lord never comes to an end: it never ceases; it is fresh every morning and all through the day, all because of the faithfulness of God. Blessedness is receiving and reproducing mercy.

Great is thy faithfulness; morning by morning new mercies I see.

—Thomas O. Chisholm

June 23

To Will One Thing

Matthew 21:28-32; Matthew 5:8

And he came to the second and said likewise. And he answered and said, "I go, sir," and he did not go (Matthew 21:30).

Blessed are the pure in heart, for they shall see God (Matthew 5:8).

WHAT DOES IT MEAN TO have a pure heart? The sixth beatitude challenges us! The *heart* in Hebrew thought meant the whole personality. Purity in the New Testament is usually interpreted not just as cleanness but as singleness of nature. Jesus abhorred the double-mindedness of the Pharisees. Duplicity caused confusion and moral sickness. Hypocrisy is to go double. Jesus wanted people who willed one thing: to know God and do His will.

A truly joyous, blessed person is one who has finally discovered that he has no other purpose than to be faithful and obedient to God. He has a basis of deciding the value, priority, and purpose of all that he does. He lives to glorify and enjoy Him.

The spiritual sickness of contemporary Christianity is ambivalence—the inability to decide between alternatives. The word "pure" means unmixed, unadulterated, unalloyed. Purity of heart is freedom from mixed motives. Our basic loyalty is to God, above and beyond all other people and groups.

Purity of heart is a constant struggle. Every day, every situation, every choice presents a renewed opportunity to seek first God's purpose and plan. Our motives are never perfect. We must confess to God our desire to serve and obey and commit ourselves anew to understand and do His will. We are all like the son who says he will go and then does not go. Purity of heart is to put word and action into marshaled obedience to purity of motive to love and obey God.

Purity of heart is to will one thing.

June 24

The Tools of Our Trade

Romans 14:19

Therefore let us pursue the things which make for peace and the things by which one may edify another (Romans 14:19).

PAUL CHALLENGES US TO pursue what makes for peace. What are the elements which contribute to peace?

Basic to all ingredients of peace is love. "Perfect love casts out fear." Fear of each other and fear between groups robs us of peace. Peace is usually closely combined with grace in the greetings and benedictions of the New Testament letters. Grace is free, unreserved love. There can be no lasting peace without a gracious spirit which accepts the inadequacies, failures, and weaknesses of others. There is no negative judgment in grace. People can live in peace with us because they are accepted and released.

Honesty and openness are crucial to peace. Hostility grows from unexpressed and repressed anger or resentment. Peace can be maintained only if we say what we think when we think it and allow no day to end with inner feelings burning within.

Forgiveness makes for peace. We forgive because we have been forgiven by God. Our task as Christians is to be as forgiving as the Lord has been to us.

Mutual upbuilding is absolutely necessary for peace. We are to contribute to each other's feeling of security and stability. Peace grows among people who are trying to find ways to express affirmation of each other in language and actions each can understand. These things make for peace and are the tools of the peacemaker.

Christ provides us with the tools of the trade of peacemaking.

June
25

Healing the Wounds

2 Corinthians 5:11-21

Therefore we are ambassadors for Christ, as though God were pleading by us: we implore you in Christ's behalf, be reconciled to God (2 Corinthians 5:20).

PEACEMAKING IS AN ACTIVE task! It is a vital ministry of reconciliation which is never finished. Paul gives us the motive, perspective, example, message, and commission for our peacemaking task.

The love of Christ is our motive. There can be no peace apart from a right relationship with Christ in our mind and emotions. As long as we are unsettled with guilt, frustrated by ambivalence, or confused of purpose, we cannot be at peace or discover peace in our relationships or situations. Controlled by the love of Christ, we seek to communicate His peace. We no longer see people from a competitive point of view. We affirm what Christ has given others to use as the gifts of life. We can become a new person altogether when we are "in Christ." The war between self and Christ can come to an end, and a new person emerges. We are challenged to share what we have found. We are to actively seek to bring reconciliation.

This ministry is helping separated parties rediscover the point of view of the other. It uncovers hostilities needing to be healed and aids in communicating forgiveness. We see ourselves as ambassadors of peace: God constantly making an appeal through us to others. We are to listen and interpret, understand and share the hurt, express and transmit forgiveness. Wherever there is a wound in the world, we are Christ's healing corpuscles sent to bring healing.

We are partners with Christ in peacemaking.

June 26

The Peace of a Deathless Life
Colossians 1:1-29

And by Him to reconcile all things to Himself, by Him, whether things on earth or things in heaven, having made peace through the blood of His cross (Colossians 1:20).

IN A WORLD LIKE THIS, we are called to be peacemakers. But how can we share peace if we have no peace? Peace must become a reality in each of our lives before we can be involved in bringing peace in our relationships, in groups, between nations, and in the world. There can be no peace until we are different.

Paul spoke of Jesus as our Peace, the One who brings the hostility to an end. Paul found a peace which enabled him to be a peacemaker. Jesus Christ had broken down the dividing wall of hostility between Him and others. The peace of Christ is to be ours through what Christ has done and is doing. His death and resurrection is the basis of our peace.

Jesus Christ has forgiven the disturbing and distressing memories which rob us of deep, inner peace. We are forgiven and free. The cost of a peaceful soul is that we confess to Him in painful specifics the memories and fears of the past and let Him deal with them with the same love that brought Him to Calvary. But that is in the past. Jesus Christ is alive and present with us to give us peace as a gift of His Spirit. He does this by giving us the courage to place our ultimate trust and security in Him above and beyond family, friends, position, and power.

Christ is Lord of the future. There is latent within most of us a fear of death. Our uncertainties of the future are all rooted in the question of our future existence. Christ is our Peace because we know that in Him we have a deathless life. We can now expend our energies bringing His peace to others because we have been liberated from frustrating fear. We are alive in eternity; heaven has begun. His peace gives us courage!

Christ Himself is our Peace.

June 27

The Zest of the World

Mark 9:50; Luke 14:34-35; Matthew 5:13

You are the salt of the earth; but if the salt loses its flavor, how shall it be seasoned? It is then good for nothing but to be thrown out and trampled underfoot by men (Matthew 5:13).

WE ARE TO BE ZEST FOR the world. This is what Jesus meant when He told His disciples that they were to be the salt of the earth. Salt is so common and inexpensive to us that we do not value the full intent of what Jesus was saying. Salt was extremely expensive in Jesus' day: a man's life was valued about as much as a bag of salt. Salt was cherished and used carefully. To be called the salt of the earth indicated value and worth. But for what purpose? To bring tang back into the bland, tasteless experience which most people had made of living!

Christians are to be the source of vitality in the world. So often our style of life is just the opposite. In history, we can mark the profound misunderstanding of Jesus on this point. Piety has often equaled caution, restriction, and negation. The Christian life has been defined by what a believer should not do! Not so with Jesus! He called His disciples to outlive, out-love, and out-serve the whole world. He wanted the pagan world to stop with a start and say, "Why, that's living!" The joy of the Christian is his saltiness. He is alive with a tremendous vitality because he has been loved, forgiven, cherished, and empowered.

A good way to deal with the challenge to be the zesty salt of the earth is to question, "Do I want the whole world to be like me? Have I found an exciting, adventuresome faith that I want everyone to have? Who would want to know Christ because of what he sees in me?" The world around us is deciding whether to take Christ seriously because of what people see that He has done for us.

A Christian is salt to a tasteless world.

June 28

Sheer Sparkle

Psalm 150:1-6

Let everything that has breath praise the Lord. Praise the Lord! (Psalm 150:6).

"I HAVE BEEN TO CHURCH today, and I am not depressed." These words by Robert Louis Stevenson were recorded as if what happened was an extraordinary phenomenon.

What can be said of our worship today? It may not depress, but does it *impress* by its vitality and power?

William Barclay said, "There should be a sheer sparkle about the Christian life; and too often the Christian dresses like a mourner at a funeral, and talks like a spectre at a feast." How about us? Are we alive with joy?

Ibsen's Emperor Julian makes a cutting comment about Christians: "Have you looked at the Christians closely? Hollow-eyed, pale-cheeked, flat-breasted all; they brood their lives away, unspurred by ambition; the sun shines for them, but they do not see it; the earth offers them its fullness, but they do not deserve it; all their desire is to renounce and suffer that they may come to die." Grim criticism, that!

Oliver Wendell Holmes once said, "I might have entered the ministry if certain clergymen I knew had not looked and acted like undertakers." That may be an unfair analysis of the clergy, but we all must ask: What will people find today in our lives?

Samuel Chadwick said, "God is love; God is fire. The two are one. The Holy Spirit baptizes with fire. Spirit-filled souls are ablaze for God. They love with a love which glows. They believe with a faith that kindles. They serve with a devotion that consumes. They hate sin with a fierceness that burns. They rejoice with a joy that radiates. Love is perfected in the fire of God." How would people define what it means to be a Christian from our lives?

Christ came to give us an abundant life.

June 29

A Light in the Darkness

Matthew 5:14-16; 1 John 1:1-10; Ephesians 5:8

You are the light of the world. A city that is set on a hill cannot be hidden (Matthew 5:14).

I REMEMBER SEEING THE CITY set on a hill to which Jesus supposedly referred. It was late at night. I was traveling by car along the winding road to the Sea of Galilee. The lights of the city vividly twinkled against the dark sky. It was daylight when I passed that way again. Even in the daytime, I could not miss the city. It could not be hidden.

A Christian is to be like that. The purpose of his life is to be a commanding witness for Jesus Christ in a dark world. What we believe, what Christ means to us, and what He has done in our character cannot be hidden.

The technological achievements of our day have tended to make us subdued witnesses. We are afraid to share the simplicity of the gospel in such a complex world as ours. We forget that our complicated, computerized life has only intensified our personal need. Today, for all our advancement, there are more people in mental institutions and under psychiatric care than ever before.

A creative witness earns the right to be heard by living a dynamic life in the light. You can't miss a living Christian any more than I could miss that city. Our challenge is to keep our minds filled with the truth of Christ and our emotions fired with the warmth of Christ, so that we will attract the people around us with His quality of life. There is no such thing as secret discipleship. That is a contradiction of terms. Disciples cannot be hidden.

An authentic witness cannot be overlooked.

June 30

A Hand, Not a Chip, on Our Shoulder

John 9:1-17

As long as I am in the world, I am the light of the world (John 9:5).

WHEN JESUS SAID, "You are the light of the world," He identified His disciples with Himself. He said, "I am the Light of the world." This was one of the greatest compliments He could have paid His disciples. They were to understand His ministry and do what He had done.

How were they to do this? Jesus Christ's light would illuminate them. We all admire radiant people. There is something about the sparkle of their eyes, the vitality of their countenance, and the excitement of their expression. The disciples became radiant men after the Resurrection when, at Pentecost, Jesus Christ made His postresurrection home in their minds, emotions, and words.

Jesus Christ was the Truth which illuminated the darkness of the misunderstanding of the world. As the disciples lived with Jesus, the Light of the World cast His brightness and dispelled the doubts and fears and confusion of their minds. The light of Jesus' love infused their emotions. His light brought brightness to their relationships with others.

As long as the apostles kept in fellowship with Jesus Christ, they were able to bring light to the world. The Christian church is God's light in a dark world. We are to proclaim truth, live in a quality of life, and communicate a power of love which will be light in a dark age.

E. Stanley Jones gave us good advice on how to be light in darkness today: "In the pure, strong hours of the morning, when the soul of the day is at its best, lean upon the windowsill of the Lord and look into His face, and get orders for the day. Then go out into the world with a sense of a Hand upon your shoulder and not a chip."

We are to reflect the light of Jesus Christ.

July 1

By All Means Witness

1 Corinthians 1:22-23

For the Jews request a sign, and the Greeks seek after wisdom; but we preach Christ crucified, to the Jews a stumbling block and to the Greeks foolishness (1 Corinthians 1:22-23).

"HOW CAN I BECOME a witness?" a man asked me the other day. "You are already," I said. "The question is, what kind?" He was startled, and so I went on to explain that we are all witnessing all the time about what Christ has or has not done in us. The way we live, how we react, and what we say or fail to say about what Christ means to us is a telling witness.

What kind of witness would you say you are on that basis? Paul presses us beyond that. He tells how the love of Christ in his heart prompted him to practice what I have called the four "I's" of authentic witness: identification, involvement, intercession, and incisiveness. Becoming "all things to all people" does not mean compromising our beliefs. Rather, it implies that we should use all our previous experience to identify with people who need Christ. Often, the things we've been through, learned, achieved, or attained by the Lord's grace give us a point of contact. Christ will use everything we've been through in both successes and failures.

The human identification can enable empathy and understanding. When we pray for a person, Christ's power is released. He or she is prepared by the Lord to hear an incisive sharing of the gospel. All we need to be is ready for the people the Lord has made ready!

All that I have and am, what I have experienced and discovered, enables me to be whatever people need in order to witness to what Christ can mean to them.

July 2

What an Example!

Philippians 3:17; Acts 26:24-29

Brethren, join in following my example, and note those who so walk, as you have us for a pattern (Philippians 3:17).

"HOW CAN WE COMMUNICATE the faith with all our hang-ups?" many people ask.

If we don't believe that what's happened to us in our relationship to Christ ought to happen to everyone, then probably too little has happened to us. But Paul goes even deeper than this. With alarming audacity he says, "Keep on imitating me." Now I believe that's a great test of the Christian life. If we are not so excited about what we have found that we want everyone to experience it, then we have not found very much.

When Paul appeared before Agrippa, he proclaimed the winsome power of his life in Christ. Agrippa responded, knowing full well that Paul was seeking to have him find the faith Paul had experienced, "In this short time, you think you will make me a Christian?" To this Paul said, "Whether a short time or a long time, my prayer to God is that you and all the rest of you who are listening to me today might become what I am." Here again, the same confidence: imitate me! Can you say that—at home, at work, with your friends? If not, why not?

But the question which has probably come to your mind as you read this is, "How can I, with a knowledge of all my imperfections, set myself up as an example?" That is to misunderstand Paul. He was very honest with people about his hang-ups. What he wanted them to imitate was the same experience of God's grace and forgiveness. How he handled his failures was an invaluable part of his witness. He didn't want people to know how great he was, but how great God had been in his life!

Every day people are deciding about Christ by what they see of Him in us.

July 3

A Full Set of Keys

Matthew 16:13-20; Revelation 1:18

And I will give you the keys of the kingdom of heaven,
and whatever you bind on earth will be bound in heaven,
and whatever you loose on earth will be loosed in heaven (Matthew 16:19).

IF WE ONLY TRUSTED OURSELVES as much as Jesus does! What tremendous things would happen if we relinquished our own negative view of ourselves and saw ourselves as Jesus sees us. What an amazing confidence He has in us!

He has given us the keys of the kingdom. This means that we can admit or block others from the kingdom, depending upon whether we will share what we have found.

Many of us find it difficult to talk about our faith. This self-consciousness is an expensive luxury. Jesus tells us that it could result in someone never knowing the joy and peace that is available in fellowship with Him. When we refuse to share, we lock the door for someone else He desires to reach through it.

Note that there are keys. There is the key of listening, the key of caring, the key of discussion, the key of witness, the key of prayer for another, the key of unchanging love. He has given us a full key ring, so that we may unlock the varied, different doors of each kind of person we meet. We have been given power to forgive in His name and to assure people of His love. What a trust! What an opportunity!

A multitude of laymen are in serious danger. It is positively perilous for them to hear more sermons, attend more Bible classes and read more religious and ethical works, unless accompanying it all there be afforded day by day an adequate outlet for their newfound truth.

—John R. Mott

July 4

Dependence Day

2 Chronicles 7:11-22

If…My people who are called by My name humble themselves and pray, and seek My face and turn from their wicked ways, then I will hear from heaven, will forgive their sin, and will heal their land (2 Chronicles 7:14).

PATRIOTISM HAS NOT GONE out of style. For a Christian it has very special implications. Independence Day is really dependence day for us. It is a day to reaffirm God's vision for America, the dream He gave to our founding forefathers, and the unique place that our nation has in His strategy for history. The Fourth of July is more than a day for picnics, firecrackers, and parades. It is a day for prayer for our nation, our leaders, and God's blessing on us.

Our Scripture today holds out a grand promise with a great "if." It is a pledge by God to His people in our land. If we humble ourselves, turn from the things which contradict His vision for our nation, and earnestly pray, He will forgive and heal our ills. The words "one nation under God" in our Pledge of Allegiance are a commitment to work for His righteousness and justice in every part of society.

But just as what distorts our nation is caused by evil people, so too the solutions must come through good people in leadership in all levels of government. So for each of us, this is a day of commitment to correct anything in our personal behavior which denigrates the American dream, and to pray for our President, our Congress, and our local leaders that they would be courageous in social righteousness. There is a vital interrelationship between our prayers and their courage. The hope of America is not in her military might or natural resources, but in God's people, you and me, as our prayers become a channel through which He can bless our land. Goodness and greatness are inseparable. America's supernatural resource for greatness is humble prayer on "Dependence Day."

The greatest expression of patriotism is prayer.

July 5

An Influential Person

Ephesians 6:10-20

Therefore take up the whole armor of God, that you may be able to withstand in the evil day, and having done all, to stand (Ephesians 6:13).

YOU ARE AN INFLUENTIAL person! Do you believe in your awesome power? Christ does. Every day, in hundreds of ways, you and I are influencing people about what it means (or does not mean!) to live the abundant life in Christ. If the people of our lives had to write a definition of Christianity from what they see and hear from us, what would they write? Our influence is either positive or negative. People are reading the signals all the time. What kind of salt and light have we been?

People and their needs are our agenda. Our faith is to pack a wallop for others. Everything Jesus gives us is for our influence on others. When we settle that, life becomes blessed indeed! We were meant to have impact, influence, and inspiration in the lives of the people we touch. What stands in the way of people seeing Christ's light burning in us? For some, it's our personalities, which need Christ's transformation; for others, it's privatism, which keeps us from sharing our faith; for still others, it is simply lack of loving concern. The Psalmist reminds us of our calling: "Let the redeemed of the Lord say so!" (Psalm 107:2).

Paul gives us the vivid description of the equipment which is given to us for our witnessing. It is moving to picture him in chains at the end of his life in Rome. But not even imprisonment debilitated his witness. The guards were led to Christ while guarding him. The ambassador in chains spoke boldly, and many people, even in Caesar's household, became Christians because of the contagious faith he communicated.

Christ is ready to use us wherever we are.

July 6

"My" Gospel

Romans 16:25-27

According to my gospel (Romans 16:25).

AUTHENTIC WITNESSING REQUIRES a gospel which is personally and passionately ours. Paul spoke of "my gospel." What is yours?

The word "gospel" means "good news." The word in Greek, *euaggelion*, had three uses in ancient times. It meant the bearer of good news, the good news itself, and the reward given to the bearer of the good news. All three have meaning for us. We are the communicators of the good news of the life, message, death, reconciliation, and resurrection of Jesus Christ. What He accomplished for our salvation, eternal life, and abundant living is the content of our good news. He Himself is our reward.

The gospel contains the truth of what Christ did and does. It is the declaration of the promise of life as it was meant to be. The content of the gospel is the message of the New Testament. It is to become my gospel and your gospel. The gospel according to you and me is the gospel which has been ingrained into our thinking, understanding, action, and attitude—biblical truth passed through the tempering of experience until it is an integrated part of us. We are not only to believe the good news, but are to be good news incarnate—the gospel on two legs walking. Only "our" gospel can make us contagious witnesses today!

Only what we constantly rediscover can be consistently reproduced.

July 7

Dealing with Anger

Matthew 5:21-26; Exodus 20:13; Deuteronomy 5:17; Mark 3:1-6

Therefore if you bring your gift to the altar, and there remember that your brother has something against you, leave your gift there before the altar, and go your way. First be reconciled to your brother, and then come and offer your gift (Matthew 5:23-24).

THE PASSAGE DEALING WITH anger is the first of six antitheses Jesus makes between the written code and the deeper righteousness of the heart. The Lord forbids anger "without cause." He is concerned about the free-floating hostility which is caused by lack of the experience of God's healing love for ourselves. Where anger is uncreatively expressed, it eventually is turned on ourselves and is the major cause of anxiety. We also have a responsibility of diffusing anger in others. When we are the cause, we have the obligation to seek forgiveness and reconciliation.

Anger is not bad. It can be an expression of profound caring. But the Pharisees were more concerned about a regulation than they were about human need. Jesus' anger was an expression of love. He loved both the man with the withered hand and the Pharisees who were trying to trap Him. Anger must be expressed in a context of love in which people know that there is nothing which can make us stop loving them.

We all feel anger at times. How can we deal with it? There's no such thing as unexpressed anger. In expressing our anger, we must be sure we do not cut off other people. Do they know how much we love them? A second test of creative anger is that we keep short accounts by expressing our feelings in daytight compartments. Our task is to do everything we can to open the channels for love to flow between us and other people. Before the day ends.

The continuance of anger is hatred.

—Frances Quarles

July 8

Straight Arrows

Matthew 5:33-37; 21:28-32

But let your "Yes" be "Yes," and your "No," "No." For whatever is more than these is from the evil one (Matthew 5:37).

OUR LORD CHALLENGES US to be "straight arrows." He wants us to be people on whom others can depend to speak the truth in love. He calls for integrity in our speech. In His time, oaths would be used to fortify the veracity of a person's statement because words could no longer be trusted as consistently true. The method of swearing by something or someone sacred was to alert others to the fact that the statement was absolutely true. Jesus demanded complete honesty and directness. All that was needed was a simple "Yes" or "No" without any embellishment.

Think of the ways that we can shade, confuse, or distort the truth by the way we say something or by what we leave out. We are to be people who are known for unvarnished, unambiguous truth. There's no need to swear by anything if we are known as people who mean what we say and say what we mean. What a great way to live!

The key to that quality of life is earnestness in our relationship with God and one another. Many of us promise more than we intend or can produce. Often we are people-pleasers who want to get off the hook by easy promises. The Lord honors an honest "No" that is open to be changed more than a facile "Yes" that we won't do. His will for us is to have us long to know and do His will. The only answer is "Yes!" with the obedience of follow-through.

Let's make today a day for earnestness with God and other people. Ask the Lord to show you what you are to do and say in today's responsibilities. Say, "Yes, Lord!" then do it!

July 9

An Artesian Flow

John 7:37-39; James 3:6-18

He who believes in Me, as the Scripture has said,
out of his heart will flow rivers of living water (John 7:38).

WHAT COMES OUT OF OUR mouths is dependent on what's in our hearts. We can speak no more than we've allowed the Lord to impute to our hearts. Jesus promises us that out of our hearts will flow rivers of living water—the Holy Spirit. When we allow the Spirit to live in us, He will speak through us. Our words take on power and love which we cannot produce by ourselves. If we lack warmth and affirmation for people, the trouble is probably in our hearts. If words are used to manipulate and control, it's because we need the Holy Spirit to fill our hearts and flow through our words.

James startles us with the power of our words. They can be used to heal or hurt, build up or destroy, encourage or dishearten. What a frightening power the Lord has entrusted to us! The key to this passage is in the gift of wisdom from the Holy Spirit. When we invite the Holy Spirit to dwell in us, we are given the gift of wise speech. But that comes from times of prolonged prayer. How often do we talk to God about what we are going to say? When we ask for His wisdom, He gives it in abundance. We will be able to see with discernment and speak with directness.

Read verse 17 again. That's the kind of wisdom the Lord wants to give us for what we are to say. Today is the day to claim Jesus' promise. What you say can come from a heart overflowing with joy and peace. Tell the Lord you want and need His indwelling Spirit.

The way from God to a human heart
is through a human heart.
—S.D. Gordon

July 10

A Wordless Denial

Matthew 26:31-35, 69-75; 1 Peter 3:13-17

But sanctify the Lord God in your hearts, and always be ready to give a defense to everyone who asks you a reason for the hope that is in you, with meekness and fear (1 Peter 3:15).

THE ACCOUNT OF PETER'S denial is an alarming reminder of how we can use words to deny our Lord. Often we do it in what we refuse to say as much as by what we say. When we have an opportunity to witness but remain silent, that's denial. Or think of the ways we contradict what we believe by the way we talk! The very fact that we talk so little about what we believe gives the impression that we believe very little. This is an eloquent, wordless denial. There's more than one way of saying, "I do not know the Man!" It's then that the cock crows. But it is exciting to read Peter's own challenge many years later in his letter to the early church. The disciple who denied the Lord by what he didn't say, as much as by what he said, later became a bold apostle and encouraged others to be ready to give an account for the hope that Christ had placed within them.

The world is filled with people longing to have someone they respect take a stand. Speak out! When we are silent about what the Lord means to us or about crucial issues of justice where our faith is at stake, we deny our Lord. It is comforting to note that when the Lord appeared to Peter on the Sea of Galilee after the Resurrection, He gave him an opportunity to affirm his love for the Lord three times. He does the same for us.

Often I hear people say, "My witness is my life. I don't talk with others about my faith." That is making quite a claim for our life! But it is also a denial of people's right to know what is behind our quality of life. Let's make today a day to share the reason for the hope that is within us.

A silent witness is a denial.
I will not deny my Lord today!

July 11

A Talent of Words

Matthew 25:14-30

And to one he gave five talents, to another two, and to another one, to each according to his own ability; and right away he went on a journey (Matthew 25:15).

TODAY LET'S THINK OF THE gift of words in the context of the parable of the talents. Our words can be used to multiply the kingdom of God—words of love, forgiveness, encouragement, and hope. We can use the talent of what He's done for us to share the adventure of new life with other people. They will listen to what Christ can do for them if there has been authenticity in our life and words.

We are to be people who can be trusted; people will share their needs and dreams with a person who has used the gift of words to affirm them. We can also break down trust by using words for gossip, negative criticism, and backbiting. Our witness will become tarnished, and we will not be the people others will trust with their deepest concerns. We will all have to make an accounting of what we did with the precious gift of words. The talent can be multiplied if we use words to share Christ's love.

The parable of the talents, when considered in the context of our opportunities to use words to share Christ's love, gives us little excuse. There may be some of us who are more capable in communicating our faith, but we all have at least one talent. We need to dig it up and begin using it. The Lord has arranged relationships for all of us with people He wants to love through our expressions of words of love and explanations of what He means to us and can mean to them. I am a Christian because two friends in college used their gift of words to communicate affirmation and then tell me about the Savior. Think of all the people who may not live forever because our talent of words is buried!

Today is the day to dig up our talent of words and invest it in sharing love and hope with others.

July 12

Get to the Point!

Job 11:1-8

Shall a multitude of words go unanswered, and a talkative man be acquitted? (Job 11:2).

JESUS WAS NEVER IMPRESSED with long, formal prayers which were prayed to be heard and admired by people. He exposed and condemned people who misused the dynamic of prayer to gain spiritual status with others. We all know people whose oratory in prayer must offend God. We do not pray to convince God, but to converse with Him. Our prayer is a response to His Spirit at work within us, creating the desire to pray. A multitude of words makes little difference. Get to the point! Be simple and direct!

Note the people who arrested Jesus' attention. He was always utterly available to the person in need who cried out the brief, honest prayer, "Master, have mercy—help me!" A person full of talk did not win Jesus' approval. He often shocked the verbose and loquacious pretenders to piety who tried to create an impression with words. He pressed them beyond their words to their moral condition. His radical moral demand brought reality and honesty to the easy, word-oriented followers. Jesus demanded integrity of words and life.

Peter Berger has given careful analysis to the cultural, political, and social forms of much of American religion. It adds up to something like this: "Have faith in faith—it's of great therapeutic value. Get up in the morning and stand in front of the window, head back, breathe deeply three times, every time with the words, 'I believe, I believe, I believe.' "

But what do we believe? That's more important than words. Jesus wants life, not just words.

Most of us talk beyond where we are willing to live.

July 13

Giving and Forgiving Love

Matthew 5:38-40

You have heard that it has been said, "An eye for an eye and a tooth for a tooth" (Matthew 5:38).

DON'T MISS THE RADICAL challenge that Jesus made in this passage. The Hebrews were very proud of their distinctive application of the *lex talionis*, the practice of exact retribution. It had brought sanity in the measurement of what a person could do to someone who harmed or hurt him.

But Jesus outdistanced that a million miles. He called for no retribution at all! It was no longer to be eye-for-eye, and tooth-for-tooth retaliation. The Master went way beyond the equal expression of anger and resentment. He drives home His point with three very pointed illustrations: a blow with the back of the hand (that's what happens when you turn your right cheek after your left one has been struck with the palm of a right-handed person!), giving a person who sues you for your tunic your only cloak, and going a second mile with someone who compels you to go one.

The only way to live the way Jesus called us to live is by His power. The life He challenges us to live, He more than exemplified Himself. When He lives in us, we are given His capacity for millionth-mile living. We are to be to each other what Christ has been to us. That's the test of a Christian. We are to love as we've been loved. Think of how Christ has loved us! His love is unchanging, unqualified, and unlimited. It is giving and forgiving. To what extent have we loved like this? Who in your life needs that quality of love from you today? The distinguishing mark of a Christian is that he or she loves with the same power that Christ has loved him or her. By that love, the world will know that we are Christ's disciples.

What the Lord requires, He inspires. We are to be channels of His love. Our challenge is to allow Him to love us so that we can love others. That's the exciting adventure of being a Christian!

July 14

Second-Mile Living

Matthew 5:41-42

And whoever shall compel you to go one mile, go with him two (Matthew 5:41).

THE SECOND MILE HAS A fascinating background. We miss the meaning unless we take time to understand the background of the words. This parable is based on a picture of an occupied country. The word to compel is from the Greek verb *aggareuein.* The noun form comes from the Persian word meaning a courier of the ancient postal system. Each road was divided into stages which took about a day to travel. There was food, water, and lodging provided for the courier at the end of each stage.

The custom was that a private citizen and his horse could be pressed into service to go a stage of the way. The word *aggareuein* is the word for such compulsive enlistment. Through the years the word was used to indicate forced labor or giving of supplies by people in an occupied land. The occupying troops could demand the response of people by force and might. In Palestine, a Jew could be pressed into service at any moment. He had no recourse but to cooperate and fulfill what was demanded of him.

What Jesus seems to be saying is that if a person asks you to go one mile and you do it, you are only fulfilling what is required in an occupied country. If, however, you keep the load and indicate willingness to go on in service, you surprise and impress others with your loving openness. The irreducible minimum does not impress Jesus. He calls His people to keep the load and press on.

This has a practical implication for resentment. Instead of resenting being pressed into service, Jesus suggests practical love for the person whom we resent. Go on beyond all expectations! Give yourself beyond your limit and you will find the second breath of the Holy Spirit infusing life, energy, love, and forgiveness.

Christ calls us to second-mile living with people.

July 15

Get Cracking!

Matthew 5:43-48

Therefore you shall be perfect, just as your Father in heaven is perfect (Matthew 5:48).

A MAN WHO CELEBRATED his 95th birthday asserted that he had no enemies. "How do you live 95 years and have no enemies?" someone asked. "I've outlived them all!" was his answer. We laugh. But then we begin to wonder. Most of us are not that fortunate. We have people who disturb and distress us all through life. Who are your enemies? Think of them. Now consider Jesus' demanding words about loving our enemies. He went way beyond that commandment to love people we like. We are to love, bless, and do good to people who hate and misuse us.

The secret of doing that is in becoming like Him. We are sons and daughters of the Lord. His nature is given to us. That's why He came: to transform our inner nature and enable us to love as He loves. Focus on your enemies and then ask, "What does love demand?" We are to outlive our enemies, not in length of years, but in the quality of the Lord's gracious acceptance and reconciliation. This is a day to love our enemies.

What an awesome challenge! We are to be perfect even as our heavenly Father is perfect. The Greek word used to translate Jesus' Aramaic word is *telios*, meaning purpose. To be perfect is to accomplish our purpose. Just as our heavenly Father continually accomplishes His purpose moment by moment, so can we. That forces us to consider the reason we are alive. We were created to be loved and to love. Our goal is not perfectionism on our own strength, but to set our ultimate goal to receive and communicate God's love. That's top priority. All other lesser goals of life must fit into this purpose. What in your life gets in the way of this primary goal?

Today is a day to get cracking
in accomplishing my real purpose.

Love Becomes Involved

Luke 10:25-37

But he, wanting to justify himself, said to Jesus, "And who is my neighbor?" (Luke 10:29).

THE GOOD SAMARITAN expressed practical love. He did not give pious words of comfort and pass by on the other side. He helped the man change his painful condition and got him the help he needed. His love got him involved.

Words of love are cheap. Involvement which costs time, privacy, and money is love which counts. God got involved in Christ in the suffering of the world. It cost the cross. God did more than say that He sympathized. He took our sorrow on Himself and suffered for us. That's the cost of true love.

When is the last time you were inconvenienced because of the needs of someone else? When has your pleasure of privacy been altered to give specific, costly love? When did you set your own plans aside to spend time with someone in need?

Most of us are like the Levite and the Priest. We say, "I sympathize." But do we? How much? The Good Samaritan gave what he had: wine and oil for the wound, his beast for transportation, his money for lodging in the inn. Also note that he knew the value of follow-up: he said he would come back. The need placed in his path had to be seen through to final healing, not just a passing concern.

Many of the major problems which face people today need practical help. We can show love as we help them through their particular problem. We earn the right to share our convictions by sharing their difficulty.

Love spells involvement.

July 17

When God Is Our Audience

Matthew 6:1-4

You have no reward from your Father who is in heaven (Matthew 6:1).

IT IS DANGEROUS TO PLAY to the wrong audience. Jesus was concerned about people who played their lives for the approval of others rather than God. The target of this passage was the hypocrites who did charitable deeds, giving alms for the adulation and approval of people rather than God. The classical meaning of the word hypocrite is an actor in a play who played more than one part. The hypocritical Pharisees were play-acting at religion for the wrong audience. Charitable deeds should be done out of praise to God for His grace and love, not for the applause of people.

We laugh at the picture of a person going to the Temple to give alms with a brass band leading the way to call attention to the gift and the giver. He will have the reward of people, but not of God. All that we have and are is a gift from God. The question is, "Who gets the glory?" We can never outgive God. The more we give to Him and His work in the world, the more He can entrust to us.

It is our responsibility to meet and know the person inside us. Give that person to the lordship of Christ. Allow Him to reshape the hopes and dreams of your life. Then get that vision out in the open for others to see. We owe it to ourselves and others to clarify what is no longer negotiable for us because of our commitment to Christ. Dishonesty about that or debilitating duality of being one thing on the outside and hiding another on the inside will cause more pressure than all our friends, people for whom we work, or loved ones in life's intimate relationships could ever produce.

Write out a description of the person you want to be in Christ. List your personal goals. Then outline how you will be that person, completely free of hypocrisy. Now we are ready to receive the Lord's power to be an authentic person. For us, to live is Christ!

When Our Own Horn Is Flat

Matthew 6:2

Therefore, when you do a charitable deed, do not sound a trumpet before you as the hypocrites do in the synagogues and in the streets, that they may have glory from men. Assuredly, I say to you, they have their reward (Matthew 6:2).

"DON'T BLOW YOUR OWN horn" is a colloquial saying with which we are familiar. It means...don't draw attention to yourself, your good deeds, your own accomplishments. We all have worked out subtle ways of letting people know whom we know, what we've done, and where we've been. We drop names, places, and possessions in our conversations.

Jesus uses a metaphorical image: "When you give alms, sound no trumpet before you!" A trumpet had been used to call people to worship or to announce the times of prayer. Jesus had a sense of humor. His listeners could picture a man on the way to the Temple to give alms with a trumpeter going before him to announce to everyone that he was on his way to be piously generous. He was concerned about ostentatious almsgiving. The hyperbole drives home the point.

Almsgiving was one of the most sacred tasks of a pious Jew—so much so that the same word is used for almsgiving and righteousness. The word "alms" means good works or acts of charity. It is closely connected with God's righteousness and mercy.

But ostentation gives illegitimate birth to the right thing for the wrong reason. Jesus was concerned about motive. He knew that our real motive for benevolence could be exposed, cleansed, and healed only if we give without any concern for reward. When Christ's love is our only motive, then the giving is itself our reward. Who needs more than that?

Any note blown from your own horn is flat!

July 19

An Uninformed Left Hand

Matthew 6:3

But when you do a charitable deed, do not let your left hand know what your right hand is doing (Matthew 6:3).

HOW CAN WE FOLLOW Jesus' advice to let our lights shine that men may see our good works (Matthew 5:16) if we do not even let our left hand know what our right hand is doing? Is this a contradiction? Not when deeply understood.

W. Robertson McCall has an interesting statement: "Show when tempted to hide; hide when tempted to show." The key is found in giving God the glory. There are some things which we do which we should freely share with others, while there are other things which would only be ostentations to rehearse. The question is…who gets the credit? Do people praise us or God at work in us? We often hide our motivating faith and parade its manifestation. The result is that people think that we are what we are by our own strength and do what we do by our own self-generated graciousness.

We ought to be living in such a quality of giving that people will want to know why we are the way we are and have given of ourselves. What we give with our right hand should not quickly be recorded for praise by our left hand.

Let's experiment today. Every time we are tempted to hide our faith, let's make a concerted effort to share the hope of our life, and every time we are tempted to draw attention to what we have done, let's consciously seek anonymity. The silent gift will radiate in our being, and the outward gift will deepen our radiance.

Be willing to share what God has done for you and be willing to be silent about what you have done about it.

July 20

Praying to People

Matthew 6:5-6

And when you pray, you shall not be like the hypocrites. For they love to pray standing in the synagogues and on the corners of the streets, that they may be seen by men. Assuredly, I say to you, they have their reward (Matthew 6:5).

PRAYER IS THE HEART OF fellowship with God. In it we open our total self to God in adoration, confession, thanksgiving, and supplication. Prayer is communion with God in which He speaks to us through the thoughts engendered in our minds and the decisions of our wills. How wonderful: we can share life with the Lord and Creator of the universe!

Prayer was absolutely central in the life and message of Jesus. But it is more than a monologue to satisfy ourselves or impress others. It is a profound kind of listening.

This is why Jesus was so critical of hypocrisy in attention-oriented public prayers. Three times a day a good Jew would stop his work and turn toward Jerusalem and pray. The professionally pious arranged it so that at the time of prayer they could be seen by others. Prayer became a formal duty used to gain the approval of others. Dr. W.D. Maxwell said, "The efficacy of prayer was measured by its ardor and its fluency, and not least by its fervid lengthiness."

John B. Coburn said, "God is a Person. He is infinitely more than this, but He is at least this. And this is the place to begin, for if you think of God primarily as a Person, then when you speak to Him you can say 'You' and 'I.' When He addresses you, He in turn speaks to a person and also says 'You.' Thus a two-way personal conversation, set in personal relationship, can be set up." This personal conversation is the essence of prayer.

Prayer is conversation with God.

July 21

The Secret Place

Matthew 6:5-8; Isaiah 65:24

But when you pray, do not use vain repetitions, as the heathen do. For they think that they will be heard for their many words (Matthew 6:7).

FACE THE QUESTIONS HONESTLY: Why do so few people pray in any consistent, rewarding way? Why is there time for everything except profound times of listening to God? Why are the best hours of our days given to other pursuits? Luther prayed three to four hours a day. Could it be that his effectiveness and original thought can be traced back to those hours?

We know the answer. The great saints of all ages received their original thought from times in prayer. Prayer is the only source of authentic originality and creativity. Jesus said that we are to pray in secret. The idea behind this challenge was that people of wealth often had a place where their treasures and valuables were stored. They would go to this room to count their accumulations and to do their private business affairs. This suggests that Jesus wanted people to talk to God in the place where their real security was hidden.

Our inner hearts are our secret place. That's where Jesus wants to meet us. He was not talking about a place, but a quality. The "room" of which He spoke is more than a location. It is the dwelling place of real, personal self-purpose, plans, and perspective. The Lord wants to communicate with us there about who we are and where we are going. The reason many prayers are empty and ineffective is that they seldom come from the "secret place." And the reason we avoid prolonged prayer is that we fear opening the door of that inner citadel to God—or even to ourselves.

I will invite the Lord into the secret place where the real decisions about my life and values are made.

July 22

The Model Prayer

Matthew 6:9-15

In this manner, therefore, pray (Matthew 6:9).

WHAT WE CALL THE LORD'S PRAYER is really a disciple's prayer. We misunderstand its content and its intended use when we use it liturgically so much that it no longer has meaning. Actually, it is a prayer of awesome depth for those who have come to know Christ, have turned the control of their lives over to Him, and are motivated by His indwelling Spirit to pray this radical prayer.

Elton Trueblood said, "The best-known prayer of our Lord is almost universally misnamed. It is called the Lord's Prayer when it is clearly a prayer designed for use of His followers. If we did not know this in any other way, we should know it because of the fact that it includes a request for forgiveness of sin. If Christ needed to ask for forgiveness, we have been entirely mistaken in our general judgment about Him."

This prayer was meant as a model of prayer, not just as a memorized prayer. In it Jesus taught His disciples how to reverence God, how to pray for His rule in all things, how to acknowledge Him as the source of life, and how to ask for forgiveness and help in testing times. Our public worship and our private prayers should be guided by this prayer, but we wonder if we do not press people who are not committed to Christ to pray beyond their experience and belief by using it in public ritual. Its revolutionary content is soon blended into the general religious words and practices which most people do not take very seriously. Go over each word and phrase and ask, "What would it mean to live this prayer today?"

Stop aimlessly repeating the Lord's Prayer and begin praying according to its guidelines.

July 23

The Fatherhood of God

Matthew 6:9; Galatians 4:1-7

In this manner, therefore, pray: Our Father in heaven, Hallowed be Your name (Matthew 6:9).

THE SAVIOR TAUGHT US TO call God our Father. The designation is seldom used in the Old Testament. Our Lord came not to tell us that God is like our fathers but to reveal a quality of love which heightens and stretches our appreciation of what it means to be a father. All that Jesus taught, lived, died, and was raised up to mediate is focused in this term "Father"—Limitless love, forgiveness before we ask, interventions when we need them most, hope for a million new beginnings. That's how much our Father loves us and why He sent Christ so we could know Him as He is.

When we pray "Who art in heaven," we affirm that God is beyond us and other than we are, and yet He chooses to be with us in Christ. Heaven is the realm in which God is praised unreservedly and known completely. To know the Father in heaven is to have heaven begin now and know that death will be only a transition to complete union with Him. That enables us to hallow His name. The word "hallow" means holy. A name signifies the character, nature, and power of a person. The name "Father" is holy. When we pray, "Our Father in heaven, hallowed be Your name," we are saying, "We accept Your unique place, affirm Your unlimited power, and are assured of Your nature of grace toward us. We will live in that confidence today."

There is no need to plead for the love of God to fill our hearts, as though He were unwilling to fill us. He is as willing as water is willing to flow into an empty channel. Love is pressing around as on all sides like air.

July 24

The Key to Power

Matthew 6:10; 1 Corinthians 4:20; Luke 13:18-21; John 3:1-5

Your kingdom come. Your will be done on earth as it is in heaven (Matthew 6:10).

THE KINGDOM OF GOD is the reign and rule of God in us, in our relationships with others, in our circumstances, in society, and in all future eventualities. This is an awesome prayer which only a disciple can pray. It means that we want to surrender our minds, emotions, wills, bodies, relationships, and responsibilities to God for His will to be done.

When we do His will, the kingdom of God becomes a reality. This sentence in Jesus' model prayer is a promise and an admonition. We are assured that we can know and receive power to do God's will. Our task is to ask, seek, and knock until we have the inner assurance of God's best for us. In every situation, there are usually three pressing possibilities: what we want, what others want for us, and what God wants of us. To pray "Your will be done" is to take the kingdom of God as Jesus revealed it as our charter and make our decisions on that basis. That's how heaven can begin on earth for us. Give the Lord a chance. He will show us what we are to do and give us the courage to do it.

Jesus told Nicodemus that he had to be born again in order to see the kingdom. The word for "again" in the Greek records Jesus' Aramaic word which means both from above as well as a second time—the miracle of a totally new and radically fresh beginning. When we surrender our wills to our Lord, accept His love and forgiveness through the cross, and invite Him to live in us, we begin life all over. Christ in us guides us in each decision and shapes our character in His image. The beginning is small, like a mustard seed, but grows to full stature in Christlikeness. That's what happens when we really desire the rule of God in us and around us.

Today I want God's will and His kingdom to come in my life in fullness of power.

July 25

Daily!

Matthew 6:11; John 6:1-58

Give us this day our daily bread (Matthew 6:11).

WE ARE DEPENDENT ON GOD for everything. We could not breathe a breath, think a thought, move a muscle, work a day, or develop our lives without His moment-by-moment provision. Put your finger on your pulse; thank God for your life. Breathe in, saying "Bless the Lord, O my soul;" breathe out, saying "And all that is within me, bless His holy name." List what is yours from God's gracious provision. Praise Him for food, your body, the people of your life, the opportunities and challenges of today. Daily bread is more than food to eat. Through the Bread of Life, Jesus Christ, all things we have and are become an evidence of unmerited favor from a Lord who knows our needs. Make this a day for "flash prayers" in which you repeatedly say "Thank You, Lord" for the abundant mercies in every moment of life.

The word "daily" reminds us that yesterday's blessings are not sufficient for today. We cannot live on the stale grace of our yesterdays. All they do is remind us that God met our needs for His glory and our growth in a way that was His best for our life. Yesterday's confidence is not enough for today's challenges. The Lord gives the day and shows the way. That's why we must seek His guidance and power for each new day. Andrew Murray said, "I have learned to place myself before God everyday as a vessel to be filled with His Holy Spirit. He has filled me with the blessed assurance that He, as the everlasting God, has guaranteed His own work in me." Thanking God in advance for His blessing for today frees us to live to the fullest today without worry over tomorrow. Open the vessel and have a great day!

The night is given us to take breath, to pray,
to drink deeply at the fountain of power. The day,
to use the strength which has been given us
to go forth to work with it till the evening.
—Florence Nightingale

July 26

Let God Forgive You

Matthew 6:12,14-15; Mark 11:25-26

And forgive us our debts, as we forgive our debtors (Matthew 6:12).

THIS IS THE ONLY SEGMENT of the Disciple's Prayer that Jesus found it necessary to explain and reemphasize. And with good reason. Forgiveness is costly—it was for God on the cross and it is for us. But true forgiveness from us to others is not possible unless we have had fresh experiences of God's forgiveness. This is one of those "You can't give away what you haven't experienced" challenges so familiar in Jesus' teaching. To be able to forgive, we need to let God forgive us. Out of gratitude for His forgiving love, we will want to make things right with others. The only person who is hurt by unforgiven hurts is us!

That leads us to some very serious thinking about three groups of people: those who need our forgiveness, those from whom we need to seek forgiveness, and those who need our help in forgiving others. Make a list of people in all three categories. Chances are that our longest list will be of people whom we need to forgive. It is frightening to ponder Jesus' words that we cannot be forgiven unless we forgive.

Our spiritual lives are like channels which get clogged. As long as there is an unforgiven hurt, however great, we will not be able to openly receive the Lord's forgiveness for us. It is a spiritual law: unforgiving people cannot receive forgiveness. We all know people who are hardened by people's actions and words. Jesus does not say that we should not feel the wound. What He does say is that we need forgiveness from Him for similar things which disturb us about other people. The years have taught me that when I'm really upset by others there is usually a need in me for fresh grace. When I receive it, then I'm ready to become a reconciler with and between people. What about you?

As a forgiven person, I will forgive—today!

July 27

Lord, Help Me!

Matthew 6:13; Hebrews 2:17-18; 1 Corinthians 10:13; James 1:13-14

And do not lead us into temptation, but deliver us from the evil one (Matthew 6:13).

GOD WOULD NOT LEAD US into temptation. Then what does this petition mean? The implication is: keep us away from temptation; be with us when we are tempted; strengthen us in life's temptations. The second portion of the petition helps us understand the first. It should read, "Deliver us from the Evil One." Evil is not abstract. It is rooted in Satan, who is in opposition to our Lord and uses situations and people to entice us. But we belong to Christ, who has overcome Satan through His death and resurrection. We become "overcomers" through Christ. He has sealed us from the power of evil and temptation which could entangle us. But we must cooperate with the Lord and accept His overcoming strength. When we pray this petition of the Disciple's Prayer, we admit our need and receive daily strength for life's temptations.

Hebrews 2:18 reminds us that Christ is able to aid us in temptation because He faced temptation and won. Note also the assurance of Hebrews 4:14-16. We have a High Priest who can sympathize with our weaknesses. He's been through it. There is nothing we can face that didn't face Him. He was victorious and so can we be through Him. When we are tempted we can pray boldly and obtain mercy and find grace to help us in a time of need. That was Paul's assurance when he assured the Corinthians that there would always be a way of escape from temptation. God will keep watch over us today. When the pressures are beyond us, He will intervene. Trust Him. All we need to do is cry out for help, and He will give us strength equal to the temptation.

When we do ill, the Devil tempts us;
when we do nothing, we tempt him.
—Thomas Fuller

July 28

All That We Need

Matthew 6:13; Jude 24-25; Philippians 4:13

For Yours is the kingdom and the power and the glory forever. Amen (Matthew 6:13).

THE LAST SENTENCE OF THE Disciple's Prayer is an adoration and assurance. It ascribes to God the kingdom, power, and glory which are aspects of His nature. He is Lord of all, the source of all power, the One who manifests Himself in life. These three great qualities about God meet the three greatest needs of our lives. We need to accept the absolute rule of the Lord over all of life; we need to receive the power of the Holy Spirit; we need to behold, experience, and live by the manifestations (glory) of His presence.

We have said these last words of this model prayer so often that they are dulled by familiarity. Actually they are a promise of what is ours because we belong to our Lord. We belong to the kingdom, we can receive power for daily pressures, and we can expect breakthroughs of our Lord into our problems. We can claim what is God's and then claim what is ours. Pray: "Praise the Lord, His will is my will; the power to do it comes from Him; and glory goes to Him." The antidote to pride is praise.

To pray "Yours is the kingdom" is to make the Lord the King of our lives. It is an act of sublime submission. When we do that, power begins to flow through us. We become the riverbed of the Spirit of God. The word in Greek for power is *dunamis,* from which our words "dynamite" and "dynamic" come. The same power that raised Jesus from the dead is ours. We are no longer helpless victims of life. But the power is given to us to know and do God's will. We have come full circle in our prayer. Now we are ready to live for God's glory in all that we say and do. There is no limit of power available to a person who is willing to give God the glory and leave the results to Him.

To say "Amen" is to say "so be it" and really mean it.

July 29

A Disciple's Prayer

Matthew 6:9-15; 7:7-12

Ask, and it will be given to you; seek, and you will find; knock, and it will be opened to you (Matthew 7:7).

LET'S RECAP WHAT WE'VE learned about how and what to pray from our study of the Disciple's Prayer. The first section deals with how we are to praise God, the hallowing of His name, the desire for His kingdom, and the doing of His will. Only then can we consider our needs. God must be put at the center before we can lift up our petitions. All-powerful praying begins by a commitment to the majesty, purpose, and will of God. The second section of the prayer deals with our petitions of supplication: food and daily provision for today, forgiveness for the past, intervention for the future. All our needs will be satisfied when they are surrendered completely to our Lord.

The third section is a commitment to God. To pray "Yours is the kingdom and the power and the glory forever" is to declare our ultimate purpose. Thus we see that prayer is adoration, confession, intercession, supplication, and a dedication. Like the five fingers of our hand, each is necessary to grasp and hold the promise of prayer.

Some time ago I was asked to give a prayer at a civic gathering. Just before I went to the rostrum, a woman stopped me and said, "This is a mixed gathering of many faiths. Not everyone is a Christian. Just pray the Lord's Prayer." The emphasis was on the word "just." The woman thought this awesome prayer of commitment Jesus taught the disciples to pray would be the lowest common denominator. Actually it should not be called the "Lord's" Prayer. It is a prayer for disciples who want to be faithful and obedient. When we surrender our total self to our Lord, then we are ready to pray and live His model prayer.

Today is a day to dare to live the Disciple's prayer by the Lord's power.

July 30

The Window of the Heart

Matthew 6:6-18

Do not be like the hypocrites, with a sad countenance (Matthew 6:16).

OUR FACE IS THE WINDOW of our heart. Or it should be. In our world of cosmetics and plastic surgery, we are not always able to look through the window. Even more serious, many of us develop a duality, so that our faces contradict our hearts. It is true when we are sad and pretend to be glad. But it is true when our joy is not expressed in radiance on our faces. What is on our faces, not our words, is the medium of our message. Often our faces deny our faith. Our faces may be an introduction for others to Christ or a negation of what He could mean in their lives. Who would want to know Christ personally because of what is on your face?

We will consider Jesus' teaching on fasting, from the perspective of the Pharisees. Some of them disfigured their faces or even smeared ashes on them to be sure people knew they were fasting. Fasting should have brought them closer to God and thus brought a radiance to their faces. The purpose of fasting had been so distorted that it was identified by a grim face. They had lost the joy! That leaves us with a question: How should our faces look because we have talked to God?

In Hebrew the word for "face" and "presence" is the same. When the Lord promised Moses "My presence shall go with you" (Exodus 33:14), it also meant "My face shall go with you." Near the end of his ministry, Moses gave a benediction which included an assurance that God's face would shine upon the people. God's face in Christ is the source of our radiant faces.

The Lord bless you and keep you; the Lord make His face shine on you, and be gracious to you.

—Numbers 6:24-25

July 31

Joy's Secret Place

Matthew 6:18; James 1:1-9

And your Father who sees in secret will reward you openly (Matthew 6:18).

IT WAS OBLIGATORY FOR ALL Jews to fast on Yom Kippur and Rosh Hashanah. The Pharisees exceeded that by fasting on Monday and Thursday, the days they believed Moses ascended and descended Mount Sinai. The original purpose of fasting was self-denial and deeper communion with God. For many of the Pharisees, it became an outward display of piety and holiness. When the purpose of fasting was lost, the pretense of piousness began. Communion with God was displayed as a grim, unhappy thing. Religion is considered to be that by many people. That's why it is so important to show on our face what is in our heart. The dominant note of Christianity is joy, an outward expression of the grace of God in our heart.

The truth is that joy is the unassailable, undisturbable, undeniable experience of those who know Christ in the midst of difficulty. Happiness is always dependent on our circumstances. Joy is way beyond that; it is the outward expression of the inner experience of God's grace in the new vortex of difficulty.

Note the magnificent progression in James' thought. Trials test our faith, this test produces steadfastness, and steadfastness develops us toward our goal. To be "perfect and complete" is the purpose of God in our lives. This means that we accomplish our reason for being: to glorify God and enjoy Him forever. But we get to that point only as the difficulties of life throw us back in absolute dependence on Christ. As we trust Him, we learn that He is utterly reliable. Our faith grows and becomes steadfast. His steadfast love produces a steadfast endurance. We are no longer pushed around by life. It is no longer what life does to us but what we do in life; not what happens to us, but what we cause to happen because of our faith.

Thank the Lord for the difficulties which make it possible to discover joy in communion with Him.

August 1

Someone Is Watching You

Acts 6:8-15

And all who sat in the council, looking steadfastly at him, saw his face as the face of an angel (Acts 6:15).

"HE'S GOT AN AUTHENTIC FACE!" That was a compliment paid a friend of mine. What was meant was that he wore his heart on his face, not on his sleeve. There was no face cover-up. But what if our hearts ache with grief, suffering, or disappointment? It is then that joy, which is consistent through pain, shines through. The radiance of a Christian is not a "happy mask." We can be honest about what we're going through but also open to communicate what the Lord is doing in us through what we are experiencing. The issue is not pretending a joy but allowing our Lord to give us a reason for joy in spite of what we are going through. The world is not interested in how we look when everything is easy. It wants to know what God can do in a life fully surrendered to Him.

The elders and scribes at Stephen's trial and subsequent martyrdom could not take their eyes off him. And Saul of Tarsus would never forget. I have often wondered whether Stephen's radiant face remained in the gallery of Saul's mind as he set off to Damascus to further harass the Christians. He had seen what the living Christ could do for a person. I am convinced that the vision of Christ in the human heart and splendidly radiant on the face of a faithful disciple contributed to Saul's conversion. When he had a vision of the Lord, he saw the source of Stephen's face. That leaves us with a question: Who in our life would want to know Christ because of what's on our face? Paul Tournier said, "Our task as laymen is to live our personal communion with Christ with such intensity as to make it contagious."

Someone's first look at Christ will be on your face.

August

2

When the Lord Smiles at You

Psalm 27:1-14; 2 Corinthians 4:6

When Thou didst say "Seek My face," my heart said to Thee, "Thy face, O LORD, I shall seek" (Psalm 27:8).

SEEKING THE FACE OF the Lord transforms our faces. The only way to have a radiant face is to meet the Lord face to face. The expression "Seek ye My face" in this psalm means to seek the communion with the Lord for which we were created. What is on our faces will come naturally from that. The Psalmist deliberately took his eyes off his enemies and difficulties and turned to the face of the Lord. We behold God in the face of Jesus Christ. The more we know of Christ, the more we know of God and what we were meant to be. If we want a face that alerts people to what life was meant to be, we will need to turn our eyes upon Jesus. Helen Lemmel was right: "Turn your eyes upon Jesus, look full in His wonderful face; and the things of earth will grow strangely dim in the light of His glory and grace."

What has your attention? What in your life takes your eyes off the Lord? Whom are you trying to please? What gives your life security and meaning?

Turning our eyes on Jesus means looking to what He has done and does for us. Look at the way He dealt with people. Put yourself in the skin of those who pressed through the crowd to see Him. Feel His unchanging acceptance. Now look at the cross. He died for each of us! We are loved and forgiven. Then look at Pentecost and see impotent people fully alive and empowered by His indwelling Spirit. That's the way we were meant to live. Finally, close your eyes and see Christ's face looking at you in tender mercy and confident assurance.

Whene'er I shut my eyes to pray,
Then let me see Thy gentle face
That smiles upon me all the day,
So full of love and grace.

August 3

The Anointed Heart

1 John 2:18-29

But you have an anointing from the Holy One, and you know all things (1 John 2:20).

THE ANCIENT CUSTOM WAS TO anoint with oil as a symbol of joy and the Lord's blessing. What Jesus suggested was in direct conflict with Jewish custom. Anointing was forbidden on fast days and particularly on the Day of Atonement. His admonition must have shocked the Pharisees and startled the disciples. In essence, He was saying that radiant joy is to be the result of any spiritual activity. We can know an even deeper anointing. The anointing of the heart by the Holy Spirit results in extraordinary power, wisdom, and love. The anointing of the Holy Spirit enables confidence, courage, and conviction. When we refer to an anointed person, we speak of one who has been blessed, infilled, and empowered by the Spirit of God. May it be said of us, "You have an anointing from the Holy One, and you know all things."

Then we will know life's greatest satisfaction. We will realize that for each problem and potential there is an anointing. We will astonish ourselves and amaze others by what the Lord has done with a human being completely yielded to Him.

For me 'twas not the truth you taught,
To you so clear, to me so dim,
But when you came to me, you brought
A sense of Him.
And from your eyes He beckons me
And from your heart His love is shed,
Till I lose sight of you and see
The Christ instead.

—Anonymous

August 4

Treasuring the Right Treasure

Matthew 6:19-21

For where your treasure is, there your heart will be also (Matthew 6:21).

WE WILL LIVE FOREVER. But where, with whom, and how? Jesus speaks to that portion of us that will not perish. What kind of heart (or soul) will we have developed during the years of this life? That determines our eternal destiny. If we have not wanted Him and His kingdom now, why should our hearts change at death? That's the alarming, frightening challenge of this passage. If we "treasure the wrong treasure," our hearts will be fashioned around our dominant desire. No one can serve the internal and the external as equal. The condition of the heart shapes what we do with our possessions. Material wealth is not condemned unless it keeps us from having a wealthy heart.

What we do with the earthly treasure will determine our heavenly treasure. Our life here is the container of the life which goes on forever. The word "treasure" meant the container, not the valued articles themselves. When Jesus said, "Do not lay up for yourself treasures on earth," He meant, "Do not invest your life in those things which debilitate and frustrate when you come to the demarcation point of death. Don't get so entangled that the one thing you will take with you...your true self...will be stunted and unfit for life forever." A surrender of our life to Christ will call for a daily death to our own will for our life and possessions. We are to die to our control and bring all *things* under His control.

John Wesley said, "Make all you can, keep all you can, save all you can, give all you can." The last aspect of that determines everything else. At the last we only have what we have given away. The character which has been developed through giving is what lasts forever. Christ is our true treasure. Is life with Him, doing His will, most important to you?

My faith in Christ is the one treasure laid up in heaven that can be enjoyed on earth.

August 5

What's Really Important?

Luke 16:10-13

Therefore if you have not been faithful in the unrighteous mammon, who will commit to your trust the true riches? (Luke 16:11).

LIFE IS A TIME FOR GATHERING of wealth, but what kind? Treasure for earth or treasure for heaven? Christ uses three types of wealth that people tried to amass in Palestine at that time, and He shows the temporality of all three.

There are things which a moth can destroy. A portion of a man's wealth consisted of fabrics in rugs, hangings, and clothing. Vermin and moths threatened this treasure. The beauty was easily destroyed. We still spend an enormous amount of money on our household furniture and decorating. Our clothing is an extension of our ego, and we spend hundreds of dollars every year for variety and attractive apparel. But styles change and things wear out.

There are things that rust can destroy. The Greek word *brosis* actually means "eating away." This meant the invasion of barns and storehouses by rats and mice. For us, the word "rust" is more applicable. Look at the junkheaps filled with old and smashed cars which once were the pride and joy of some family.

Then there are things which can be stolen. Thieves break in and steal. Homes and protective walls were made of baked clay; entry to steal had to be done by digging through. There is no protection against thieves for all our vaults. In this false category are all the treasures we collect in money, stocks, and bonds. If Jesus were to repeat His parable to us, He would talk about depression, market fluctuation, and financial insecurity. The point, however, would have been the same: our values are distorted. The one thing we will take with us—our soul—often has the least of our care and concern.

What is really important to you?

The Indestructible Treasure

Titus 3:1-11

But when the kindness and the love of God our Savior toward man appeared, not by works of righteousness which we have done, but according to His mercy He saved us, by the washing of regeneration and renewing of the Holy Spirit (Titus 3:4-5).

WHAT ARE TREASURES in heaven? This phrase communicated more to Jesus' listeners than it does to us. A treasure in heaven for a good Jew meant the accumulation of good deeds recorded for him in heaven. This idea is not altogether dead among us. We often think of God as a tally keeper recording our good deeds against our failures. But we know that this is not true according to Jesus' message on forgiveness. Our good deeds flow from our experience of His love, and not to assure our eternal life. Yet it is interesting that often at Christian funerals we fall back into assuring a family that their loved one is with God because of his good life.

William Barclay tells the story of persecution in the early church. The Roman prefect demanded of Laurentius, the deacon, "Show me your treasures at once." Laurentius pointed to the widows and orphans who were being fed, the sick who were being nursed, the poor whose needs were being supplied. "These," he said, "are the treasures of the church." But not *for* eternal life, but *because of it!*

The other aspect of Jewish belief was that character was treasure in heaven. That comes closer to Jesus' teaching, but He went deeper. He concerned Himself with character in the depth of the soul. He believed that when a person lived in fellowship with God, God's own nature was imparted in him. The relationship of love and forgiveness nurtures a person's total being. Anything which encourages, depends, and develops this relationship is treasure in heaven, for this is the one thing which cannot be destroyed.

Our most valuable treasure is in our soul.

August 7

The Kingdom of Thingdom

Colossians 3:1-4; Hebrews 13:5; 1 Timothy 6:17-19

Let your conduct be without covetousness, and be content with such things as you have. For He Himself has said, "I will never leave you nor forsake you" (Hebrews 13:5).

WE LIVE IN A KINGDOM OF thingdom! Much of our security is in things, large and small. We work and save and spend (often overspend) to keep our lives stabilized by things. Our properties and possessions become our source of pleasure and meaning in life.

A friend of ours recently had an experience which put things into perspective. On the way to a conference her bag was misplaced by the airline. She was frantic, not because she had no change of clothing for two days, but because she had foolishly placed her most precious jewelry in the inside pocket of the bag. Pearls given her by her parents before they died, a valuable brooch from her husband, several diamond rings, and some costume jewelry were all packed in the lost bag. The airline called and said the bag had been found, but also had been burglarized.

On the way to the airport our friend had to face how important these things had become. When she got her bag, she quickly checked to see what was missing. The thieves had taken everything of monetary value but had missed the pearls and the brooch, the only things of spiritual value, because of their sentimental value. The insurance company settled for the other things, but in the meantime the woman had learned an important lesson: things were too important, and life collapsed when they were lost. The crisis had focused her false master which kept her from a deeper loyalty to Christ. What things dominate you? If they were lost or stolen, what would it do to you? What things in your life have become too important?

Things can be a false master.

August 8

What Do You See?

Matthew 6:22-23

If your eye is good, your whole body will be full of light (Matthew 6:22).

WE HAVE A SAYING, "What you see is what you get." In this passage Jesus is saying, "What you get is what you see!" What we receive from Him is what enables the eyes of our hearts to see clearly. When we accept Him as absolute Lord of our lives, then we can see all that we have and are as His gracious provision. We can worship the Giver and not the gifts. Our material possessions will be seen as the generosity of God and not as false gods.

That gives us the key to understanding good and bad eyes. The word for "good" in Greek means both single and generous. When we are single-minded in our commitment, we see generously, with love and gratitude. The word for "bad" means grudging and stingy. Sick spiritual eyes will make us judgmental and negative. How does this relate to the previous thought about treasuring the right treasure? How do you look with the eyes of your heart at what you have and have accomplished? What do you see? How does that make your eyes generous toward others?

Paul knew what that meant. He gave himself away to people with abandonment because of all that Christ had done for him. His eye was both single and generous. He shared his secret with the Corinthians: "Do you remember the generosity of Jesus Christ, the Lord of us all? He was rich, yet He became poor for your sakes so that His poverty might make you rich" (2 Corinthians 8:9 PHILLIPS).

Absolute commitment to Jesus Christ makes us generous people. We can give ourselves away.

How would you act today if gratitude and generosity were in your eye?

August 9

The Mammon Membrane

Matthew 6:24; Luke 16:1-8

No one can serve two masters; for either he will hate the one and love the other, or else he will hold to the one and despise the other. You cannot serve God and mammon (Matthew 6:24).

THE WORD "MAMMON" IN Hebrew means material possessions. Originally it meant money or possessions entrusted to someone else. The root of the word means to entrust. As the years passed, the word changed from that which was entrusted to that in which a person puts his or her trust. Both aspects of the evolution of the meaning of the word help us to understand Jesus' incisive challenge about trying to serve two masters. All we have has been entrusted to us by God. Our distortion is that we put our trust in it rather than in God. What would it mean to put the Lord first in our lives and trust Him as our Master in the use of what He has entrusted to us?

One place to start is with our money. Few things are as close to us or are as much an extension of our egos as our possessions. What we earn, the value of our estate, and the power of our financial position are all such a part of us that we cannot talk about putting God first until all expenditures, savings, investments, and financial arrangements are put squarely under His will.

How often do we ask God's direction in financial matters? Do we pray about our budget? Do we give as much for the need of the community and world as we spend on our vacations, alcohol, personal appearance, and unnecessary comforts?

Do we follow the biblical admonition of the tithe? In our budgeting, are God's causes through the church and benevolent organizations in the world at the top of our budget? Do we take care of our tithe before anything else?

Well, how did you do in that inventory? We wonder on one hand why our faith is not vital and on the other why we have financial problems. The answer is probably that we have never broken through the mammon membrane.

Do I put my trust in anything that God has entrusted?

August 10

When Possessions Posses Us

Luke 12:13-21

But God said to him, "You fool! This night your soul will be required of you; then whose will those things be which you have provided?" (Luke 12:20).

POSSESSIONS EVENTUALLY POSSESS US if they become our reason for being. The danger is that they become our "life," our dominant desire. The Lord becomes an addendum to our already full life. This parable flashes with meaning when we contrast verses 15 and 19. The word for life is *zoe,* meaning essential life, eternal life as contrasted with death. The word for soul is *psuche,* referring to mental capacity. The rich fool was talking to his thinking process, not his soul. What he was really saying was, "Just think what I have achieved." His voice of self-assurance came from within himself, an echo of his frenzied accumulation. The voice of God interrupted his self-accolade: "Fool! Tonight you will die. Now who will get all you have acquired?"

What does that have to say to us? Is it possible to miss eternal life by making gods of the material possessions of life?

Here's a helpful way to answer that question with a question. What dominates our thought most of the time? Our god is whatever controls our thinking and demands our allegiance. If we were to ask a member of our family or a really close friend to answer, what would be the response?

The problem most of us face is that we believe in God and draw our identity and security from our possessions or financial security. But we can be like the "fool" in Jesus' parable even if we don't have full barns. If our worry over their emptiness dominates us to the point of anxiety, we are still worshiping the barns. We can become distracted by getting when we have little and hoarding when we have much. The challenge is to surrender all that we have and are and ask the Lord to guide us in using it for His glory.

If I worry over too much or too little,
I am a fool with full barns and an empty heart.

August 11

Who Is Running Your Life?

James 4:13-17

For what is your life? (James 4:14).

WHAT IS YOUR LIFE? This question from James will not go away. Each of us must answer. He stresses the brevity of life on earth. There's an old saying, "You can't take it with you." Not true. We will take one thing with us—ourselves! Belief in Christ as Lord and Savior is the determining factor. But what if our divided loyalties have made someone or something the lord of our lives? How is the phrase "If the Lord wills" a good corrective? How can that guide us in preparing now to live forever?

I talked to a man the other day who was at a standstill spiritually. He believed in Christ, loved his church, and was a fine, responsible Christian businessman. Yet he had an anchor in the mud. We talked late into the night. What was wrong? He was uneasy and found little joy in his faith. He was dissatisfied with his job, the community, and his family. Everything seemed to be out of sorts.

The more we talked, the more we realized that he had only half the truth. He believed in Christ as Savior of his life but not as Lord of his life.

"What are the values which drive and shape your life? How do you decide between alternatives for your life? Just how much does Christ have to say about your daily life?" I asked.

"Very little!" he said. "I decide things according to what I think is best for everyone. But seldom, if ever, do I ask for specific direction. I feel that's my business. God gave me some intelligence to work things out for Him."

That attitude is exactly what James is talking about in today's Scripture. He notes that most of his readers are deciding things for themselves. Life is brief and fleeting; during the brief span of life here we are to discover a relationship with Christ that will go on forever.

When we open ourselves to His guiding power, exciting things begin to happen and we are released from the tension of running our own lives.

I will allow the Lord to run my life today.

August 12

Strangling the Soul

Matthew 6:25-29

Therefore I say to you, do not worry about your life (Matthew 6:25).

WORRY IS THINKING TURNED toxic, the imagination picturing the worst. The word "worry" comes from the root "to choke or strangle." Incisive insight! Worry does choke and strangle our creative capacity to think, hope, and dream. It twists the joy out of life. We get dressed up like mountain climbers and climb over molehills. Worry changes nothing except the worrier. It becomes a habit.

At the core, it is a low-grade fever of agnosticism. When we worry, we express a lurking form of doubt that God either knows, cares, or is able to do anything. It is a form of loneliness—facing eventualities by ourselves on our meager strength. Worry is a distortion of our capacity to care.

In verses 31-34 is Jesus' description of worry and His diagnosis of what to do about it. Three sources of worry are enumerated: what we eat, drink, and wear. The list could be endless for most of us. What causes you to worry? Jesus does an amazing thing in this passage. He tells us to exchange secondary worries with one great concern; He shows us the anxiety which can cure anxiety.

Our only concern should be to put God first in our lives. Then our only anxiety will be that we may miss the real reason we were born: to seek first the kingdom of God and to be right with Him. From your experience, how does putting God first banish worries? Why, after we say we have committed our lives to Christ and accepted His righteousness through the cross, do some of us still worry?

Worry is interest paid on trouble before it becomes due.
—William R. Inge

August 13

God Really Cares

Matthew 6:30-33

For your heavenly Father knows that you need all these things (Matthew 6:32).

MORRIS BISHOP HAS CAUGHT THE yearning of human nature for identity in the midst of the secularized anonymity of our life in the poem *The Perforated Spirit.*

The fellows up in Personnel,
They have a set of cards on me.
The sprinkled perforations tell
My individuality.

And what am I? I am a chart
Upon the card of IBM;
The secret places of the heart
Have little secrecy for them.

Monday my brain began to buzz,
I was in agony all night.
I found out what the trouble was—
They had my paper clip too tight.

Ever feel like that? In so much of life we are little more than a number. To the government we are a Social Security number, to our political party we are a vote, to our employer we are a person who can get things done, to our church we are one of a large congregation, to our families we are a breadwinner, a mealmaker, and allowance provider. But who are we really? Does anyone care?

God does. One of the most profound affirmations of Scripture is that the same God who is Creator and Lord of the universe, and the Source of all life, knows about each of us personally. He loves us as if there were only one of us.

God knows about each of us and our needs.

August 14

The Father's Good Pleasure

Luke 12:22-34

Do not fear, little flock, for it is your Father's good pleasure to give you the kingdom (Luke 12:32).

RECENTLY A MAN ASKED ONE of my sons a personal question: "What's your dad really like?" The man wanted inside information about me that only a member of the family could know.

Jesus gives us that kind of intimate information about God in today's Scripture. Only the Father's Son could know and share His inner heart. And what He tells us has the power to change our lives. Be sure to listen to the amazing promise made in verse 32.

We are to seek first the kingdom of God. But Jesus tells us that it is the Father's good pleasure to give us what He wants us to seek. Both the desire to seek and the reward of our seeking are a gift. Savor the word *pleasure*. The same Father who said about Jesus, "This is my beloved Son, in whom I am well pleased," is pleased to give us life in His kingdom. As we have said, the kingdom is the reign and rule of God in our hearts and in all our relationships and responsibilities. Knowing ourselves as we do, the capacity to put God first in our lives is not easy.

But Jesus assures us that we will be given the desire and the capacity to want God's will and way in our lives. We get the feeling from Jesus that God is hovering over us, longing for us to want what He wants for us. He is not against us, waiting for us to measure up. Rather, He multiplies the least response so that, as His children, we might know the fullness of His power and love. We are His beloved.

Therefore, we need not worry. What we need will be given at the time and in the way that is best for us.

Today I will live in the wondrous truth that in spite of all that I might have done or said, the Father is unqualifiedly pleased and wills to give me the kingdom. So why worry?

August 15

What Can I Say?

Matthew 10:1-42

Do not worry about how or what you will speak. But it will be given you in that hour what you will speak, for it is not you who speak, but the Spirit of your Father who speaks in you (Matthew 10:19-20).

ONE OF THE GREAT SOURCES OF worry for all of us is what we will say in life's challenging moments. This passage is Jesus' assurance that the Holy Spirit will give us the thoughts, words, and courage to speak. Our only task is to open our minds in calm expectation of wisdom beyond our own capacity. We were never meant to be adequate on our own. It is when we think we are adequate that we get into trouble. A Christian is not one who works *for* the Lord but one in whom and through whom the Lord works. We are not to speak for God but to yield our tongues to express the thoughts the Lord has implanted. We need not worry. The Lord will never let us down!

Note the progression in Jesus' challenge. The Spirit speaks in us before He speaks through us. He gives us X-ray vision in discerning situations and people. When we calmly ask what He has to say, He will speak in the deepest regions of our inner self. He will infuse thoughts into the tissue of our brains, love in our emotions so that we can "speak the truth in love," and incisiveness in our wills to dare to communicate what He has revealed to us.

The people in our lives today will need us to be open channels of the Spirit's discernment. But what we have to say will be heard only if we have expressed loving concern for them. People feel intuitively whether we are really for them or not.

The Spirit-filled Christian has supernatural capacities. We are equipped by the Lord for life's knotty problems and complexities. Surrender the situation to Him, saying, "Lord, speak to me that I may speak." And He will!

I will listen to the Lord before I speak and then speak with boldness and love.

August 16

Love Is the Antidote to Fear

John 6:15-21

It is I; do not be afraid (John 6:20).

THE ACCOUNT OF THE DISCIPLES in the storm at sea is an actual record of what happened, but also a parable of our life. How like these disciples we are. We struggle on the sea of life. The waves of problems and perplexities threaten to engulf us. Life seems like a perpetual night waiting for dawn. Then Jesus comes. What He said to the disciples He says to us. The actual translation of verse 20 is "I am. Have no fear!" This is one of the great "I am" statements of our Lord. It is Jesus' undeniable claim to be Yahweh, God Himself. He could calm the water He had created. He is in charge of our lives. Nothing can happen to us that He cannot use for His glory and our growth. If we believe this and trust Him, worry is cut at the taproot. Watch! He is coming. Listen to Him: "I am. Have no fear." On the basis of that, we can stop worrying and start living!

The Apostle John had been with the other disciples that early morning when Jesus conquered their fear. Near the end of life he wrote, "There is no fear in love; but perfect love casts out fear, because fear involves torment. But he who fears has not been made perfect in love. We love Him because He first loved us" (1 John 4:18-19). The way to overcome fear is to grow in a love relationship with the Savior. The more of His love we experience, the less fear will strangle our hearts. One of my favorite quotes is by F.B. Meyer: "God incarnate is the end of fear; and the heart that realizes that He is in the midst, that He takes heed to the assurance of His loving presence, will be quiet in the midst of alarm! No weapon that is focused against thee shall prosper. Only be patient and be quiet."

I will conquer fear by receiving more of Christ's love.

August 17

Sure Anchors in the Storm

Acts 27:13-44

Then, fearing lest we should run aground on the rocks, they dropped four anchors from the stern, and prayed for day to come (Acts 27:29).

WHAT ARE YOUR ANCHORS FOR the storm? What do you have within you to stabilize the ship of life through the winds of doubt, sorrow's bitter sea, temptation's jagged rocks? It's what happens to us in the storm, not in the calm or the quiet of life's ports, that tests what we believe.

Paul started for Rome under Roman guard. On the voyage from Crete to Malta a northeaster called the Euroclydon blew down from the mountains of Crete, caught hold of the ship, and tossed it for days. Paul alone was confident in the midst of frenzy. While the ship drifted across the sea nearing the coast of Malta, the sailors sounded the fathoms and, fearing for rocks, let out four anchors. And Paul prayed for day to come. Life is like that. What four anchors would stabilize our souls for time's turbulent sea? Paul had more than the physical anchors in the sea. In prayer he lowered the true anchors of life.

He had the anchor of *trust* in the present help of God. Through his ministry God had been faithful in each new crisis. He could trust Him now. then he had the anchor of *hope*. Paul's hope was based in the Lord of history who was faithful—He had seen the Apostle through each crisis faithfully. The Psalmist was right: "Hope in the LORD."

But Paul also had the anchor of *purpose*. He knew his work was not finished. He was to stand before Caesar. God would finish what He had begun. A purpose liberates our fears and gives us courage. Our purpose is to glorify God and enjoy Him forever, in spite of what happens or what people say. Lastly, there was the anchor of *fellowship*: "God has granted you all these who sail with you." those who responded to Paul's message were responsible for him. God always provides some person who knows and understands, listens and loves. These are our anchors until the dawn of a new day.

There are anchors for the storm!

August 18

Creative Anxiety

Luke 15:11-24

I will arise and go to my father, and will say to him: Father, I have sinned against heaven and before you (Luke 15:18).

THERE IS A CREATIVE ANXIETY. Jesus seems to be saying that we ought to be much more anxious about living in the kingdom under God's guidance than anxious about things which do not ultimately count.

Jesus' listeners thought they had it made spiritually. They took God for granted and misused their election to be His people. They had grown careless and had tried to manipulate God for their own purposes. They had shelved Him, and they took Him off the shelf only when they needed Him.

We do much the same. We treat God like an adjunct to a full life. We use prayer for crises and times of need and think of Him and His will only when we are pressed against the wall of an insurmountable problem. The whole drift and direction of our lives is under our own control.

Jesus seems to be saying, "Don't be so sure that you can use God that way; without knowing it your anxiety about little things is really caused by the anxiety of separation from God." Anxiety of this deeper kind is God's gift. It tells us something is wrong, missing, out of joint. The uneasiness we feel in quiet moments, our disquiet inside when all is quiet around us, our loneliness in a crowd, our deep insecurity even when all seems outwardly in order—that's creative anxiety because it presses us back to God. What finally occurred to the Prodigal Son can happen to us. Why live the way we are when the Father is waiting?

There is a creative anxiety which is God's gift.

August 19

Today Is All We Have

Matthew 6:34

Therefore do not worry about tomorrow, for tomorrow will worry about its own things. Sufficient for the day is its own trouble (Matthew 6:34).

ONE OF THE MOST DISTURBING aspects of anxiety is concern for the future. Soren Kierkegaard said, "What is anxiety? It is the next day." It is the unwritten chapter of our lives which distresses most of us. Jesus gives us the key: let tomorrow take care of itself; live today to the full. The point is that if we live the way He suggested today, tomorrow will be more glorious than we ever dared to imagine. The reason for this is that what we do today will be inseparably related to what can happen tomorrow. We can have something to say about what will happen by how we handle what's happening. Jesus' advice is that there is sufficient opportunity today to see His power at work over evil. Concentrate on that, and tomorrow will be a succeeding opportunity. Once our ultimate "tomorrow" or eternal life is secure, we can live without reservation each day.

Most of us get so tomorrow-oriented that we do not enjoy the present moment. We are preoccupied by what is coming, and we fail to experience what is. We press on in preparation as if some new plan, relationship, or opportunity will make everything different. It is good to plan but not to the point that we miss what God is saying in the difficult or unpleasant thing we may now be living through.

The seeds of tomorrow's harvest are today. How we cultivate them will determine what we will reap. Don't forget to live...today!

Today is all we have. Don't forget to live!

August 20

The Boomerang of Judgments

Matthew 7:1

Judge not, that you be not judged (Matthew 7:1).

TODAY WE ARE GOING TO consider Jesus' teaching on judgments. We must approach the subject with real care because we could easily misunderstand what our Lord is trying to say to us.

What's wrong with judging? We can't help making judgments. Evaluations, appraisals, and ethical verdicts are a part of every day's life. Are we to overlook wrong in society or people in some kind of sentimental, mushy acceptance of evil? Are we not responsible for ourselves and those for whom we care, to see things for what they are and speak truth about them? What did Jesus mean?

He was concerned about judgments of condemnation. Whenever our judgment depreciates another human being, it is wrong. This happens when we write off another person for what he has said or done. We judge him as useless.

Also, Jesus wanted us to know that we are judged by God. If we can be as gracious to others as God has been to us, our criticism will be creative. If we first examine our own hearts before God on the same subject, we will not be as anxious to blast another person. What we give we will get. That's the boomerang of censure!

Then too, Jesus reminds us that we do not know all the facts of any situation. The things of which we are critical are only part of what's disturbing a person. Burns was right:

> "What's done we partly may compute,
> But know not what's resisted."

We can say with Masefield, "O God, Thou knowest I'm as blind as he."

Judgments are a boomerang.

August 21

Plankated Vision

Matthew 7:3-5

You hypocrite! First remove the plank from your own eye, and then you will see clearly to take the speck out of your brother's eye (Matthew 7:5).

JESUS HAD A SENSE OF HUMOR. We see this in His use of hyperbole, an overstatement to drive home a basic truth. One of the best examples of this is our Scripture today. For Jesus' listeners, this must have been a source of laughter.

The word "speck" is really the word for a splinter of wood. "Log" would better be translated as "beam." "The figure is purposely grotesque," Sherman E. Johnson suggests. Jesus exposed the reformer who purposely covers up his own failures in criticism of others.

The truth is underlined. A log of timber is grossly bigger than a splinter. The sin in us is more serious to God than the sin in another which we criticize. The sin of negative judgment, in God's eyes, is larger than the sin in the person we criticize. It is easy to criticize if we have never comprehended how deadly a sin this is. It eats away at us and breaks down not only our relationship with the people criticized, but with God.

The point of this pithy parable is that if we busy ourselves with the log in our own eye, we will have less time and inclination to criticize. If our sour minds are sweetened by God's forgiveness, we will have less negativism about others.

According to Jesus, people who are overcritical are hypocrites. This strong word means to play a part, to pretend, to be one thing outwardly and another inwardly. F.D. Maurice said, "Looking for the faults in others which I had a secret consciousness were in myself...has more hindered my progress in love and gentleness than all things else." Disturbing words!

We cannot see in compassion because of the log in our eye!

August 22

When Analysis Brings Paralysis

Matthew 7:2

With the same measure you use, it will be measured back to you (Matthew 7:2).

JESUS DOES NOT CONDEMN honest value-judgments between truth and falsehood, right and wrong. He does not counsel us to abandon analysis and evaluation. We have been given powers of discernment to know what is right and to do it. The question is, "With what kind of spirit do we evaluate the lives of others?" What Jesus condemns in this passage is a censoriousness which ends up in playing God. When we become censorious judges of others, we constantly find fault and are negative and debilitating. We have plankated vision.

The only way to develop a nonjudgmental, noncensorious spirit is to consider what we have done with the gift of life ourselves. Jesus is very humorous in His parables of illustrations—a speck in someone's eye, a plank in our own. A censorious spirit is an unloved and unlovely spirit. We are condemnatory in our judgments when we have refused to allow God to love us sufficiently. A gracious person is one who has been loved profoundly by God and then by himself or herself.

The other day I had to be analytical of a friend's performance. It was interpreted as judgmental. A strain came into the relationship. I felt I was right; he felt I was overly critical. There was no way to break the bind except to go to him and reestablish the relationship. There was no way he could appropriate however much I had said that was creative until he was sure that I loved him as a brother in Christ. The experience makes me wonder about how to communicate truth in love so that the other person can appropriate what we say. Christ can give us that quality of love and will enable a person to know that our insights are not a put-down. Who needs that in your life? Who needs you to go back and reestablish trust?

I will take responsibility for the way I share my insights so that there will be no question of the depth of my love.

August 23

The Context of Criticism

Ecclesiastes 3:7

A time to be silent and a time to speak (Ecclesiastes 3:7).

CREATIVE JUDGMENT REQUIRES timing and relationship. We dare not blurt out our judgments without a context of mutual acceptance, love, and sensitive timing.

In every relationship there are those things which disturb us about others. However happy a marriage, family, friendship, or business association may be, eventually there will be some friction. That's natural. We are all different and bring to every relationship all that we have been and are. The deeper two people grow together, the more of their individuality is exposed. The problems which arise between people may not indicate an inadequate relationship but may indicate that love is being expressed enough for people to take off their masks in self-disclosure. There must be some helpful way for each person to say what he thinks and observes about the other so that both may grow.

This is done through affirmation and timing. When we know that nothing can break our relationship with a person, we are free to say what we think. But at the right time! There are times when we are more open than others. Often when we are exhausted or troubled about other things, we react to criticism with the steam of those emotions and not with honest reaction to the criticism. We need to be sensitive and patient to not be so urgent about our own feelings that we must unload on a person who is already overloaded. If we ask God to judge our judgment and guide our timing, our insights can open a new stage of growth for another person.

There is a right time for criticism in a creative context.

August 24

Before You Criticize

James 2:8-13

So speak and so do as those who will be judged by the law of liberty (James 2:12).

JUDGMENTS OFTEN RELIEVE us of responsibility. We categorize people in limiting preconception, expose their weakness, condemn their failure, ridicule their inadequacy, and go on our way. Judging is creative only if its analysis and insight are a prelude to doing something about the person or situation we have focused. Judgments are careless unless we are willing to be part of God's solution. If not, we become part of the multiplication of the problem.

"All right, what are you going to do about it?" should be our response to ourselves and critical others. Talk and analysis are cheap: action is costly; caring is demanding. What constructive thing can you do and say about the need you have cut open?

This gives us pause to think! How can we say what we have to say in such a way that people will feel our love and willingness to help? Judgments debilitate and often leave people immobilized for any constructive action. We add to the burden rather than lift it. Conversely, the way we word our insight, the spirit of love with which we communicate, can enable a person to say, "Well, I'd never thought of that! Thank you."

We need to know much more about what we want people to become in the whole of their lives before we criticize some aspect. We can unsettle people about the things they do but give little help with the kind of persons they are. Most of us do what we do because of what we are. Criticism of doing demands responsibility for being. We need to be cautious that our judgments do not make people so hostile that we cannot share with them the love of God, which is the only thing which will ultimately change them.

How responsible are your judgments?

August
25

Stumbling Block

Romans 14:1-13

Therefore let us not judge one another anymore, but rather resolve this, that no one put a stumbling block or a cause to fall in his brother's way (Romans 14:13).

PAUL GIVES US A FORMULA for freedom from negative judgmentalism. The thrust of his admonitions is that God alone can be the ultimate Judge of other people. That means that our task is to help people find a healing relationship with God. This will give them a perspective and receive the power of His Spirit to change and grow. If we spend as much time enabling people to experience grace as we do criticizing them, we could transform people, churches, and the places where we work. Why is it usually easier for us to criticize than help a person become a changed person?

The thing Paul wants us to be sure about is that Christ, and not we, is the stumbling block. He talked about Christ as a stumbling block. "Why? Because they did not seek it by faith, but as it were by the works of the law. For they stumbled at that stumbling stone" (Romans 9:32). The Greek word *skandalon* means a snare, a trap, or a cause of tripping. Christ tripped up our efforts at self-justification. The cross short-circuits our desire to be right with God on our own adequacy and performance. We must trip before we can fall into His arms of loving forgiveness. Our pride must be snared.

Once we have stumbled and been caught up in the everlasting arms, our task is to be sure that there is nothing in our personalities, character, or attitudes which are a stumbling block as people move toward Christ. It is frightening to consider all the people who may never stumble creatively over Christ because they stumbled over us!

I will not be a stumbling block today so people can stumble into the Lord's arms.

August 26

The Cure of Negativism

Romans 14:14-23

Happy is he who does not condemn himself (Romans 14:22).

THE SIN OF CENSORIOUSNESS is really the sin of unbelief. God has told us that only He is the Judge of people. Are we afraid that He cannot or will not do His job? We play God when we decide the value or usefulness of another person. We can love people, knowing that, like us, the Lord is not finished with them. We are all in process, and we are to be as patient with others as God has been with us. You cannot love someone else until you love yourself!

I shall never forget the time I discovered that I could never love anyone deeply until I learned to love myself. I had always been taught that self-appreciation was conceit and was to be avoided at all costs. An inverted pride of pretentious selflessness and self-negation filled the void. I could not take real delight in being myself and enjoying the gifts and opportunities God had given.

What a joy it was to begin to appreciate myself! When I accepted Christ's uncalculated, unchanging love for me, I found that I had a new patience with myself and a new excitement at being me! Lots of people had greater gifts, many had superior skills, and most outdistanced my ability, but suddenly I was overcome with the realization of the tremendous potential that God placed within me. I decided to use all I had as loved by Christ and to stop negating what He had given.

The result was a new appreciation for others. I was aware of their potential and found that a radical transfer of interest and concern had taken place. My energies were less focused on myself and increasingly zeroed in on others. I had new love because I had learned to love myself. Judgmentalism was worked out of my soul by forgiving and affirming love. I longed to be to others what Christ had been to me.

Negativism about others begins with negativism about ourselves rooted in lack of trust in what the Lord can do with us and then with others.

August 27

A Major Cause of Criticism

Romans 2:1

Therefore you are inexcusable, O man, whoever you are who judge, for in whatever you judge another you condemn yourself; for you who judge do the same things.

A FATHER PACED THE BEDROOM floor while his daughter took what he thought was far too long to say good night to her boyfriend in the living room below. "I don't see why it takes that young man so long to say good night. I don't know about this younger generation!" he said. "Oh, come to bed," his wife said. "Weren't you young once?" "Yes, I was, and that's just why I'm worried and can't come to bed!" We laughed at that. The humor enables us to consider a very serious truth.

The overworried father's statement expressed real insight into himself. His judgment of his daughter and her young man was based on his own memories of what he had done in living rooms a generation before. The problem was that he had projected these memories into worry in the present. His judgment did not fit the new situation but was based on his own concern.

Judgments often are exposures of our own needs. The things we judge in others are often the things which are troubling us deeply within. Righteous indignation may be caused by something not so righteous in us. Something we have done or wished we had had the courage to do, something unresolved or unforgiven, something hidden or unhealed will cause the judgment of someone else.

Whenever we are overly critical we should ask ourselves and each other, "Why does that bother you?" There are some things which need to be questioned in loving concern for another person, but when our judgments are rash or emotional or severe, it usually indicates that part of the problem is still within us.

What we criticize in others may be unresolved in us.

August 28

Mercy Triumphs over Judgment

2 Timothy 4:1-5; James 2:1-13

For judgment is without mercy to the one who has shown no mercy. Mercy triumphs over judgment (James 2:13).

OUR LORD HAS HIS WORK to do, and we have ours! He is the Judge of the living and the dead. We are ministers of His grace. When we are set free of censoriousness, we can put the focus on the good news of the gospel. The only way to overcome negativism is to fill the vacuum of our hearts with positive love. When people know we love them, they will hear what we have to say. The key is communicating how great the Lord is, not how bad people are. They know about their faults and need someone who will believe in them. Will you be that person?

Mercy triumphs over judgment! That's the answer to the judgmental times in which we live. In fact anyone who has true mercy will have little condemnatory judgment. We all make judgments about things, situations, and people, but the deprecatory judgments which relegate and debilitate are healed by the expulsive power of mercy.

Mercy is the very nature of God. It is His love in action. In Christ, God has identified with us in our plight. He does not condemn us, but comes that we might have life. This kind of identification cuts negative judgment at the taproot. Once we feel with another person what he is going through, our judgments will be less severe.

A good test of the extent of mercy in our lives is how much we judge others. We will know that something is amiss in our relationship with Christ if this urge to undercut others is present in our hearts.

The only way to overcome judging is to go deeper in God's mercy. Calculate anew what God has put up with, gone through, forgiven, repaired, and healed in your own life. Then you will find that a renewed sense of mercy will inadvertently fill you with mercy for others.

Judging is a telltale sign that we are out of touch with Christ's mercy.

August 29

Spiritual Snobs

Romans 2:1-11

And do you think this, O man, you who judge those who do such things, and do the same, that you will escape the judgment of God? (Romans 2:3).

WE WILL BE JUDGED FOR our judgments! The impact of Paul's words unsettles us. We will be accountable for the judgments we have made which relieved us of caring and responsibility. What upsets you about other people to the extent that you can write them off? What if God's patience were that weak and His temper that short with us?

"What a snob I am!" a woman cried out in a moment of honest confession and contrition. "I am beginning to realize that one area that my faith in Christ has never touched is my prejudice and reserve with people who don't meet my standards. I just seem to gravitate to people with education, Ivy League clothing, and culture. I don't dislike others, but I just never get around to them. I must admit that people in power, with popularity and position, are the ones I am attracted to. I used to say that they need Christ's love as much as others so why fight it? Now I am beginning to wonder why I can't love people who don't measure up."

Well, what do you think of that? Sound familiar? Ever feel that way? Most of us have, in one way or another. And think of the people we miss because of it! God's surprises often come in people with strange wrappings. He has a great deal to give us from unusual people, many of whom are not great by the world's standards.

Grace is a great leveler. In matters of the faith we are all the same. We all need God's love and forgiveness. As an act of will, we need to break out of our preconceived categories, to be used by God with all sorts of people. A great church should never represent only one social stratum, rich or poor, educated or uneducated. We are God's people and need each other. What is lacking in one of us God fulfills in another. Together we are complete and whole.

I resign from being a spiritual snob!

August 30

Lifting Up Each Other

Galatians 6:1-10; 5:22-23

Bear one another's burdens, and so fulfill the law of Christ (Galatians 6:2).

HERE IS A GUIDE FOR creative concern for others. After Paul listed the fruit of the Spirit in Galatians 5:22-23, he went on to show how these qualities are lived out in our relationships. Love, joy, peace, long-suffering, kindness, goodness, faithfulness, gentleness, and self-control are the qualities of Christ. When the indwelling Christ lives in us, we are given His character. It is impossible to be the kind of person Paul describes in Galatians 6 without the fruit of the Spirit. Compare each fruit of the Spirit with each challenge. The result of Christ's indwelling will be extraordinary love to live an extraordinary life. We will discover a mutual ministry in times of need. But that's often blocked by false pride.

"Why should I tell anyone else my troubles? I caused them, I am responsible, and I must work it out for myself. Anyway, who can I trust?" is an often repeated statement. Not unlike it is the statement of another; "I am afraid to let people know about my sins. If people really knew what I am like, they wouldn't like me!"

These statements hit wide of the mark of Christian fellowship. Paul is talking about an openness with each other which does not pretend by leading from strength all the time. This does not mean that we are to go around telling people how bad we are.

What it does say is that when we have failed or sinned, another person is needed to mediate and communicate God's grace. We were never made to know God alone. His word of assurance is to be given by another.

The other day a man poured out his heart to me. After we talked I said, "My friend, God loves you and forgives you." Then he said, "You know, I knew that, but I needed to hear it from someone else."

I will be a mediation of grace and hope today.

August 31

The Danger of Too Much Self-Criticism

Romans 8:1-5

There is therefore now no condemnation to those who are in Christ Jesus, who do not walk according to the flesh, but according to the Spirit (Romans 8:1).

THE YOUNG WOMAN WAS critical of her grades even though they indicated real improvement. Her father's comments were encouraging and enthusiastic. He was delighted with her progress. Each time he said something complimentary, she countered with a self-depreciating, self-critical comment. Self-judgment had become so natural for her that she did not know how to be positive.

"How can you be so hard on someone I think is so great?" the father asked his daughter. "Well, Daddy," she said, "You don't have to live with me all the time like I do."

In the past few days we have considered judgments. No analysis is complete without thinking of self-judgment. Some of us are harder on ourselves than others, or even God, would be. We are critical of our best efforts and can't believe in ourselves. We negate God's love for us and can't believe that He accepts us as we are. Only if we measure up to our impossible standards could He or anyone else love us. This is just another way of running our own lives. We are still in control, however bad we think we are.

We have not accepted ourselves as forgiven. This becomes a sick pattern of life and keeps us from loving others. It is self-centeredness in the worst form. We become inverted on ourselves. Be careful that genuine self-analysis and healthy introspection do not turn into self-condemnation.

It is dangerous when self-analysis becomes self-condemnation. Being down on ourselves becomes a habit and a way of escaping our potential and of lovingly helping others realize theirs.

September 1

When to Offer the Pearl

Matthew 7:6

Do not give what is holy to the dogs; nor cast your pearls before swine, lest they trample them under their feet, and turn and tear you in pieces (Matthew 7:6).

THE PARABLE OF THE PEARLS and the swine in this verse is an example of Jesus' illustrative use of hyperbole—an overstatement of contrast to make a point. The point is that we all have evaluative insights and creative criticisms, but we must earn the right to be heard. A pearl has no nutritional value for a pig. That's the issue. Not until a person knows our love and God's acceptance can we communicate what He, the Lord, has given us for them.

We all have a problem with censoriousness when it prompts us to write another person off as hopeless. How can we become creative communicators of what God can do in people's lives? What people do is caused by what they are. And only God can change that!

The parable has further meaning for our witness to others. The pearls of our advanced thinking experience of Christ cannot be digested by those who have not met Christ. So often we become esoteric in our language and obscure in our theology. We major in the minors. Our witness is a postgraduate presentation of theology rather than a freshman's course in basics. We need to be simple, but not simplistic. People are yearning to see how Christ can make stepping-stones out of their struggles. What they need to hear and see is the difference Christ can make in a person's life. There is a winsome contagion in a person who shares the adventure of life in Christ. But there will be times when a person is resistant and hostile. That's the time to lovingly witness with affirmation and assurance. There will be a time when the person is ready and receptive. God will make sure of that!

I will share my faith on the Lord's timing and under His remarkable guidance.

September 2

God's Best Gift for My Life

Matthew 7:7-12; Luke 11:13

If you then, being evil, know how to give good gifts to your children, how much more will your Father in heaven give good things to those who ask Him! (*Matthew 7:11*).

THE DEEP MEANING OF this passage is unlocked when it is studied with Luke 11:13: "If you then, being evil, know how to give good gifts to your children, how much more will your heavenly Father give the Holy Spirit to those who ask Him!" the emphasis in both renderings (Luke and Matthew) is on the amazing generosity of God. He longs to give His best Gift—Himself—the Holy Spirit. But only to those who ask, seek, and knock. This is more than an exercise in importunity; it is the expression of a dominant desire. To ask is to have our needs clarified by God; to seek is to have those needs corrected in keeping with His will; to knock is to seek entrance into the abundant life filled with His Spirit. We come with our wants; the Lord shows us our deepest need; then we can knock with assurance.

The impact of this passage is that the will and desire to ask, seek, and knock are all gifts of God! He motivates us to desire what He is waiting to give. Why then the three steps? Why knock on a door that's standing open? Because God wants people who want Him more than His secondary gifts. Frederick W. Faber said, "We must wait for God, long and meekly, in the wind and wet, in the thunder and lightning, in the cold and the dark. Wait, and He will come. He never comes to those who do not wait." But the waiting is part of His caring. He waits to be wanted. He will not burglarize the will. Ask, seek, knock!

Prayer enlarges the heart until it is capable of containing God's gift of Himself.
—Mother Teresa of Calcutta

September

3

Fruitfulness

Matthew 7:15-20

Therefore by their fruits you will know them (Matthew 7:20).

THIS IS AN AWESOME PASSAGE. It is more than a warning against false prophets or wolves in sheep's clothing. The bottom line of the whole impact is that every one of us is a prophet. We are all models to others of what we believe in our actions, attitudes, words, and lifestyles. Inadvertently we are reproducing our quality of Christianity, or lack of it, in the people who observe us. Before we smack our lips or wring our hands in consternation over the false prophets of easy religion or the sects of pseudo-Christianity, we need to hear what Jesus is saying to us. Beware of being a false prophet! That's the message that thundered through as I reflected on this passage. A first reading of the passage prompts an initial question: "Do I know any false prophets?" then the laser beam of a deeper question burns into our consciousness: "What kind of prophet am I?"

This passage leads to an honest evaluation of our fruitfulness. In the New Testament, fruit is used in several ways: the character of Christ reproduced in us; the fruit of the Spirit; the fruit of the branch connected to Christ the Vine; the fruit of good works; the fruit of new life in others through witness and evangelism. Eventually we must confront the issue that the people in our lives are beholding in us what it means to be a Christian. We can lead people only as far as we have gone ourselves. They are deciding for or against Christ by what they observe that He means to us.

What kind of prophet will I be today?

September 4

God's Best Enables Our Best

Matthew 7:21-23

Not everyone who says to Me, "Lord, Lord," will enter the kingdom of heaven, but he who does the will of My Father who is in heaven (Matthew 7:21).

OUR LORD IS DEEPLY CONCERNED about our influence on others. His great concern is that we will expose to others a mediocre level of discipleship that honors Him with words while we run our own lives. The contradiction between what we say and are is the focus of this passage. Is it possible to call Jesus "Lord" and not allow Him to be Lord of our lives? Look at history. Look at the church through the ages. Look at yourself! The secret of producing good fruit of authentic Christianity is the words, "but he who does the will of My Father who is in heaven." What areas, situations, circumstances, relationships in your life need to be brought under radical obedience to the will of God?

There is a powerful story told of Leonardo da Vinci. One day in his studio he started work on a large canvas. He labored on it, choosing the subject carefully, arranging the perspective, sketching the outline, applying the colors, and developing the background. Then for some unknown reason he stopped, with the painting still unfinished. He called one of his students and asked him to finish it. The student was flabbergasted. How could he finish a painting by one of the world's truly great masters? He protested his inadequacy and insufficiency for so challenging a task. But the great artist silenced him: "Will not what I have done inspire you to do your best?" he asked.

That's really Jesus' question, isn't it? He began it all 2000 years ago. His life, message, death, resurrection, and living presence started the great painting of the redemption of the world. He has given us the task to finish the painting. But there's a difference. Da Vinci left his student alone; Jesus never does that. He has given us the color palette, and He whispers His guiding insight to us at each uncertain stroke.

When the will is ready, the feet are light.

—George Herbert

September 5

Productive Branches

Luke 3:7-20; John 15:1-8

Therefore bear fruits worthy of repentance, and do not begin to say to yourselves, "We have Abraham as our father." For I say to you that God is able to raise up children to Abraham from these stones (Luke 3:8).

WAS JESUS CONCERNED ABOUT results? The Scripture clearly says that He was: "You shall know them by their fruits." He was not very easy on the people who said, "Lord, Lord" but did not do the will of God. Jesus was not concerned about results as an end in themselves, as a source of pious pride. But He was profoundly concerned that faith in Him should result in moral, ethical, and spiritual implications.

Our Scripture today is both a warning and a promise. But Jesus and John warn that those who do not bear fruit will be cut off. Jesus prunes the dead branches from the tree of the church so that the tree can grow. What is the fruit of which He speaks? The fruit of one Christian is another. We were meant to be reproductive. Can you look to any one person as your child of the faith? Have you ever helped someone else know Christ and trust his life to Him? The function of an ethical life and service to others is to put us in the position of sharing with another person the source of life we have in Jesus Christ. We do not draw attention to ourselves so that others will say, "My, what a fine person you have made of yourself!" but rather, "Now that's the way I want to live! What's the secret of your joy?"

Jesus' promise is that if we draw the power of life from Him, by abiding in Him, we will be productive branches, and fruit will come as a natural result. That leads us to want to pray: "Lord Christ, I can look to so few people who have come to know you because of Your life in me. Help me to be reproductive! Make me sensitive today to all the people who are anxious to know You if I would only point the way. Amen."

The fruit of one Christian is another.

September 6

Faith on the Job

Ephesians 6:5-9

Not with eyeservice, as men-pleasers, but as servants of Christ, doing the will of God from the heart (Ephesians 6:6).

THE KEY TO BEING A CHRISTIAN on the job is to bring meaning to our work, not to try to find life's ultimate meaning in our work. For example, the major cause of vocational burnout is that men and women make work their god. Titles, positions, salaries, and recognition become a lust of life. We work all the harder to assure success and power. Fear of failure grips us. Then exhaustion and fatigue creep up on us. Usually when we are run down, we take on more. The love of work becomes a compulsion. Overburdened, we become irritable, defensive, cynical, paranoid, and depressed. Creativity eludes us. It happens so subtly that we do not know it's happening until it's too late.

And yet, for a Christian, it's never too late. The Lord is ready to begin again whenever we realize that our work has become more important to us than our relationship with God. He helps us to draw back and get things into perspective. Then we can surrender our work to Him and ask Him to guide us in making our work an expression of, rather than an exception to, our faith. Any job in which we cannot honestly live out our faith is the wrong job. Work done well can be a glory to God. Effectiveness earns us credibility to share our faith with fellow workers. God's strategy may have placed you where you work, not just for the work to be done, but for the influence you will have on the people with whom you do the work.

We are to find our security and purpose in the Lord, and then bring that to our work.

September 7

Our Wills to Make Them God's

Psalm 40:1-17; 143:1-12

I delight to do Thy will, O my God; Thy Law is within my heart (Psalm 40:8).

Teach me to do Thy will, for Thou art my God; Let Thy good Spirit lead me on level ground (Psalm 143:10).

IF WE ARE TO BE CHRISTIANS who do more than say "Lord, Lord" in wordy religiosity, we will need to desire God's will more than anything else. The Psalmist shows us how to have a passion for God's will. Memorize these key verses. Repeat them in times of indecision and uncertainty. Make this a day to focus your consciousness in deliberate longing for God's direction and determination to follow through. Tennyson was right: "Our wills are ours, we know not how; our wills are ours, to make them Thine."

Augustine confessed to God, "when I vacillated about my decision to serve the Lord my God, it was I who willed and I who willed not, and nobody else. I was fighting myself....All You asked was that I cease to want what I willed and begin to want what You willed." That's it! To want what God wants is the secret of true happiness. If we want that with all our hearts, specific guidance in our decisions will not be long in coming. Robert Louis Stevenson said, "I came about like a well-handled ship. There stood at the wheel that steersman whom we call God."

It fortifies my soul to know
That though I perish, Truth is so:
That, howsoe'er I stray and range,
What'er I do, Thou dost not change.
I steadier step when I recall
That, if I slip, Thou dost not fall.
—Arthur Hugh Clough

Lord, What do You Want Me to Say?

Mark 13:9-13

But when they arrest you and deliver you up, do not worry beforehand, or premeditate what you will speak. But whatever is given you in that hour, speak that; for it is not you who speak, but the Holy Spirit (Mark 13:11).

"WHAT CAN I POSSIBLY SAY in a situation like this? How will I ever find the words to explain, give comfort, offer challenge, and express love in a circumstance like that? What should I say?"

Ever feel that way? We all have! We all sense our inadequacy to speak a word of truth in love when it is needed most. When we anticipate the crises of life, we admit our lack of wisdom, insight, and discernment.

Jesus gave us a promise which dispels our fears.

Preparation for times of trial and testing comes long before the situation. Jesus Christ, who knows what we will face, is at work imputing into us the wisdom which will give birth to the right words for each troublesome and challenging time. When the moment comes and we are on the spot, we will have power to speak with maturity beyond our years, love beyond our capacities, and insight beyond our knowledge.

The fact is that He will speak through us. He will use us to speak the right word which will convict, comfort, and challenge. We will be amazed! All He needs from us is the willing mind and tongue. If we dare to pray, "Lord, what do You want me to say?" He will answer, and we will know what to say.

If we trust Him, Christ will guide what we say in life's difficult situations.

September 9

True Stability

Matthew 7:24-25

Therefore whoever hears these sayings of Mine, and does them, I will liken him to a wise man who built his house on the rock (Matthew 7:24).

HOW WOULD YOU DESCRIBE a stable person? What words would you use? At the conclusion of the Sermon on the Mount, Jesus gave a parable to illustrate a stable person whose life was built on a rocklike foundation. The man who built his house upon a rock was one who heard the Master's words and did them. Hearing and doing were the inseparable combination for great character.

We all know people who talk beyond what they live. We are never sure of them. Jesus Christ is able to help us hear His message and live it. The result will be stability. Each time we dare to live out an aspect of the gospel as we know it, it becomes part of our character. Consistency and congruity between what we believe and what we do will build the house of our life on a firm foundation.

That kind of stability will show in our countenance, be reflected in our voices, and radiate in our convictions. The world desperately needs established, stable Christians who know who they are, Whose they are, and what they are to be and do. The storms of life may beat on us, but we do not change. The winds of change blast away, but we do not collapse because the One who is able has taken control of our minds so we can think His thoughts, of our emotions so we can be calm in life's distresses, of our wills so that we can discover and do His will, and of our bodies so that they can be strengthened by His Spirit.

Training and conditioning make a stable person. It begins in life's little things and prepares us for the big crises.

No one ever gets ready for a crisis in the midst of one. Moment by moment, Christ is laying an indestructible foundation. Let the storms and the winds come! He is able!

September 10

Not What But Whom

Matthew 7:26-27

And everyone who hears these sayings of Mine, and does not do them, will be like a foolish man who built his house on the sand (Matthew 7:26).

APPLICATION IS THE FINAL STEP of learning. We know only so much as we can live. Jesus lived in a time not unlike our own: great beliefs were held but not applied. That's why He ended the Sermon on the Mount with a "Do it now!" thrust. The parable of the foundations—one on rock, the other on sand—teaches us the integration of hearing and doing. The Lord's conclusion to His message from the Mount is very direct: What are you going to do about it? Take an inventory—how have your actions and behavior been changed by the days of this in-depth review of Jesus' teaching on the Sermon on the Mount?

John Oxenham in *Bees in Amber* reminds us that Christ and obedience to Him comprise the only sure foundation of a great life.

Not what, but whom!
  For Christ is more than all the creeds,
And His full life of gentle deeds
  Shall all the creeds outlive.
Not what I do believe but whom!
  Who walks beside me in the gloom?
Who shares the burden wearisome?
  Who all the dim way doth illume,
And bids me look beyond the tomb
  The larger life to live?
Not what I do believe
  But whom!
Not what but whom!

Today is a day to hear and do!

September 11

An Astonishing Life

Matthew 7:28-29

For He taught them as one having authority, and not as the scribes (Matthew 7:29).

THE CHURCH IN AMERICA IS like Israel at the time of Jesus' ministry. We hear great truths every Sunday. What if we lived them with obedience? The difference between Jesus and the scribes was that He demanded action. Ultimately He was crucified not for what He said but for what He did. He didn't just talk about love; He loved. He not only proclaimed God's power to heal; He healed the people. He didn't say the kingdom of God would come someday; He announced its reality as present and called people to live in it presently. He did more than theorize about forgiveness; He forgave. That's why people were "astonished at His teaching."

The astonishing life will be one in which word and deed, idea and character, thought and action, belief and obedience are one. The words "astonished" and "amazed" are used often in the Gospels to describe people's reactions to Jesus' life and message. As we noted before, the Greek word actually means to be driven out of oneself. The Lord did just that to people: He drove them out of self-containment, caution, and constriction. We are to live in Christ in such an abandoned way that people will be astonished by what we are and do. The test of how astonished they are will be the urgency with which they desire to know our secret of true happiness. Who has asked you lately?

A Christian should be an anointed question mark prompting people to ask how we became the astounding people we are.

September 12

Over the Rainbow

Genesis 9:1-17

I will set my bow in the cloud, and it shall be for a sign of a covenant between Me and the earth (Genesis 9:13).

THE RAINBOW IS A SIGN OF the end of the storm. It has been a special symbol of God's faithfulness for His people through the ages. Noah had been obedient before the flood. He followed the Lord's instructions completely and was the source of the survival of mankind. In affirmation, the Lord gave the rainbow as the sign of the covenant. I never see a rainbow without remembering what God can do with people who do what He says.

It is in the storms of life that we need to remember the rainbow. When the rains fall and the winds blow in the adversities of life, we need the courage to remember that the storm will end and the rainbow will appear. Only the covenant God has made with us can give us that kind of fortitude. God is committed to be our God. Our hope is not that we can be adequate enough to deserve His love, but rather that He has chosen to be our God.

Over the rainbow is the cross. Greater than a sign in the heavens, the cross is the establishment of a new covenant of grace and forgiveness. The cross tells us how much God loves us and the extent to which He was willing to go to make us His own. When we look at the cross, we know that at the center of the universe there is a giving, forgiving, unchanging, unlimited love which will never let us go.

O Love that wilt not let me go,
I rest my weary soul in thee;
I give thee back the life I owe,
That in Thine ocean depths its flow
may richer, fuller be.
—George Matheson

September 13

Dare to Risk

Genesis 12:1-9

And the LORD appeared to Abram and said "To your descendants I will give this land." So he built an altar there to the LORD who had appeared to him (Genesis 12:7).

IT WAS AN AWESOME PROMISE that required audacious risk. The Lord astounded Abram with the promise that he would be the father of a great nation. All the families of the earth were to be blessed through him. But the cost was high. He had to leave Ur of the Chaldeans, security, familiar surroundings, and prosperity. Abram became the patron of people who discover that being obedient means risk.

The Lord is constantly calling us out. He wants to get us to the place where He is our only security and assurance. Think of how hard we work to eliminate the risks of life. We labor, save, plan, and invest ourselves with safe responsibilities. Then we settle into the ruts of sameness and complain that life is no longer exciting.

As long as we are alive, there will be a next step in our adventure with the Lord. He constantly calls us out from where we are to a new level of risk. There will never be a time when what we've done or been can be our security. We were programmed to always be on the growing edge of new adventure. Where is the element of creative risk in your life? What would you do if you trusted God completely?

The crucial element in risking for the Lord is guidance from Him. Our challenge is to discover where the Lord is leading and launch out with His daily direction, risking with the knowledge that He imputes strength for what He inspires us to do.

A life without risk is like a bird without wings.

September 14

Old Ways in a New Life

Genesis 12:10-20

Then Pharaoh called Abram and said, "What is this you have done to me?" (Genesis 2:18).

IT IS DIFFICULT TO IMAGINE that the adventuresome Abram, willing to take the great risk we met in yesterday's Scripture, could so quickly forget the Lord's promise to take care of him. The initial risk of leaving Ur of the Chaldeans was to be followed by constant challenges to trust the Lord in the realization of His promise.

Abram failed the first opportunity to discover God's intervening power. He was afraid of what might happen to Sarai in Egypt, and he fell back on his old methods of manipulation and lying. How very honest the Bible is about its heroes! Abram fled and implicated Sarai in his lack of trust in God. His fear was that the Egyptians would see how beautiful Sarai was, take her, and kill him. He told his wife to lie and tell the Egyptians that she was his sister.

Everything happened as he had suggested. Sarai was taken to the Pharaoh, and Abram was treated like royalty. But the Lord had greater plans for Sarai than to be one of the many women of the Pharaoh. God sent a plague on the ruler's house, and he sent the two dissemblers away from Egypt. Our lack of trust in God's power to do His work always causes suffering for us and others.

Why is an exposing story like that in the Bible? How can the knowledge of Abram's weakness help us? We can all identify with Abram's false dependence on human conniving. Our form of human self-reliance may not be the same as Abram's, but all of us have some difficulty living the new life in Christ, with vestiges of the old person still controlling our responses. Raw dependence on the Lord to take care of us is a moment-by-moment risk. But He's worthy of the trust. He will step in and make old ways unnecessary.

Daily risk requires daily dependence.

September 15

The Parable of the Red Volkswagen

2 Timothy 3:1-9

They will maintain a façade of religion, but their life denies its truth (2 Timothy 3:5 PHILLIPS).

A FRIEND TELLS A DELIGHTFUL story of a woman who bought a new red Volkswagen. One day she took her children to the zoo. She left her car in the parking lot near the elephant show. When she returned, late in the afternoon, she was dismayed to learn that her car was badly smashed on the roof and sides.

What she was alarmed to hear was that, during the day, an elephant had gotten loose. It had been trained, as part of the act, to put its foot on a big red drum. Dutifully, after years of training, it had put its great foot right down on top of the VW! The woman was frantic. The zoo authorities assured her that they would assume the expense of the repairs.

On the way home she was stopped by a policeman, who accused her of having left the scene of an accident. He saw the damage but did not know the unusual circumstances. "But officer, I have not been in an accident!" she explained. "An elephant put his foot on my car." His response to this was to give her a drinking test and take her to the nearest police station. "But you don't understand! Please call the zoo!" was the woman's plea to the desk sergeant. Finally he did and was assured by the zoo authorities that she was telling the truth. Chagrined, he released her with apologies.

How wide the believability gap often becomes! Things are not the way they seem. We say one thing but the evidence seems so contrary. Our talk about God's power of love in the cross is not matched by the observable facts of our lives. The woman's story is an extreme example of the breakdown of communication, but some of the contradictions of our own words and life are no less startling!

To be and not to seem—that is the issue.

September 16

Oh, Really?

1 Corinthians 4:6-13

For who sees anything different in you? (1 Corinthians 4:7 RSV).

SOME YEARS AGO, WHEN the science of voice amplification was in its infancy, a church I was serving equipped me with a remotely controlled lavaliere microphone with no cords attached. A power pack, which I wore in my hip pocket, was fed through an FM sending set which broadcast my voice on the public-address system of the sanctuary. That gave me freedom to move about the chancel and in the pulpit with freedom and be heard by the people. What we did not know was that the same band on the FM dial had been also assigned to some ham radio operators.

One Sunday I finished my sermon with a flourish, with my hand outstretched in a triumphant gesture. At that very moment a ham radio operator was carrying on a conversation which invaded the public-address system in the sanctuary. As I stood before my people finishing my sermon, his voice was heard all over the sanctuary. "Oh, really?" he said to the person with whom he was carrying on a conversation. We all laughed.

That's not a bad question to ask at the conclusion of any sermon or anything we do in the church. "Oh, really?" points us to the credibility gaps of what we say so eloquently and forcefully from the pulpit and throughout the life of a church. What difference will it make?

The same question needs to be asked about the follow-through of our grand beliefs in daily discipleship. "Who sees any difference in you?" is another way of asking "Oh, really?" Who could tell that Christ lives in you because of your attitudes, actions, and reactions in life's tight places?

The world is watching and listening.
Is what I say congruent with the way I live?

September 17

Walk Through the Promise!

Genesis 13:1-18

Arise, walk about the land through its depth and breadth; for I will give it to you (Genesis 13:17).

WE WONDER WHY the Lord wanted Abram to walk through the land He had shown him that would be his and his descendants! Wasn't seeing enough? No, the Lord wanted Abram to relish each acre of His gift, claiming what He had promised as true.

The same is true for the Christian life. When we read through the Gospels we are amazed by what our Lord had told us He would do for us. He promised an abundant life now and an eternal life forever. All power would be given to us. He would be with us. Our hearts were to become His home. The things He had done we were to do, and even greater things. Through Him we would be able to love, forgive, heal the needs of people, and introduce them to Him. Our problems would be the prelude to receiving fresh power. He would make us like Him in our character and actions. Death would be a transition in living, and heaven would be our eternal home.

Amazing? Yes! We capture how Abram must have felt as he began to walk through the promise God had made. To claim what Christ has offered is our challenge. We live as spiritual paupers when unlimited resources are placed at our disposal. There is nothing left out. All we need, now and for eternity, has been given to us.

There's a great difference between sitting on our problems and standing on the promises!

September 18

It's Going to Be a Great day!

Psalm 118:1-29

This is the day which the LORD has made; let us rejoice and be glad in it (Psalm 118:24).

I GREETED A CAB DRIVER early in the morning in Austin, Texas. "How are you?" I asked sleepily as he drove me to the airport. "Just great and it's going to be a mighty fine day!" I asked him why he was so hopeful about the day ahead. "The way it began," was his reply. He had come to work at 4:00 A.M. and had made several trips already. "When a day starts right, it stays right. If it starts slow, it stays slow," he said prophetically.

The Lord never sleeps. He's awake waiting for us to talk to Him and give Him our day. Jeremiah discovered that the mercies of God are new every morning. God has divided our time into days and nights so that we can ask for fresh power for each day. When we begin the day with a quiet time with the Lord, it's like reporting in for duty, getting the strategy for the day, and hooking into power to make each day maximum. Job discovered that the morning stars sing together. We can join in that song.

Attitudes determine so much of how we handle life's pressures and challenges. When we surrender a day to the Lord and spread out before Him all that we anticipate, suddenly the day is a delight and not a drudgery.

Some people are morning people and are wide awake the moment their feet hit the floor. Others are night people, whose best hours are after midnight. But whichever we are, the daytime is when most of the world does its business and makes its crucial decisions. We need to be wide awake for the Lord's incredible possibilities in each potential that masquerades as a problem.

*God's best for my life makes any day
the best day of my life.*

September 19

By Faith Alone

Genesis 15:1-21

Then he believed in the LORD; and He reckoned it to him as righteousness (Genesis 15:6).

WE ALL HAVE AN INNER longing to know God and be in a relationship with Him. There is no inner peace without being right with God. Even those people who make no claim to know God or show any interest in Him have an inbred quest, an unsatisfied hunger. They try desperately to fill the emptiness with substitutes, but the hunger persists. It is called by many names: insecurity, anxiety, fear, frustration, lack of fulfillment, and loneliness, but the real cause is missing the relationship with God for which we were born.

But what if we realize our need? What can we do? Our key verse for today is one of the most crucial verses in Scripture. Two words in it are interdependent: *believed* and *righteousness.* Abram believed that God existed, and he trusted his life to His guidance in accomplishing the promise He had made. Faith in God is the only basis of righteousness. Abram was made right with God, not on the basis of character refinement or what he did for God, but by faith alone. That faith spurred him on in obeying God, but his goodness was not his status with God.

Paul used Abram's faith as the example of what God requires of us in his epistle to the Romans. He showed the Christians that it was not good works but faith that made a person righteous. He looked back on Abram's faith from the other side of Calvary.

Our faith is also a response to love revealed on the cross.

I can live righteously because I am right with God through faith.

September 20

Marching to a Different Drummer

Romans 3:1-31; 1 Corinthians 12:6-11

Where is boasting then? It is excluded. By what law?
Of works? No, but by the law of faith (Romans 3:27).

AUTHENTIC FAITH IS THE WORK of the Holy Spirit in us. He alerts us to the emptiness inside our souls, creates a hunger for truth, empowers the communication of the gospel to us, and gives us the power to respond. True faith is the Spirit's power in us releasing us to surrender our mind, soul, and will to the Lord. We accept God's control over all our affairs. We march to a different drummer. Nothing but this complete relinquishment will satisfy God. Our efforts at righteousness, morality, religious observances, or goodness cannot make us right with God. There is only one way to the heart of God: faith in what He has done for us in Christ. That truth is hard for many of us to swallow both before and after becoming Christians. There is a lingering desire to be accepted for something we are or have done. But righteousness by faith alone is God's way and the only way.

Is there a difference between the gift of faith to believe and faith that is one of the gifts of the Spirit in 1 Corinthians 12? Yes. The difference is that one provides a right relationship with God, and the other equips us to minister for God. The quality of faith given to us in the beginning is to believe in God; the special gift of faith after we've become a Christian is to trust God courageously with situations, circumstances, people, and impossibilities. Faith as the gift of the Holy Spirit is the capacity to dare to believe that all things are possible if willed by God. We should pray for it and thank God in advance for it. The gift gives us a daring, all-stops-out boldness to expect miracles.

I will follow the cadences of Christ, my new Drummer.

September 21

When and When Not to Laugh

Genesis 17:1–18:33

And the LORD said to Abraham, "Why did Sarah laugh, saying, 'Shall I indeed bear a child when I am old?' Is there anything too difficult for the LORD?" (Genesis 18:13-14).

THERE'S A GREAT DIFFERENCE between laughing *at* God and laughing *with* Him in joy over what He is able to do with life's seemingly impossible situations. Abraham and Sarah laughed at God over the promise that they would have a son to carry on the Lord's legacy of blessing. Sarah was 90 years old! No wonder they laughed. What would your response have been?

Once again the Lord had to convince Abraham that God is able. The question must be answered. Is anything too difficult for the Lord? No, not if He wills it and we are willing to accept it. When confronted with that, Sarah claimed she had not laughed. Why was it important to the Lord for her to admit that she had laughed? Why did He retort with the demand for honesty: "But you did laugh"? Only when we confess our lack of faith is the Lord willing to do what He has promised.

There are times in all of our lives when we laugh at God rather than laughing in delight with Him. The birth of a child of promise was absolutely necessary for the fulfillment of God's plan for His people. Sarah's age was secondary to that. God does not squander His miracles. He can, and will, do anything which is strategic for our eternal welfare.

I will stop laughing at God's possibilities so that I can hear His laughter and laugh with Him.

September 22

Who or What Is Your Isaac?

Genesis 22:1-13

And Abraham said, "God will provide for Himself the lamb for the burnt offering, my son." So the two of them walked on together (Genesis 22:8).

THERE IS NO BETTER PERSPECTIVE from which I view Abraham's willingness to offer Isaac, his only son, as a sacrifice than from within his heart. Imagine the panic which gripped him when the Lord made this ultimate test of his obedience and unquestioning faithfulness. We feel with Abraham the years of longing and then the gift of a son. Identify the most precious person in your life, and put his or her name in the place of Isaac, and you begin to feel the anguish.

Now trudge up Mount Moriah. What was going through Abraham's mind? What turbulence tumbled about in his heart? What was God doing? Why would He ask for the sacrifice of the only hope of the fulfillment of His promise?

Listen to the imploring love of Isaac. He trusted his father implicitly. His question,"Behold, the fire and the wood, but where is the lamb for the burnt offering?" must have cut Abraham to the core. He ached with pain in his heart too great to bear as he bound his son. Did he protest? Was there a cry of anguished struggle? No. Isaac trusted his father as Abraham trusted God.

It was just as Abraham was about to thrust the sharp blade into his beloved son's chest that the Lord intervened:"Abraham, Abraham!" The commanding voice from heaven so shattered and shocked Abraham that he dropped the knife. Then he saw the ram the Lord had provided for the sacrifice.

Why did God put Abraham through it? It was because He wanted Abraham, not Isaac.

Our Isaac is not ours until surrendered to the Lord.

September 23

The Lord Will Provide

Genesis 22:14-24

And Abraham called the name of that place The LORD Will Provide, as it is said to this day, "In the mount of the LORD it will be provided" (Genesis 22:14).

ABRAHAM HAD BEEN FAITHFUL and obedient. He had been willing to give up his cherished son. The Lord intervened at just the right moment and provided the ram for the sacrifice. He had all of Abraham that there was. The altar he built in memory of the crisis of obedience and the Lord's intervention gives us one of the greatest names for our God: YHWH-jireh, Yahweh will provide.

On another mount called Calvary, the Lord provided a Lamb for the sacrifice for the sins of the world: Jesus Christ, our Lord. He is the ultimate provision when all our self-justification and human effort fails. We trudge up our mount to offer God an oblation of obedience only to find that there is a cross towering there with a Savior who takes upon Himself all our rebellion and willful disobedience. We are free to live indeed!

I once had a frightening dream. In it, the Lord asked me to hand over all my loved ones, my church, and my ministry as if never to have them again. I felt the anguish of the loneliness and depletion of all my efforts to serve the Lord. It seemed like an eternity before He returned them to me. I will never forget the words He spoke in my dream: "All that you have and are are mine! I entrust them back to you as My gifts. Never again think of them as your possessions. They are a trust from Me to you. As long as you put Me first in your life, and keep the cross as your only security, you can enjoy them for My glory." I know in some small way what Abraham went through and that the Lord does provide!

All of life is a gift because the Lord provided the Lamb of Calvary.

September 24

Great Parents of Great Children?

Genesis 25:1–26:35

So he built an altar there, and called upon the name of the Lord, and pitched his tent there; and Isaac's servants dug a well (Genesis 26:25).

WOULD YOU RATHER BE a great man or the father of great children? That depends on what we mean by great. The challenge which all parents face is to communicate the vitality of their faith. The family accomplishes its purpose if children are able to hear and see in their parents the evidence of an authentic relationship with the Lord. If children can witness how parents deal with the delights and difficulties of life, with both bringing them closer to the Lord, they will discover a faith that is their own. The problem is that so often all that children receive from their parents' faith are the rules and regulations of moral behavior. Parents must discipline, establish right and wrong, and help children discover and utilize their potential. But too often the motive of an intimate, personal relationship with the Lord is not communicated. The result is that children associate the Lord with the oughts of Christian discipline without the adventure of Christian discipleship.

Abraham was both a great man and a great father. He shared the promise and destiny God had given him so that Isaac grew to be a strong, quiet, consistent man. He trusted God, acknowledged His faithfulness, stood firmly against his enemies, and worked hard in the simplicity of his pastoral life. He is remembered for little else than that he was Abraham's son and Jacob's father, and that he dug wells. There were no acts of valor or daring triumph. But a truly good life can be a great life. Isaac fulfilled his purpose in God's unfolding strategy. What parent could want more than that?

Great parents share the greatness of their faith so that in raising their children they introduce them to an authentic relationship with the Lord.

September 25

Making the Willful Willing

Genesis 27:1–33:20

So Jacob named the place Peniel, for he said, "I have seen God face to face, yet my life has been preserved" (Genesis 32:30).

THE ACCOUNT OF JACOB'S LIFE raises the old question: Are we the people we are because of heredity or environment? Yesterday's meditation on great fathers and great sons must also be considered in the light of the turbulent, restless character of Jacob. He was much more like his grandfather, Abraham, than Isaac. His father passed on the faith, but Jacob spent a lifetime accepting the Lord's sovereignty over his life and discovering the quiet trust we noted in Isaac. Jacob had a very different nature. Both heredity and environment were woven into the fiber of his soul. As we have seen in today's Scripture, he was often his worst enemy, made an enemy of his brother, and at times, even of the Lord. Jacob is like many of us—impetuous, strong-willed, and gifted, but slow to acknowledge the Lord as the source of our blessings.

Jacob could not wait for the providence of God to give him his father's blessing. Along with the connivance of his mother, he manipulated events to steal the blessing. God would have worked that out, but Jacob could not wait. When Isaac blessed him and sent him to Paddan-aram, the Lord extricated him from the syndrome of sibling rivalry so He could make him into the man He destined him to be. The blessing of the Lord in the dream at Bethel gave him the assurance he had tried to manipulate. How gracious the Lord was to him! In Laban's land, he was given Rachel and eventually great wealth. But his heart was still with Isaac, and the memory of his deception prompted him to return to make restitution with Esau. On the way, the Lord again appeared to him. Jacob wrestled in his soul with the Lord. The limp that resulted never allowed him to forget that he had to lean on God.

God loves us so much that He sometimes breaks our will to make us willing to be willing.

September 26

When Circumstances Contradict Our Vision

Genesis 37:1-36

Here comes this dreamer! (Genesis 37:19).

THE LIFE OF JOSEPH IS AN account of the intervention of God. The Lord had a great destiny for the 17-year-old dreamer. But what He had to put him through to accomplish the dream is one of the most exciting accounts of the providence of God at work in a life in all of the Old Testament.

Joseph's dream of his brothers someday bowing down before him further ignited their sibling rivalry and jealousy. Joseph was Jacob's favorite, and the brothers knew and abhorred this. Their attempted murder and subsequent sale of him to the Ishmaelites was an act of bitter hatred. And yet the Lord had plans to bring good out of their evil deed. The Ishmaelites from Gilead did not happen along the way by chance. The Lord wanted Joseph in Egypt at all costs.

So often, circumstances contradict our dreams. We get a vision of what is ahead and then seem to face difficulties which contradict the dream. While Joseph rode along on the Ishmaelites' camel, he probably felt the disappointment we all feel at times. But God was working His purposes out. When he arrived in Egypt, he was sold to Potiphar, the captain of the Pharaoh's bodyguard. There he rose to power. His natural talents, multiplied by the Lord's blessing of him, resulted in position and authority in Potiphar's household. That too was part of the plan which would lead to accomplishing God's purpose to use Joseph as a source of blessing as the one through whom He would eventually get Jacob and his sons to Egypt.

Hold fast to the vision God has given you for your life. The difficult things we go through are to prepare us for the realization of the vision on God's timing and by His power!

I will not deny the vision that God has given me even when circumstances seem to contradict it!

September 27

God Uses Everything

Genesis 39:1–41:57

But the LORD was with Joseph and extended kindness to him (Genesis 39:21).

JOSEPH WOULD NOT DENY his loyalty to Potiphar or his faithfulness to God. It landed him in jail on the charge of doing what he refused to do! But the Lord was with Joseph. That's the phrase which punctuates the amazing life of this blessed man.

The term in jail also had its purpose in God's plan. Joseph's leadership qualities were recognized again, and he was elevated to a position of authority. But there were others in that jail by divine appointment. The Pharaoh's cupbearer had fallen into disfavor and was thrown into prison along with Joseph. He had a dream which Joseph interpreted by God's power. When the cupbearer was released, he was more than ready to tell the Pharaoh about the mysterious Hebrew he had met in jail. The ruler of Egypt had had a perplexing dream about seven fat and seven lean cows and seven good and seven thin ears of grain. Joseph was called on to interpret. The dream clearly predicted seven prosperous and seven lean years ahead for Egypt and the surrounding territory. The interpretation won for Joseph the position of regent of Egypt, the next in power and command to the Pharaoh.

Amazing! At 30 years of age Joseph's dream was coming true. Who would have imagined that the evil deed which Potiphar's wife did could have brought about this result?

This portion of Joseph's story reminds us that God can weave in His plans despite the evil that people do to and around us. The hurts which people do and say are not beyond the providential workings of our God! Nothing can deter the plan of God. Just as He used everything that went seemingly against Joseph for what He had planned for him, so too He can use the difficulties we are facing right now to get us one step further in His plan. Trust the Lord.

*God is working His purposes out
in spite of what people do to us.*

September 28

Life Makes Us Bitter or Better

Genesis 42:1–49:33

I am your brother Joseph, whom you sold into Egypt. Now do not be grieved or angry with yourselves because you sold me here; for God sent me before you to preserve life (Genesis 45:4-5).

THE FAMINE WHICH STRUCK Egypt also hit Joseph's homeland of Canaan. When Jacob learned there was grain in Egypt, he sent his sons to buy grain. The account of the intrigue involved in their visits reads like a good mystery story. What Joseph put his brothers and Jacob through was so that they could share in the real purpose of his original dream. His brothers did indeed bow down before him, but he was a very different man from the one they had sold to the Ishmaelites. Note his compassion and tenderness when he finally revealed his identity to his brothers. Instead of an arrogant dreamer, he now saw himself as God's agent of preserving life. The Lord had given him the wisdom to realize that He had enabled the succession of miraculous interventions in his life to get his family to Egypt. A sense of being a cooperator in God's strategy gives us accepting love and forgiveness for people who may have blocked His plans with us.

How easy it would have been to say, "You did terrible things to me. Now don't expect any kindness from me!" Instead, Joseph's repeated expressions of God's kindness made him tender and gracious.

Life can make us either bitter or better. What happens to and around us can drive us to retaliation or reconciliation. What is life doing to you? Who would Joseph's brothers represent in your life? How have you reacted? Can you see that perhaps what they did made you stronger and more receptive to God? If so, use every opportunity to share the storehouse of the plenty God has given you when leanness brings others to you out of their need.

I will receive the "Joseph's brothers" of my life with kindness and forgiveness—today!

September 29

God Knows What He Is Doing!

Genesis 50:1-26

Do not be afraid, for am I in God's place? As for you, you meant it for evil against me, but God meant it for good, in order to bring about the present result, to preserve many people alive (Genesis 50:19-20).

ALL THAT JOSEPH HAD BEEN through had brought him to this profound conviction that God can bring good out of evil. What he said to his brothers could be a good motto for our daily living. It should be memorized and remembered when things go wrong, people hurt us, or our dreams are dashed. God does know what He's doing.

This passage affirms God's control and our free will. He loves us so much that He wants us to be people, not puppets with no freedom. The choice to give us freedom was awesome. God knew what we would do with it. Yet He also knew that there can be no freedom to choose to love Him unless we are given free will. He gave us the sublime opportunity to use our freedom of choice to choose to respond to His love and love Him and others in return.

It is with this same freedom that we choose what our attitude will be to people who have misused or mistreated us. When we are convinced that God not only gives us freedom but loves us so much that He can use our mistakes and rebellion in spite of us, then we can surrender what happens to us and thank Him that He will accomplish His purposes regardless. This leads to a profound peace and security. We can say in a prayer of relinquishment, "Okay, Lord, I'm hurting, but I believe in Your providential power to use the worst for the best. I leave this whole thing in Your hands. Teach me and help me to grow to be a person who dreams and is mature enough in You to realize the dream."

Have Thine own way, Lord,
Have Thine own way.
Thou art the Potter,
I am the clay.
—Adelaide A. Pollard

September 30

God Is Faithful

Exodus 1:1–2:25

And the sons of Israel sighed because of their bondage, and they cried out; and their cry for help because of their bondage rose up to God. So God heard their groaning; and God remembered His covenant with Abraham, Isaac, and Jacob. And God saw the sons of Israel, and God took notice of them (Exodus 2:23-25).

HAVE YOU EVER HAD THE feeling that God had forgotten you? We've all experienced it. It happens when we face difficulties, pray about them, and there seems to be no answer.

The people of Israel felt like that. Their bondage in Egypt was excruciating. And it became worse each day. Did God know or care? Had He forgotten His covenant with Abraham, Isaac, and Jacob?

At the very time the people doubted Him most, God was preparing for His big move. The passage of Exodus we read for today vividly communicates three things: the condition of the people of Israel, the faithfulness of God to His Covenant, and His preparation of Moses to be the liberator of His people. The Lord had not forgotten. We may wonder why He waited so long. The people of Israel had become accustomed to the luxuries of Egypt. Only the suffering they were now enduring at the hands of the Egyptian overlords could have gotten them prepared to want to leave. God wanted to make them a great nation. Their groaning to Him indicated that the time was right. And God was preparing Moses for what He had planned.

It is usually just before we give up that the answer comes. Probably we were not ready before. We would have used the answer as a reason for pride, thinking we had accomplished it. Be sure of this: God never forgets. We are His covenant people, people of a faithful promise. He will act when we are ready and His timing has arrived. Would we want to spoil the best that God has by getting it at the wrong time and in the wrong way?

Wait for the Lord, and let your heart take courage!

October 1

One Thing Which Is Certain

Exodus 3:1-22

Thus you shall say to the sons of Israel: "I AM has sent me to you" (Exodus 3:14).

MOSES' EXPERIENCE OF GOD in the burning bush became an indisputable discovery. He never forgot it. It introduced him to the Lord who would strengthen and sustain him all through his trials, tragedies, and triumphs of the years leading the exodus from Egypt and bringing the people of Israel to the promised land.

The encounter with God came at a time of weakness and despair in Moses. He was an exile from Egypt. He had tried to take things into his own hands, had made an effort to help his people, and had failed. He had learned about the God of his people but he did not know Him. The plight of the people was on his heart that day as he tended the sheep. Where was this God? What was He like? Why didn't He do something about the suffering of His people? It is when we are feeling the weakest and are filled with questions about the Lord that He comes to us. The burning-bush encounter is for those who have tried and failed and are ready to receive power beyond their own.

We've all said, "Who am I to go? Who will believe me? When they ask who sent you, what shall I say?" The Lord's response to Moses was, "Tell them 'I AM' sent you." It really means, "I will be what I will be." The divine name YHWH, Yahweh, signifies the One who makes things happen. That's all Moses had to go on. But what more did he need? The Creator, the Father of Abraham, Isaac, and Jacob, would be with him, and He would make things happen, indeed!

I will live this day in the power of the Lord, who makes things happen.

October 2

Be Careful What You Call Impossible

Exodus 14:1-31

But Moses said to the people, "Do not fear! Stand by and see the salvation of the LORD which He will accomplish for you today" (Exodus 14:13).

THE OPENING OF THE Red Sea and the open tomb are two crucial events in the Hebrew-Christian tradition which make the word "impossible" an unacceptable word in our lexicon. Both events are vivid reminders that the Lord is able to do what we would call impossible.

The Lord set up Moses and the people of Israel for a miracle of grace. He led them into an impossible position. Following instructions, they traveled down to the foot of the mountain range on the western shore of what we know now as the Gulf of Suez. They were trapped by the mountains on one side, Migdol (a garrison outpost of Pharaoh's troops) on another side, and the northern extremities of the Gulf of Suez. Picture the situation. Moses could not lead the people south because of the mountains, nor east because of the approaching chariots of the Pharaoh's armies, which were now in hot pursuit. The people of Israel were like a mouse in Pharaoh's trap. But the Lord had led them there.

It was when the situation reached crisis proportions that Moses, confident of the I AM of the burning bush, said, "Fear not, stand firm, see the salvation of the Lord." There's a three-point strategy for life's struggles! The Lord opened the Red Sea for the people to pass through at just the right time. He had allowed an impossible situation to teach them that if they would trust Him nothing would be impossible. That's the assurance we all need. A Red Sea is going to open for us today and the Lord of the open tomb will show the way through!

I will not fear, I will stand firm, I will wait for the salvation of the Lord, I will go forward!

October
3

Anything's Possible

Mark 6:30-56

For they had not understood about the loaves, because their heart was hardened (Mark 6:52).

HERE IS ONE OF THOSE passages which must be read in the light of how it ends. The key is what Jesus says when He comes to the disciples in a tempestuous sea when they were rowing against the wind. He walks across the water and says, "Take heart; it is I—have no fear!"

That day Jesus had fed the five thousand with five loaves and two fishes. After that they should not have believed that anything was impossible. The disciples should not have forgotten so easily...nor should we in our crises. The Lord gives His present miracles, not only to help us now, but to give us lively confidence for the future.

What impossible thing do we need to see Jesus do in our lives? Great Christians are daring. A dynamic emerges when we are capable of believing the impossible, because then it does happen! What is it that makes us pull back and say, "Everything is possible for our Lord...but not that...or this!" That then becomes the very thing we must trust to the Lord's limitless possibilities. The disciples were awestruck with the power of God in Jesus.

Mark 6:53-56 is one of those telling comparisons so effectively used by Mark. In contrast to the disciples' seeming faithlessness about impossibilities, he dramatizes the way people bring their sick to Jesus just to be able to touch even the fringe of His garment.

In which group do you find yourself today—the fearful disciples, or the needy people willing to believe that with Christ nothing is impossible?

What Christ wills is never impossible.

October 4

By Whatever Name, Remember!

1 Corinthians 11:17-26

Do this in remembrance of Me (1 Corinthians 11:24).

ON THE FIRST SUNDAY of October all of Christendom celebrates Worldwide Communion. The event falls on a different date each year, but it is crucial for us to recapture the awesome meaning of this central sacrament.

It is the Lord's Supper. We remember the historical event when Jesus celebrated the Passover meal with His disciples. There Jesus broke bread and shared the cup as a portent of His broken body and shed blood on the cross. It is the covenant in Christ's blood. Covenant means a relationship of promise. God established His first covenant with Abraham, and now, through the shedding of the blood of the Lamb of God, Christ, a new covenant of forgiveness and grace has been established. We come to the Lord's table to affirm that covenant and claim our forgiveness and new life.

It is a Eucharist. This became the official name for the sacrament from Ignatius in A.D. 115. The word means "thanksgiving." Our hearts are filled with gratitude for what our Lord has done to reconcile us and set us free from sin and guilt. It is a communion. We experience the living Christ in the broken bread and the wine. The challenge is to become fully committed to His plan, purpose, and power. It is a sacrament. The word comes from the Latin word for pledge. The Roman legions pledged themselves to Caesar with a sacramentum, an outward sign of a deep and inward bond.

No wonder the early Christians adopted the word to describe what happens when the bread is broken and the wine is given! The power of the Lord is released at that moment for those who partake. Christ is present and His people are strengthened.

I cannot take communion; communion takes me!

October 5

Stale Grace

Exodus 16:1-8

Behold, I will rain bread from heaven for you; and the people shall go out and gather a day's portion every day (Exodus 16:4).

MOST OF US LIVE ON stale grace. Old experiences, outworn ideas, tattered religious memories have become the false basis of our security, rather than a fresh realization of God's grace for each situation and each new day. We think that grace, God's unmerited love and favor, can be hoarded from the past for future experience. The difficulty, however, is that God cannot be pressed into the stereotype of previous experiences. We can learn how God has revealed Himself to us or others in previous concerns, but we cannot hold over spiritual strength from one event to the other. God gives us a new portion of His power and wisdom for each crisis so that we may discover the unique thing that He seeks to do in each situation, and with each person with whom we come in contact or for whom we are responsible.

This was the Lord's promise which was manifested in the miracle of manna. Manna was the name given to a sticky, honeylike substance which exuded in heavy drops from a shrub found in the desert in which the people were wandering. During the night under the heavy dew the manna would be provided by God. In the morning, after the dew had risen, there would be left on the ground a sweet, flaky substance which provided adequate nourishment for the people in each day.

The people of Israel discovered that if they tried to hoard the manna from one day to the next, except in preparation for the Sabbath, it would rot and be filled with worms. What the Lord sought to do was to help His people to depend on Him by giving them just enough food for each day.

God has divided time into daily units where neither the strength, nor even the insight, of one day can be carried to the next. He wants us to trust Him in each day for the strength and the particular direction that He alone can give.

Are you living on stale grace?

October 6

The Royal Order of Aaron, Hur, and Joshua

Exodus 17:8-16

So it came about when Moses held his hand up, that Israel prevailed, and when he let his hand down, Amalek prevailed (Exodus 17:11).

WE BELONG TO EACH OTHER. We are the Lord's gifts to one another in the battles of life. We were never meant to fight alone without the Lord's help and the encouragement of one another. This is the exciting message of today's Scripture. I have a friend who spurs me on with the words, "Remember, the battle is the Lord's and I'm in it with you!" He is a member of what I like to call The Royal Order of Aaron and Hur.

As the people of Israel pressed on into the wilderness, they were attacked by the Amalekites. The Lord gave Moses the secret of fighting His battles for His people. All Moses had to do was hold his rod high in the air and the armies of Israel would win against the Amalekites. The rod of God used to open the Red Sea would be the symbol of His presence and His power for victory in battle. But the battle was long and hard. Moses' arms grew weary. It was then that Aaron and Hur became strengthening agents. They held Moses' arms up while Joshua fought the battle. What a team!

The roles are interchangeable for us. Sometimes we are called to be Moses and lead; at other times Aaron and Hur to life up drooping arms of a tired leader; at still other times to fight like Joshua while others pray. It is impossible to win in life's battles without faithful friends who pray with us, uphold us, and fight our battles as if they were their own. Who holds your arms up? Who needs you to do that for him or her today? Life has its difficult times when we need friends. And the Lord provides the right person at the right time.

Lord, I am ready to join the royal order of Aaron, Hur, and Joshua today.

October 7

The Everlasting Arms

Exodus 19:1-8; Deuteronomy 32:8-12

You yourselves have seen what I did to the Egyptians, and how I bore you on eagles' wings, and brought you to Myself (Exodus 19:4).

WE WONDER IF THE LORD drew Moses' attention to the flight of an eagle as he climbed up Mount Sinai. The metaphor of the eagle as an example of God's providence never left Moses. He remembered it all through his life. God had indeed carried the people of Israel on His wings.

At the end of Moses' life, he looked back on how God had cared for His people. He had been like an eagle training its eaglets to fly. That's what Moses tried to tell the people in the Deuteronomy passage we have read. The Lord stirred up the nest in Egypt, making it so uncomfortable that they had to move on to the plans He had for them. An eagle will do whatever is necessary to get an eaglet out of the nest when it is time to fly. Then it will push the eaglet off the edge of the nest so that it can use its unfledged wings. The word "hover" in our Scripture reading is the same word in Hebrew for "broods" used in the creation account of God brooding over the waters. In this case it is the eagle's watchful eye caring for the first-flight attempts of the eaglet. And then when the eaglet is in danger of falling too far, the eagle swoops down, spreads its wings, and catches it on its pinions.

That's the way God deals with us. He will not allow us to stay in any comfortable nest. He presses us out to discover our potential. And yet He hovers close by, brooding over us, keeping us from falling too far. Moses knew that from years of experience. "The eternal God is a dwelling place, and underneath are the everlasting arms" (Deuteronomy 33:27).

The everlasting arms are for those who dare to fly.

October 8

I'll Do It His Way!

Exodus 20:1-17

You shall have no other gods before Me (Exodus 20:3).

THE WORDS OF THE POPULAR song "I'll Do It My Way!" appeal to our desire to carve out a life of independence and self-reliance. I think of the song each time I review the Ten Commandments. The Lord gave us the commandments so that we could "do it His way." There is no other way that really works. We don't just break the commandments; we break ourselves on them when we sidestep the Lord's ordained plan for living. The commandments are like natural law—they are principles by which we are able to realize the purpose for which we were created. But they were never meant to be obeyed on our own strength. The same Lord who gave them offers to give the strength to live them.

That's where people have gone wrong through the ages. We have either brashly broken the commandments or else made our efforts to follow them as a basis of our self-justification. All the commandments are part of the first—to put God first and have no other gods before Him. The world offers many substitutes, and we are tempted to worship them. Each of the subsequent nine commandments deals with the false gods of religion, self, possessions, and power over people. Take each one of them and consider the contemporary forms of breaking them. There are so many subtle expressions of our equivocation. What are yours?

When we take the commandments seriously, we realize how difficult it is not to break them in one way or another—if not in acts, so often in our thoughts. A Christian dares to live by the commandments by the power of grace through Christ. When we are faithful in "doing it His way" we realize that we fail, are forgiven, and are given strength to begin again.

With Christ's love and power, I'll do it His way!

October
9

The Cloud Where God Was

Exodus 20:18-21

So the people stood at a distance while Moses approached the thick cloud where God was (Exodus 20:21).

THERE ARE TIMES WHEN GOD seems to be clouded, beyond our reach, mysterious and aloof. Other translations use "thick darkness" for the thick cloud. Either translation identifies with our experience in times of doubt and fear.

But look at it another way: it is often in those dark times that God is most at work in our lives. The words *darkness* and *God* seem contradictory. But He uses the dark times of discouragement as well as the bright times of victory. He is with us in the dark clouds of life's difficulties.

When we accept that basic fact, we are ready to grow through what happens to us. God has not left us. The mist has come in for a time, and we must walk by faith. The mist will lift and we will look back on the experience, wondering why we questioned what God was doing. And we will know something else: the Lord never forsakes us. His answers will not always be what we think best, but the friendship He longs to have with us will be deepened.

The Holy God has come to us in Christ to reveal how He uses the darkness. The Resurrection was the assurance that He always has the last word. The only way to live with freedom and joy is to accept that there are dark, cloudy days. Without them we would never appreciate the bright days when the answer we asked for in the darkness is answered. With that confidence, we can say with the poet,

"I've found a friend; O such a friend! He loved me ere I knew Him. He drew me with the cords of love, and thus He bound me to Him. And round my heart still closely twine those ties which naught can sever: for I am His and He is mine, forever and forever!"

God is in the dark as well as the bright experiences of life.

October 10

When We Get Tired of Waiting

Exodus 32:1-29

Now when the people saw that Moses delayed to come down from the mountain, the people assembled about Aaron and said to him, "Come, make us a god" (Exodus 32:1).

ONE OF THE MOST DIFFICULT challenges in living is knowing when to act and when to wait. We all abhor lack of courage and boldness. But equally so, we are disturbed by people who constantly take things in their own hands and act without guidance from the Lord. The secret is to discover how to act in God's timing, on His power, and under His guidance. And that requires waiting for the Lord. Most of us find waiting very difficult.

The people were tired of waiting for Moses. He had been on Mount Sinai for 40 days. "What are we waiting for?" they asked. "Who is this tyrant of Sinai who makes us wait? And where is the Moses who spends his time praying on the mountain? Other nations have gods they can see and touch; our God is an invisible, thundering power. We want a god to live on our level, go before us, and lead us to our destination when we want it. We are tired of waiting around!" Impatience is the illegitimate child of faithlessness and willfulness.

The golden calf was the result.

Anything we do without waiting for God's guidance and timing becomes a golden calf. All that God had done for the people of Israel had been forgotten in their impatience. The same is true for us. We overlook the fact that God has promptly met our needs and graciously denied any wants that would hurt us.

The full-time vocation of living is to seek and know the Lord and His will and act on His timing, strategy, and power.

October 11

A Broken Sentence from a Broken Heart

Exodus 32:30-35

Moses returned to the LORD and said, "Alas, this people has committed a great sin, and they have made a god of gold for themselves. But now, if Thou wilt, forgive their sin—and if not, please blot me out from Thy book which Thou hast written!" (Exodus 32:31-32).

WE KNOW HOW MOSES felt. We've all experienced times when we wish we could step in and take the consequences of some failure for a loved one who has failed. We find it difficult to stand by helplessly while someone we love faces the result of wrong choices. Who is there who has not wanted to say, "Lord, judge me, put the blame on me. Let my loved one go!"

We can empathize with Moses during that long night of the soul when he contemplated the sin of his people who had built and worshiped the golden calf. What could be done? Three undeniable realities burned in his soul: the righteous holiness of God, the idolatrous sin of his people, and the judgment of God on the sin. He wondered—had it all been for nothing? The battle for freedom from Egypt, the struggle in the wilderness, the high adventure of pressing on to the promised land—was this all lost? Then he remembered a new word the Lord had used 11 times in the instructions about the Day of Atonement. The thought of the sacrifices for the sins of the people seized his mind. He would offer himself!

When Moses came before the Lord, he blurted out the possibility which had grown in him. It has been called literature's most pathetic broken sentence. We wonder how long it took him to finish by offering himself as a sacrifice.

God did not seem to be impressed. No person can assume the sins of another. Our efforts to atone for others do not work. Only God can do that. And that's exactly what He did when He came in Jesus Christ. This passage presses us on to the Incarnation and the ultimate atonement on the cross. What we cannot do for others or ourselves, God has done for us.

I will stop trying to atone for people and spend myself communicating the atonement.

October 12

The Ultimate Prayer

Exodus 33:12-23; 34:29-35

Moses said, "I pray Thee, show me Thy glory!" (Exodus 33:18).

IT WAS A DIFFICULT TIME for Moses. The people were difficult to lead. The Lord called them a "stiff-necked" people. To stiffen one's neck requires setting the jaw in defiant stubbornness. The jaw must be protruded rigidly. What could Moses do?

He does the only thing any of us can do when life becomes difficult and people around us are problems: he goes to God with all his troubles. He tells the Lord that he wants to know Him better and understand His ways. He reminds Him that the people are His people. Then the Lord promises that His presence will go with them. Moses is shocked. He had never considered leading the people without the Lord. "If Thy presence does not go with us, do not lead us up from there." He wanted nothing to do with leading the stiff-necked people without God!

Then Moses felt the courage and confidence to pray the ultimate prayer. "Show me Thy glory!" he pleaded. The Hebrew word for glory means presence. It is the total impact of the person and power of God. That was Moses' greatest need. With God's glorious presence, he could attempt anything.

We all need deep times with our Lord in which His glory is infused into us. The ultimate prayer, "Show me Thy glory!" is always answered. The way is perfectly fitted to our need. Any answer to prayer which does not bring us into the Presence is no answer at all. More than answers, we need *the* Answer: the glory of God.

Today I will seek God's glory and not my own.

October 13

Face to Face

2 Corinthians 3:2–4:6

But we all, with unveiled faces, beholding as in a mirror the glory of the Lord, are being transformed into the same image from glory to glory, just as by the Spirit of the Lord (2 Corinthians 3:18).

PAUL UNDERLINES THE ASTOUNDING difference between Moses and our experience of the glory of God. We can remove the veil and look the Lord in the face through Jesus Christ. God has graciously revealed His presence, His glory, for us to behold in Christ. And the result is that we can be changed into Christ's image from one degree of glory to another. The Christian life is transformation into Christlikeness!

That's what we all need, isn't it? We all long to be more like Christ in character, attitude, action, and reaction. Human personality can be changed. Day by day, as we pray Moses' prayer "Show me Thy glory!" we can know Paul's assurance that the "glory of God in the face of Jesus Christ" can have lasting radiance on our faces. We do not have to wear a veil to hide a fading radiance.

And the process of being glorified in Christ never stops. We are not the persons we were and we are not what we will be. The Lord is up to a great work in us. Our only task is to give Him full sway, complete control, absolute obedience and attention. The more we concentrate on Christ, the more, by His grace, we are refashioned into His image.

Do you really want that? Tell the Lord. He is more ready to answer that prayer than we are to ask. But when we do, we will notice the difference in our relationships and the way we handle the pressures of our responsibilities. Christ's love and forgiveness, peace and power, hope and courage will be unmistakable.

I am being transformed into Christ's image from glory to glory.

October 14

Things Become What They Seem

Numbers 13:25-33

Then Caleb quieted the people before Moses, and said, "We should by all means go up and take possession of it, for we shall surely overcome it" (Numbers 13:30).

THERE WAS A MAJORITY report of fear and a minority report of courage. The majority report of the spies sent in to survey the land of Canaan was grim. Notice how these negative reporters viewed themselves as grasshoppers in comparison to the Canaanites and actually became that in their sight. Things do become what we imagine. Most of all, we have the tendency to picture the worst and put our energies into achieving it. These frightened people transferred their own image to their enemies. What they had forgotten was that they belonged to a mighty God who had destined them to go in and possess the land. They multiplied their meager lack of confidence with zero and ended up with panic.

Now listen to Caleb's courage. He saw the same giant warriors in Canaan, but he also knew that the Lord was with His people. Praise God for people like Caleb! They have the capacity to multiply limited human resources by the unlimited power of God and turn it into vision and hope.

We face challenges of life, and in this particular day which faces us with the alternatives of the majority report or the minority report. There are more than enough people around us who are afraid and negative. We need a Caleb to give us assurance that, with the Lord, we can move forward. Now the crucial question: are you more like Caleb or more like the men who became grasshoppers in their own image? How would your family, church, the people with whom you work, answer that?

I will become whatever image I hold of myself and life, and therefore I will picture what I can be when filled with the Lord's power.

October 15

Willing to Receive Wonders

Joshua 3:1-7

Consecrate yourselves, for tomorrow the LORD will do wonders among you (Joshua 3:5).

THERE'S AN INSEPARABLE relationship between today's consecration and tomorrow's wonders. The people of Israel were on the edge of the River Jordan about to cross over into the Promised Land of Canaan. The Lord was ready to do wonders. What He needed was the unreserved consecration of the people to His plans and purposes. Consecration is yielding all we know of ourselves and our resources to all we know of God and His plan and purpose. There is no limitation on what He can do with people who have given Him control of their total lives.

Joshua was elevated into an awesome position of leadership as Moses' successor because the Lord had all of Joshua that there was. The Lord was his passion and purpose. Joshua was completely sold out in a surrender of his will to the Lord. He had learned his lessons well from Moses. The leader of the exodus had given him the secret of power: absolute obedience.

What wonder would you long for the Lord to do tomorrow? He gives us today to be willing to be made willing. When we relinquish our tenacious control of our future, the Lord can step in and do wonders beyond our imagination.

Relinquishment is the only way. We have been given a free will in order to have the capacity to choose to love the Lord and allow Him to love us. But our will becomes a citadel, a bastion of imperious self-control. It is possible to believe in the Lord and still control our own tomorrows.

Tomorrow's miracles begin with today's consecration.

October 16

The First Step Is the Hardest

Joshua 3:8-17

And it shall come about when the soles of the feet of the priests who carry the ark of the LORD, the Lord of all the earth, shall rest in the waters of the Jordan... (Joshua 3:13).

THAT'S A GREAT PROMISE! The priests carrying the ark of the Lord held the key to realizing it. They represented the tribes of Israel and were to be participants in the realization of a great miracle. All they had to do was get their feet wet! They had to take the first step into the Jordan River, and then the Lord would roll back the waters so the people could pass through. The first step was the hardest; the Lord did the rest.

How like life! The Lord wants to do tremendous things in our lives, but He graciously gives us the opportunity of participating. He wants to know how serious we are about crossing our Jordan River and claiming the promised land He has prepared. There is no limit to what He can do if we will dare to get the soles of our feet wet. Imagine the trust and commitment those priests had to have to take that first step!

Often the first step to realizing a miracle of God in our lives is to ask for guidance, receive a promise, and then act as if it were ours. I find that the formula of asking what to ask for, then asking, and thanking the Lord with praise really works. The crucial thing about the miracle of the rolling back of the waters of the Jordan is that this is exactly what the Lord told Joshua would happen if the priests were courageous enough to believe and take Him at His word.

There will be no miracle until we get the soles of our feet wet. Have you acted on what He's told you to do? If you loved Him with all your heart, what would you do? Do it today!

Today I will take the first step, knowing that God will honor my obedience.

October 17

Take Courage!

Matthew 9:2; Mark 10:49; Psalm 31:1-24

Be strong, and let your heart take courage, all you who hope in the LORD (Psalm 31:24).

COURAGE GROWS FROM FAITH. Courage is ours for the taking. The Psalmist discovered that. The Lord said to him, "Be strong, and let your heart *take courage.*" It must be claimed and appropriated. This is the salient thrust of Jesus' offer to His disciples on the night before the crucifixion. I like the accurate rendering of the Greek in the New American Standard Bible: "These things I have spoken to you, that in Me you may have peace. In the world you have tribulation, but *take courage;* I have overcome the world" (John 16:33 NASB, emphasis added). This translation is stronger than others which say, "Be of good cheer." We can take courage only because the Lord has taken us. He has a tight grip on us. Then we will have courage to discover and do the Lord's will.

"How can I know that what I want is what the Lord wants for me?" There is only one way: the conversion of your "wanter." The issue is, have we asked the Holy Spirit to truly fill us? If we have, then we should dare to be much more confident about our wants and His will. A deep self-distrust can be overcome with a Holy-Spirit confidence. Questions about knowing the will of God are very exposing. They reveal a great need for intimacy with God's Spirit: prayer; Bible study; prolonged periods of friendship with the Lord. We should be in constant conversation with Him. Would we have to ask what a close, trusted human friend believed about or would do in a situation? Probably not! Longing for the will of God is really longing for Him!

If God is on our side, who can ever be against us?

—Romans 8:31 TLB

October 18

The Secret of Spiritual Power

Judges 6:1-27

Surely I will be with you (Judges 6:16).

GOD USES ORDINARY PEOPLE to do extraordinary things. We look with amazement at the power some people have. We wonder what secret to receiving God's strength they have discovered. They obviously have the same human frailties we have, but spectacular things happen to and around them. Why? What do they have that we've missed?

The story of Gideon gives us the answer. The Bible delights in telling us about the human inadequacies of its heroes. When we see what they accomplished, we are astounded by what God can do with a willing person totally committed to Him.

Gideon was pressed into the Lord's service at a very difficult time in Israel's history. The people had entered the Promised Land and began to learn the disciplines of being an agricultural people. They made a fatal mistake. They adopted the local fertility worship and placed Baal shrines in their fields. Their agrarian success was short-lived. The Midianites swept down at harvest-time to rape and ravage the products of their pluralistic religion. Israel had become syncretistic—they worshiped Yahweh and the Baal gods all at the same time. Syncretism is the worship of more than one god, the blending of religious loyalties. At a time when everything seemed hopeless because of the Midianite attacks, the people cried out to God, but they kept the Baal shrine intact.

That's when God stepped in. He came to Gideon with a promise and a command. He promised to go with him and He told him to tear down his family's Baal shrine and its female counterpart, the Asherah.

God always begins a reformation in us before He can use us to accomplish one around us. Gideon had to take a stand. And so do we.

God can accomplish great things through a person who puts Him first in his or her life.

October 19

Contagious Courage

Judges 6:28-33

And they said to one another, "Who did this thing?" And when they searched about and inquired, they said, "Gideon the son of Joash did this thing" (Judges 6:29).

GIDEON HAD TAKEN HIS STAND for the Lord. The Baal and Asherah of his family were in shambles. The people in the area were enraged. That always happens when false gods are exposed and dismantled. Gideon was a hero for the Lord God, but not for the frightened neighbors. But there is another hero in the story—Joash, Gideon's father. He stepped in and defended his son. Could it be that Gideon gave him courage to take a stand that he had wanted to take for a long time?

Courage is contagious. We need more parents like that today who are willing to support their children's obedience to God, even if it exposes their own lack of faith. Joash stood with his son and the Lord against the people who wanted their false gods kept intact. His ridicule of Baal's impotence was magnificent. If Baal was as strong as the people thought, let him defend himself against Gideon. The father's affirmation was expressed in giving his son a new name, Jerubbaal, meaning "Let Baal contend against him." He released his son to battle for the Lord.

We all have false gods which we syncretize with the Lord. We believe in Him and yet we draw our meaning and purpose from people, possessions, positions, and our human power. We worship at the shrine of success, human achievement, and culture. What is it for you? What competes with your obedience to the Lord? The promise of His presence and power for Gideon was dependent on the tearing down of the pagan altar. When Gideon did that, the peace and power of the Lord was promised for future challenges. The magnificent things Gideon did to save Israel were accomplished because the Lord had all that there was of Gideon.

There is no limit to what God can do when He alone is Lord of our lives!

October 20

Clothed with the Spirit

Judges 6:33-35

So the Spirit of the LORD came upon Gideon; and he blew a trumpet (Judges 6:34).

THE MEANING OF THE HEBREW of our key verse for today could be translated, "The Spirit clothed Himself with Gideon and he blew a trumpet." What a vivid image! The Spirit of God comes within us, clothes Himself with us, and gives us courage to sound the trumpet, calling others to seek His best for their lives.

Whatever Gideon was able to do was because his talents were multiplied by God's Spirit. All the Lord needed was a receptive, willing, guidable person who would depend only on Him. The results were up to the Lord.

God's best for our lives is His Spirit. All that we ask Him for or ask Him to do for us in our prayers is not His best. He is the best Himself. The Lord's Spirit is all we need. The glory of God is a person fully alive through the infusion of His Spirit. We were created to receive and live by the indwelling power of the Spirit. The purpose of God all through history has been to call a people to be His people and live in them.

That's why He came in Jesus Christ. He lived, taught, suffered, and died for our sins to begin a new creation of new creatures. Christ's death and resurrection defeated the forces of evil which keep us from being open to receive His Spirit.

All that Christ said and did was to prepare a new people who would be His clothing in the world. When He clothes Himself with us, we are made like Him, given His character, and empowered to live the life He lived. That's what He meant when He promised, "These things which I do, you shall do also, and greater things." Blowing His trumpet is to call others and dare to attempt by His power. Our life should demand an explanation. How can we be the people we are? Then we can explain: Christ is our motive, message, and might.

My mind, emotions, will, and body are the wardrobe of the Spirit.

October 21

Go for It!

Ephesians 5:15-21

Be filled with the Spirit (Ephesians 5:18).

THERE ARE THREE WAYS to live. The first is to do our will on our power. That's humanism. The second is to do our will on Christ's power. That's religion. The third is to do Christ's will with Christ's power. That's the abundant life.

Paul's five-word admonition "Be filled with the Spirit" spells out the secret to power. The Greek tense is in the continuous present imperative: "Go on being filled with the Spirit." Throughout the New Testament there are two uses of being filled with the Spirit. The first is initial at the time of conversion and the second is for the challenge and opportunities of ministry.

Christ creates in us a sense of emptiness, makes the good news of the gospel impellingly clear, engenders desire to receive forgiveness and a new life, gives us the gift of faith to receive Him as our Lord and Savior, takes up residence in us, and then gives us exactly the gift we need to launch out into the adventure of the abundant life. That's why we need "to go on being filled." Each new possibility or problem presents us with an opportunity to be given fresh power for the immediate situation, circumstance, or relationship.

Today each of us faces tasks which are beyond us. We wonder how we can take what will be thrown to or at us. Don't worry! The Lord never gives us more than He can handle. Our only concern is to find out what He guides and then to step out daringly, knowing that we will have the power we need. He will give us intellectual insight, the right words to say, and the will to do His will. We need not be afraid. Our confidence is not that the Lord has joined our team, but that we have joined His.

And He never runs out of strategy, strength, or surprises. Then, in the words of our altruistic motto, we can say to ourselves, "Go for it!"

October 22

God's Peace Is Our Fleece

Judges 6:36-40

Then I will know (Judges 6:37).

IT IS SOME COMFORT TO US to know that even after Gideon's decisive encounter with the Lord, he needed further assurance that God would deliver Israel through him. How like most of us! We want to be sure. There needs to be some sign. Our lack of confidence demands an undeniable revelation before we will get on with what the Lord has told us plainly we are to do.

Gideon needed not one but *two* reaffirmations just to be surer. The amazing thing is that God was willing to meet the frightened leader at the point of his need. The fleece was wet and then dry according to the precise requirements of Gideon's two tests.

We wonder about that. What would it take to convince us that the Lord is with us and will give us power to accomplish His guidance? The point is that He loves us so much that He is willing to enter into dialogue with us in prayer and give us a sign that a particular direction or action is what He wills. He uses the thoughts of our minds, the feelings of our emotions, and the arrangement of circumstances to assure us. When we surrender our wills and ask for guidance well in advance of a major decision, He will get through to us. Be sure of that! At the right time there will be a convergence of our thinking and feeling, of what we've read in the Scriptures, and of what we discern around us.

But a fleece is secondary to close communion with the Lord. He had already told Gideon what to do. Most of us have more guidance than we've acted on. The most important thing I've learned about making crucial decisions is that the Lord draws me closer to Him in the time of uncertainty.

An inner peace is our fleece.
The Lord who gives the day will show the way!

October 23

The Rudder of Guidance

James 3:4

Look also at ships: Although they are so large and are driven by fierce winds, they are turned by a small rudder wherever the pilot desires (James 3:4).

GUIDANCE FROM THE LORD IS like a rudder of a ship. James uses the image to show the power of words. The same metaphor can be used for prayer. Following up on yesterday's meditation, I want to share some questions which have been an authentic fleece for me. I have discovered that at times when I need guidance, the Lord wants to give *Himself* as well as direction. When we grow in closer union with Him, the answers become clear.

The fleece was fine for Gideon at that stage in his spiritual development, and the Lord answered in a way to make him sure. The great difference for us is that we can have the mind of Christ. We live in a new dispensation of grace. Through the cross we are reconciled with God and have access to Him in a much more profound way. So many of our questions are answered in the message and mandate of Christ. As new people in Christ and in intimate fellowship with Him, I can ask these questions.

Will this decision enable me to grow in grace? Is it God's best for my life? Is it in keeping with the life and message of Jesus Christ? Can I do this and seek first His kingdom and His righteousness? Does it will the ultimate good for me and all around? Is it part of the long-range goals the Lord has already revealed to me? There's no better fleece than answering those questions. But finally, raw trust in the Lord is our only fleece. And not even our wrong choices are beyond His forgiveness and innovative power to provide His best for our lives.

Abiding in the presence of the Lord and asking the crucial question is a sure way for our Pilot to move the rudder in the direction we should go.

October 24

The Audacious Assumption

Proverbs 16:1-9

The mind of man plans his way, but the Lord directs his steps (Proverbs 16:9).

"ISN'T IT A BIT AUDACIOUS to think that God cares or is concerned about the decisions of our daily life?" Paul would have answered this person's question with a resounding "No!"

The word "audacious" can be taken in two ways. It can mean intrepidly daring, bold, adventurous, venturesome; it can also mean presumptuous, saucy, and impudent. The two divergent uses of the word focus the different attitudes of people about God's guidance. The rank-and-file Christians do not expect to be guided by God. They think it petulant personalism to think that God either has a plan for their lives or has the inclination or interest to communicate to individuals a particularized providence. They feel that the idea of God guiding us makes the Almighty a messenger boy, the Bible a Ouija Board, and contemplation of the implications of circumstances like reading a horoscope.

But there are others whose audacity is rooted in a humble belief that the habitual response of a God-centered mind to the total life situation in which responsibility and opportunity meet, can find guidance for the specific decisions and involvements of their lives. The result is an assurance issuing in obedience and freedom.

He leadeth me,
He leadeth me!
By His own hand He leadeth me!
His faithful follower I would be,
For by His hand He leadeth me.
—Joseph H. Gilmore

October 25

A Daring Adventure

Judges 7:1-25

And the LORD said to Gideon, "The people who are with you are too many for Me to give Midian into their hands, lest Israel become boastful, saying, 'My own power has delivered me'" (Judges 7:2).

THE ODDS WERE NOT GOOD when Gideon prepared for battle: 32,000 Israelites against 135,000 Midianites. With the Lord's help, perhaps he could win. No wonder Gideon was shocked when the Lord made two cuts in his army! He lost 22,000 when he followed the Lord's instruction to tell those who were afraid and trembling to go home.

The second test of the remaining 10,000 was to march the soldiers through the riverbed. Those who stopped, took off their armor, and put their mouths into the water to drink were eliminated. Only those who kept their eyes on Gideon while reaching down for a little water in their cupped hand, then licking it like a dog, were qualified. The issue was commitment to battle and not their own temporary thirst, and their willingness to keep their attention riveted on Gideon. Only 300 men survived this test. But with these the Lord accomplished victory over Midian.

The account tells us two things. The Lord wants loyal, committed followers who keep their eyes on Him. He can do the impossible with people whose only security is in Him. We have a greater than Gideon to lead us: Jesus Christ.

But also, the story tells us that the Lord thins the ranks so that the glory will be given to Him and not to our cleverness. What are we daring to attempt which could not be accomplished without His strength and intervention? So often we plan our lives around what we could do without Him on our own. A sure sign that we are in communion with the Lord is that we are attempting what only He can do! Can you identify that in your life?

I will dare to attempt something which only God could accomplish through me.

October 26

Criticizing After the Battle

Judges 7:24–8:3

Then the men of Ephraim said to him, "What is this thing you have done to us, not calling us when you went to fight against Midian?" And they contended with him vigorously (Judges 8:1).

AMAZING! AFTER THE WORST of the battle was over, Gideon gave the armies of Ephraim an opportunity to be a part of the mopping-up action of completely defeating Midian. They were given the chance of sharing the victory and the glory. How grateful they should have been! Not so. They complained that Gideon was able to dissuade their anger with a few well-chosen compliments. But we are left to wonder: what does it take to satisfy some people?

Ever have the problem? Of course, we all have. We do our best and we try to be considerate of the ego needs of others, but still something is always wrong. The Ephraimites were not unaware of Gideon's battle against Midian. Why did they wait to be called? Were some of their army those who were afraid, or those who could not pass the Lord's test in the river? My experience of human nature wants to read that into the account, but true or not, it would be consistent with people through the ages who can't take the heat of the battle and find some reason for complaining after the victory is secure. Know anyone like that? God forbid that anyone would ever say that of you or me!

But we need both compassion and a sense of humor for those who are critical after the battle is won, even if they did little or nothing to secure the victory. When our eyes are on the Lord, and our own craftsmanship for Him, we can overlook the criticism of people who have made safety and lack of adventure their craft!

I will not criticize if I have not been in the battle, and I will ask the Lord for a sense of humor for those who do.

October 27

The Listener

1 Samuel 3:1-21

Then the LORD came and stood and called as at other times, "Samuel, Samuel!" And Samuel said, "Speak, for Thy servant is listening" (1 Samuel 3:10).

SAMUEL'S CALL TO BE A prophet reveals the essence of life and ministry. The theme of the life of this pivotal character was, "Speak, Lord; Your servant is listening." Samuel's name was interpreted by his mother to mean "God hears." Biblical scholars also suggest that the name means "The Name of God." Both were expressed throughout Samuel's life. No person in the Old Testament lived more completely in the confidence that God does hear and that in His name is power and authority for His people. The words he spoke in response to the Lord's call provide us with the secret to making this an exciting day in our lives. Because the Lord hears, we can say what's in our hearts and then say, "Speak, Lord; I'm listening."

Samuel's ministry came to the end of the period of the judges and the beginning of the monarchy. He was the architect of the rebuilding of Israel's spiritual and social life. The "Lord's Listener" was used to communicate God's call to Saul and David, and he anointed them as kings. The prophet was the father of the prophetic office in Israel's life from his time forward. He was a God-sensitive man who was so open to God that he could hear God speak and acted on what he heard.

Let's make this a day to listen—to God and then to people. God does hear our prayers and He does speak in the Scriptures, through the inner voice, and in the confirmation of a right direction in a profound peace in our feelings.

My mind and heart have ears to listen to the Lord.

October 28

Ebenezer and Jehovah-Jireh

1 Samuel 4:1–7:17

Then Samuel took a stone and set it between Mizpah and Shen, and named it Ebenezer, saying, "thus far the LORD *has helped us"* (1 Samuel 7:12).

SAMUEL BECAME A MIGHTY source of courage and guidance to the armies of Israel in their battles against the Philistines. It was a time of military crisis. The Lord met the people's need in Samuel. The prophet was totally dependent on Him to show each step of the way.

This is exposed in a beautiful way in today's key verse. After victory over the enemy, Samuel built an altar and called it Ebenezer. The Hebrew word is very significant. It means "thus far the Lord has brought us." What had been the sight of Israel's defeat was now a hallowed memory of victory. They did not have to retreat. The stone marked the place where the Lord had brought them under His watchful care and intervening strength.

The hymn "Come Thou Fount," by Robert Robinson, uses this word Ebenezer: "Here I raise my Ebenezer; hither by Thy help I've come, and I hope, by Thy good pleasure, safely to arrive at home." We are sure that generations of Christians have sung that hymn without knowing the deeper meaning of the word Ebenezer. Another verse, however, is a vivid description: "Hitherto Thy love has blessed me; Thou has brought me to this place; and I know Thy hand will bring me safely home by Thy good grace."

The Lord is gracious to give us points of resting gratitude. We can look back and say "Ebenezer!" Then we can look forward and say "Jehovah-Jireh." You remember from our meditation on Abraham's altar on Mount Moriah that this means "the Lord will provide." Samuel would need both for the challenging days ahead with Saul and David. Think about the meaning of both words for your life today.

My model today will be "Ebenezer" and "Jehovah-Jireh."

October 29

Our Awesome Power to Limit God

1 Samuel 8:1–15:35; 1 Chronicles 10:13

So Saul died for his trespass which he committed against the LORD, because of the word of the LORD which he did not keep (1 Chronicles 10:13).

SAUL HAD GREAT POTENTIAL. He was handsome, taller than any of the people, and endowed with immense talent. But the signs of his weakness were evident from the beginning. Why didn't he know about Samuel? Was he unaware of the soul-sized issues gripping his people? He was so engulfed in his own affairs that he was not a part of the struggle of Israel to be the faithful people of God. He was totally undone by the fact that the Lord would choose him to lead in a struggle he had never made his own concern. When he had a moving experience of God, the people were equally amazed. "What has come over the son of Kish? Is Saul also among the prophets?" And yet God chose him through the voice of the people. But where was he? Hiding among the baggage!

The first evidence of Saul's deeper problem was exposed when he blundererd ahead in making a sacrifice without Samuel and then led the people into battle without clear guidance. Saul found it difficult to trust God to be his only strength. He never got his heart into the rhythms of the Lord's guidance. He lived on the level of talent rather than the Lord's gifts. God was never really personal to him. In Saul we see our potential and our problem. There is no substitute to habitual obedience, constant trust, and God's resources for our needs.

The Bible gives us impelling examples of what happens when we cooperate with God and frightening examples of what happens when we don't.

October 30

God Uses the Ordinary to Do the Extraordinary

1 Samuel 16:1-23

So he sent and brought him in. Now he was ruddy, with beautiful eyes and a handsome appearance. And the LORD said, "Arise, anoint him; for this is he" (1 Samuel 16:12).

WE CAN IMAGINE THAT THERE was no small stir in Bethlehem when Samuel appeared and said that the voice of God had directed him to the house of Jesse to find a king of Israel. Jesse had eight sons, and he did not think to call David, his 14-year-old son, as a possible candidate for anointing. Surely the Lord would not want David! Yet Samuel said, "Are all your sons here?" Jesse was amazed. "There remains yet the youngest, who keeps the sheep." "Send and fetch him," said Samuel.

The moment Samuel looked at David, he knew that this was the one for whom he was searching. This lad who had roamed the hills, keeping watch over the flocks, playing to himself on the shepherd's harp, gazing at the stars at night, and dreaming of the future—this was God's chosen to lead His people. God was to make him one of the greatest men of history, but not without trial and conflict. The hammer blows of experience were to shape him into the man God wanted and needed.

The story of the life of David tells us the exciting truth of how God takes frail, ordinary human beings and makes them great for His purposes. We dare never say, "Who, me? Why me?" The God who chose David also chose humble fishermen to be His Son's disciples, and He changed the world with them. David learned what we must learn: God uses ordinary men to do what others think impossible. David was a God-dependent man. God could use him to do the extraordinary because he trusted Him completely. God can do that today with us!

God chooses and uses unspectacular people to do spectacular things in history.

October 31

A Person After God's Heart

Acts 13:16-25; Psalm 89:20; 2 Samuel 11:1–12:31; Psalm 51:1-19

And when He had removed him, He raised up David for them to be their king, to whom also He gave testimony and said, "I have found David the son of Jesse, a man after My own heart, who will do all My will" (Acts 13:22).

DAVID WAS A MAN AFTER God's heart. We wonder at this description. How could you call an adulterer, a murderer, and a man who practiced great cruelty a man after God's heart? The Scripture unsparingly announces the sins of David. But it was out of these failures that God used him in His purposes for Israel. David failed successfully because he learned of the gracious goodness of God and because he was one of the most thankful men of history.

David was a man after God's own heart because he abounded with thanksgiving. In the Psalms there is such a mixture of confession and thankfulness that David was accounted, even by God Himself, to be a man after His own heart. Only a sense of unworthiness can issue in profound thanksgiving. David's life challenges us that it is not our perfection but our thankful dependence which counts. We can identify with David in his fallible humanity, and we can see what God can do with a person who confesses and thanks God for his forgiveness.

David had been against God's heart before he was fully a man after God's heart. The Bible paints the dark story of his transgression and sin. God waited long for him to repent. After his adultery with Bathsheba and his cruel sending of her husband, Uriah, into war to die, God sent Nathan the prophet to judge his sin. A deep, penetrating parable was given and then the challenge "Thou are the man!" David knew! His repentance is for history to read in Psalm 51. And God took him at his word. The infinite mercy of God lifted him up and used him in His further purposes for Israel.

We are called to be men and women after God's heart.

November 1

Affirming the Gifts of Others

1 Samuel 17:48–18:16

Saul has slain his thousands, and David his ten thousands (1 Samuel 18:7).

"DAVID IS GREAT! Saul hath slain his thousands, and David his ten thousands!"

This is the victory chorus following David's smiting of Goliath. This is one of the most familiar Bible stories. We love it because it reveals the power of God which was now upon David. Saul's reaction to the miraculous event was very human: "Inquire whose son the stripling is." He wanted to use him to accomplish his purposes without seeking the source of his power. David was successful in battle wherever Saul sent him. And then, as David became popular and the people grew to love him, Saul became angry and jealous. This was the battle of the generations in an old focus. Saul was more concerned with his own image than with getting God's work done. What a sorry analysis Scripture gives us: "Saul was afraid of David, because the Lord was with him and had departed from Saul."

Often what we cannot use for our own purposes and manipulate for our own plans, we grow to hate. The history of God's people is black with stories of godly people who could not work together to accomplish God's will. The church, Christian groups, families, and friends are often split because we cannot bear to affirm what the Lord is doing through another. The reason in Saul was that he could well remember what it was like to be powerful in the Lord and loved by the people. David could either drive him back to the Lord or drive him mad because he was the incarnation of what Saul had been. Often we are hostile to people, not because of what they do to us, but because of what they show us about ourselves. Christian maturity leads us to care most that God's work is done; who does it is not important.

Today I will affirm others who do God's work differently from me, and I will learn what God wants to teach me that I am to do.

November 2

Saul's Problems with Saul Called David

1 Samuel 18:1-30

When Saul saw and knew that the LORD was with David...then Saul was even more afraid of David. Thus Saul was David's enemy continually (1 Samuel 18:28-29).

SAUL WAS OBSESSED WITH jealousy over David. It became a virulent poison flowing in his confused nature. But long before David became the focus of Saul's insecurity, the king had resisted God's plan and purpose for his life. He repeatedly said, "No!" to the Spirit's nudging and promptings. Saul never really appreciated Saul! Even the Lord's call and repeated interventions to help him did not heal his lack of self-esteem. He did not allow God to love him deeply and sufficiently. Until we let God love us, there will always be a David to unsettle us with jealousy—some person who has what we want or does what we wish we could do. David was a threat in Saul's mind before the unstable king put him into the category in fact. Jealousy made Saul a man God could not use.

Saul had a problem with Saul that he called David. His own insecurities became fastened on how the Lord was using David. That exposes that his greatest concern was not the battle with Israel's enemies, but with his conflict with his own status and recognition. Why couldn't he rejoice that David was victorious over the Philistines? Any wise king should be able to affirm a general's success for him. Not Saul. He could not see that David was fighting for the Lord *and* him. Saul's unstable relationship with the Lord made him jealous of one who was able to do what he could no longer do. The poison of jealousy keeps us from sharing the glory. When we do we can take delight in the way He works in others and in us. Commit this day to affirm the way God is using others, and praise God.

If a glass of poison were offered to us, we would refuse it; yet we sip the poison of jealousy day by day, and at long last our soul is dead. The old Gaelic blessing is a wonderful alternative: "Belong to God and become a wonder to yourself!"

November 3

Misplaced Praise

Song of Solomon 8:6-7

Jealousy is as severe as Sheol; its flashes are flashes of fire, the very flame of the LORD *(Song of Solomon 8:6).*

JEALOUSY. IT'S THE "what's mine is mine and what's yours ought to be mine also" attitude. Jealousy is the result of an unstable state of grace. It hits us when we are out of the flow of the Lord's grace, do not delight in our own uniqueness, and fail to express thankfulness for what we have received ourselves. Comparison of ourselves with others takes our eyes off the Lord.

Today's Scripture from the Song of Solomon gives us insight into the cause and curse of jealousy. This short book of the Bible is a love poem of Solomon for his beloved. After extolling the glory of love, Solomon depicts the grimness of jealousy. It is like hell, here called Sheol. Throughout the Old Testament, Sheol was the place where the dead continued to exist, a region of shadows, misery, and futility; there the faithless lived forever in misery and futility. Jealousy is a living hell.

Most of all, jealousy is misplaced praise. That's the meaning of "the very flame of the LORD." The flame of God in us is misspent and misused in adoration of another person or his gifts and possessions. The capacity of praise is misdirected and used to want to be or have what is someone else's. The antidote to jealousy is to focus on the Lord and His goodness and then on ourselves as blessed and loved by Him. The more we praise Him for our uniqueness, the more we can affirm another's specialness without wanting to steal for ourselves.

The Lord says to each of us, "You are meant to be an original, and no other person's copy! Take delight in Me and the special person I intend you to be, and then jealousy will trouble you no more!"

November 4

The Alarm Signal

Galatians 5:16-26; James 3:16

The works of the flesh are evident...jealousy...envy (Galatians 5:19-21). Wherever you find jealousy and rivalry you also find disharmony and all other kinds of evil (James 3:16).

THERE'S A GREAT DIFFERENCE between the works of the flesh and the fruit of the Spirit in today's passage. The works of the flesh are human nature apart from the Lord. They are what we are without the regeneration of being born again and the rejuvenation of being Spirit-filled. When we surrender our minds and emotions to the Lord, He takes up residence in us. He actually displaces the tendencies of flesh (humanity separated from Him) with His own character. It's impossible to imagine Jesus Christ being jealous! Paul lists jealousy as a work of the flesh, a natural tendency of human nature which has not been transformed. All of the fruits of the Spirit which the Apostles list tell us what Christ produces in us.

But what about jealousy after we are converted? It is an alarm signal that we are taking our measurements from other people rather than Christ. The way to win in the battle with jealousy is to go deeper into Christ and the realization of His fruit in us. Christ's love for us is the only medicine which heals jealousy. When you are jealous, take His prescription!

Here are some inventory questions to overcome jealousy with delight in our special uniqueness: How has Christ shown His love to me? When were the times I felt good about myself? How has Christ used me in the past? What are my assets as a person because of Christ? Who is enriched because of my influence? What would life be like if I pulled out all the stops and used my gifts? What stands in the way of enjoying being me? What is the Lord's picture of the person I can become? When is the last time I allowed God to exercise my unique gifts? Can I let go of false comparisons and accept the Lord's confirmation of His delight in me?

November

5

Helping People Deal with Their Feelings

James 5:13-18

Confess your trespasses to one another, and pray for one another, that you may be healed (James 5:16).

THE YOUNG WIFE STOOD talking to friends at a party. The room was jammed with wall-to-wall people. Suddenly she was distracted from the pleasantries of her conversation. Through the forest of people she spied her handsome husband talking to a very attractive young woman. She was disturbed by how much her husband seemed to be enjoying the exchange and how very attentive and saucily solicitous the smashingly dressed woman appeared. A surge of jealousy pulsed through her. She tried to work her way through the crowded room to remind her husband that she too was at the party. To no avail.

As the husband and wife drove home from the party, the wife's stony silence provoked the question which she hoped he would ask: "Is everything all right? You seem very upset about something." She tried to share with him how she had felt at the party and confessed that she was engulfed with a feeling of jealousy. He exploded with defensive consternation. "What's the matter with you?" he said angrily. "We were only talking politics!" "Well, can't you imagine how I felt?" the wife retorted. "You spent most of the evening with her. Haven't you ever felt jealousy?" The husband sidestepped the moment of honesty which could have healed the whole thing. "Of course not! Your insane jealousy is going to ruin this marriage."

We all have feelings of jealousy at times. We need to be able to get this out in the open. A true friend is not shocked or judgmental. He or she understands and empathizes. Then we can be helped to tell God. He cures our jealousy by unqualified love and a special gift of new delight in the person we are as cherished by Him.

I will be nonjudgmental when people feel jealousy so that I can help them receive the courage to give it to God.

November 6

Whom Shall I Fear?

Psalm 27:1-14

The LORD is my light and my salvation; whom shall I fear?
The LORD is the defense of my life; whom shall I dread? (Psalm 27:1).

IN THIS GREAT PSALM, DAVID reaffirms that God is his sure defense. Light for darkness and deliverance for battle were his hope. The Lord would show the way, would light the path, would give mental illumination and emotional courage. Why be afraid?

The evildoers were among God's people as well as the Philistines. David was beset from within as well as without. Yet he would be confident. He asked only one thing: fellowship with God, knowledge of Him, and growth in His love.

This is David's hope because God has promised protection in the day of trouble; He would cancel him from danger and set him above his enemies' power.

On the basis of this review of God's goodness, David is filled with hope and joy. Things looked brighter in the context of God's ultimate purpose. His only fear is that God might remove His blessing from him. Everyone else could forsake him, but not God.

Now David wants most to know God's will. Lord, what do You want me to do? False witnesses are no help; God alone can guide the human heart. The psalm ends in final exultation and praise for God's faithfulness.

Note how this psalm teaches us to pray. First it teaches us to begin with a simple review of what we know of God and His nature. Second, it shows us that we are to pour out whatever is on our minds and hearts in complete self-emptying of concern. Third, we are to affirm again that the one thing we wish above all is to do God's will and ask God to teach us His ways. Fourth, we are to leave the problem or opportunity with Him, acknowledging His goodness in the lives of men. Last, we are to wait in patient confidence to see what He directs.

Wait for the Lord; be strong and let your heart take courage. Yes, wait for the Lord!

November 7

Glorify and Enjoy God!

2 Samuel 6:1-5,12-19

And David was dancing before the LORD with all his might (2 Samuel 6:14).

THE STORY OF DAVID IS FILLED with human pathos, but it is also filled with divine joy. David knew how to rejoice. There are dark days of failure and repentance in David's story, but we must also see this man of deep emotion praising God out of sheer, uncontainable joy.

We are thankful for the picture of David dancing before the ark of God. He let himself go in unreserved praise: "And David played before the Lord and danced before the ark, and the earth shook." There's a dimension of response we too need to discover as a part of our life. The Westminster Catechism says, "Man's chief end is to glorify God and enjoy Him forever." We are to enjoy God!

But do we? Many of us are grim Christians. We have the distorted idea that being a Christian is thinking right, acting decorously, and being responsible. It is that, but much more. We need more of the foot-tapping enthusiasm of frontier religion. Everything we do is so proper and in order. When do we just let go and praise God?

The more we discover of human need, the more we realize that our problems are emotional. We have not learned to be free in expression of love and affection to God and one another. It's good for us to laugh and frolic, sing and dance. God is not a cosmic policeman looking to arrest those who enjoy themselves. The Christian faith is not dull and drab. It is delight with God, with life, and the gift of others. Let yourself go in praise and adoration. David did, and so should we.

But there are always the killjoy Michals to contend with in life. Michal was not as free as David, and she despised him for his free expression of joy. But David would not stop because of her negativism.

Let yourself go in joyous, carefree adoration!

November 8

The Affirmation of Life

Psalm 18:25-30; 1 Kings 2:1-4,10-12

I am going the way of all the earth. Be strong, therefore, and show yourself a man (1 Kings 2:2).

THE CONCLUDING WORDS OF the narration in Arthur Honegger's *King David* are: "And King David said, 'the Spirit of God is within me. One cometh after me to lead my people in the fear of the Lord. O how good it was to live! I thank You God, You, who gave me life.' "

Oh how good it was to live! Now there is an affirmation of life! David's life was filled with triumph and defeat, blessing and sin, repentance and forgiveness, joy and heartache. There is no human emotion or problem which David did not experience. He could not look back on it all without thanking God for the gift of life and say that it was good to live. Now at length the sunset and quiet of eventide had come for David. His dependence upon God was always a sure defense against evil, his victory in battle was always a fresh opportunity for praise to God, and his personal failures were always the prelude to a new sense of forgiveness and mercy. At the end of all his trials, this was still his verdict as it had been before: "This God—His way is perfect; the promise of the Lord proves true; He is a shield for those who take refuge in Him."

What is our verdict? Can we say, "How good it is to be alive!?" What do we say as we look back over the years? Can we say with Paul, "All things work together for good to those who love God"?

The only good life is the God-life. A life lived in fellowship with Him will enable us to grow in grace in the triumphs and victories as well as the failures and defeats. God is in control, and He has given us the gift of the abundant life as it was meant to be in Jesus Christ.

The good life is the God-life!

November 9

God Can Make Us Wise

1 Kings 3:1-28

And Thy servant is in the midst of Thy people which Thou hast chosen, a great people who cannot be numbered or counted for multitude (1 Kings 3:8).

IT WAS AN AWESOME THING that the Lord asked young King Solomon: "Ask what you wish me to give you." There are so many things that Solomon could have asked for: the favor of the people, military might, trusted officials, strength like his mighty father, David. But Solomon had learned the profound lesson from his father. He observed that as David "walked before the Lord in truth and righteousness and uprightness of heart," he had been richly blessed.

Solomon did not presume that he had been given the throne because of his own ability or temperament. He knew that the opportunity was a gift of God's providence. Therefore, he asked for the one gift he needed most: wisdom. "And it was pleasing in the sight of the Lord that Solomon asked for this thing."

Wisdom is the mind of God implanted in the tissues of our brain. More than the talent of a sagacity or insight, it is God's thought controlling our thought. It results in an immense discernment and knowledge beyond our own human capacity. The "understanding heart" is used by the New American Standard Bible and "understanding mind" by the Revised Standard Version. "Heart" is preferable because in the Hebrew language it encompasses intellect, emotion, and will. True wisdom begins in guided thought, infused emotions, and engendered will. All the spectacular things that Solomon was able to accomplish find their source in the headwaters of the flow of wisdom from God's Spirit.

But we know so much more about what to ask for than even Solomon. Paul said that Christ "is the wisdom of God." Dynamic Christianity is Christ living in us to think His thoughts through us.

All our needs are focused in one great need: wisdom. And our Lord is waiting for us to ask.

November 10

Let Me Go!

1 Kings 11:14-22; Matthew 19:16-21

Then Pharaoh said to him, "But what have you lacked with me, that behold, you are seeking to go to your own country?" And he answered, "Nothing; nevertheless you must surely let me go" (1 Kings 11:22).

HADAD AND THE RICH YOUNG ruler had the same problem: the kingdom of thingdom had trapped them. They both needed a metamorphosis of their materialism. Hadad found the answer. His story is vivid and exciting. He had escaped the slaughter of the males of Edom and had fled to Egypt. There the Pharaoh took a special liking to him and gave him all the material blessings that Egypt could offer. The sumptuousness of Egyptian society was at his fingertips. Yet when he learned that his people were leaderless and that God needed him in Edom, he asked the Pharaoh to release him.

The rich young ruler could not make that choice. He had conditions in his response to the Master. When Jesus discerned that the bind of materialism was upon him, He told him to go sell all he had. He could not do that, and so turned away. Jesus did not run after him to change the terms!

The implications of this are for all of us, whether rich or in need. There may be something, someone, some memory, or some uncommitted plan which Jesus would expose and demand that we surrender to Him. He loves us so much that He gives us the freedom to say "No" to Him.

Yet, like Hadad, when we consider the joy of life in Christ now and eternity with Him forever, we say, "Oh world! Only let me go!"

He is no fool who gives what he cannot keep to gain what he cannot lose.

—Jim Elliot

November 11

We Are Never Finished

1 Kings 18:1–19:3

Now Ahab told Jezebel all that Elijah had done, and how he had killed all the prophets with the sword. Then Jezebel sent a messenger to Elijah, saying, "So may the gods do to me and even more, if I do not make your life as the life of one of them by tomorrow about this time" (1 Kings 19:1-2).

THE BATTLE WITH THE PRIESTS of Baal on Mount Carmel left Elijah depleted. He had fought for the Lord and won. That should have settled the question of who was God in Israel once and for all. But what Elijah thought was the final battle with evil, Jezebel regarded as a skirmish. Elijah had only touched the peak of the iceberg of evil in the land. Jezebel was more dangerous than ever after the defeat of her priests, and Elijah was never more vulnerable to discouragement than after his spectacular victory. The emotional high of his triumphs clouded his perception of his emotional, physical, and spiritual exhaustion.

Jezebel's vitriolic threat undid him: "So may the gods do to me and more so if I do not make your life as the life of one of them by this time tomorrow." And Elijah was afraid.

We've all had times like that. We battle life's problems and win, work hard for the Lord and know superhuman effectiveness, and then suddenly a small threat or mishap throws us into a tailspin. The difficulty is that in times of pressure or challenge we forget that we are human and that immense energy has been invested. We say with Elijah, "It is enough!" or "I can't take any more. I thought I had finished the battle, and it's only begun!"

That's when we need the Lord's perspective and power. How He dealt with Elijah's discouragement is exactly what He offers us. We will consider that tomorrow.

The Lord will give us strength for each new battle.

November 12

Fire Out of the Ashes

1 Kings 18:1–19:21

It is enough; now, O LORD, take my life, for I am not better than my fathers (1 Kings 19:4).

NOTE CAREFULLY HOW THE LORD healed Elijah's depression. He gave him rest and sleep. The prophet had to be rebuilt physically. Then the Lord fed him with nourishing food. When he was rested and refortified, the Lord asked the shocking question which broke the bind: "What are you doing here, Elijah?" He wanted Elijah to get in touch with what was happening to him. Then the Lord sent outward signs of His power: wind, earthquake, and fire.

But the assurance of the Lord's presence came from within in a still, small voice. Elijah was finally quiet, rested, and ready to hear. His status with the Lord was not dependent on his spectacular feats of victory, but on the Lord's love and acceptance. The same fire which had won the victory on Mount Carmel now burned in his heart. Then He sent Elijah back to work, not on his own strength, but with the Lord's. He gave the prophet a new image of himself, a new task, and a new power. Discouragement was turned to new courage. The Lord will do the same for each of us when we take ourselves and our failures too seriously and forget to take the Lord seriously enough.

The fire of the Lord is not just for the battles of Mount Carmel, but for our burned-out hearts.

November 13

Where Is Your Nineveh?

Jonah 1:1–4:11

And should I not have compassion on Nineveh? (Jonah 4:11).

TO KNOW JONAH IS to love him. And the reason we love him is because he is so much like us in our response to God's guidance. He is the reluctant evangelist of the Old Testament. Jonah was astonished by the call from God to go to the Ninevites to proclaim the sovereignty and power of the Lord as the God of the world. Jonah lived in Gath-hepher in the Zebulun territory which is now Galilee. The Ninevites were archenemies of the Hebrews, and Nineveh was symbolic of everything they had been taught to abhor and hate. And yet the Lord told Jonah to go to these people with a message of judgment and forgiveness. He resisted the Lord at every turn. The unfolding story will have great meaning for us if we substitute the Ninevites with people we find it difficult to love because they contradict everything we believe right and true. But we belong to the Lord who called us to love our enemies.

Jonah ran away from his calling. He went to Joppa and took a ship in the opposite direction. Tarshish could not have been further away from Nineveh. Jonah heard the call and got moving, but went in the wrong direction! He didn't say "No!" to the Lord—he just didn't go where the Lord told him. And yet the Lord intervened to get him back to where He wanted him. In Nineveh the people were very responsive to the petulant prophet. From the king down, the people repented.

Jonah ran from God and got into trouble; he ran with God and had great success; and finally he ran into the loving nature of God. The message of the Book of Jonah is that we can keep our faith only when we give it away—even to people we don't like but who are infinitely loved by our Lord.

It is better to be in Nineveh with the Lord than in Tarshish without Him!

November 14

His Love Knows No Limits

Hosea 1:1–14:9

Then the LORD said to me, "Go again, love a woman who...is an adulteress, even as the LORD loves the sons of Israel, though they turn to other gods" (Hosea 3:1)

THE HEART OF GOD IS filled with limitless love. Hosea discovered that out of an excruciating personal experience in his marriage. His heartbreak put him in touch with the things that break the heart of God. Hosea's wife, Gomer, became unfaithful in the most abhorrent way. She not only became a harlot, but participated in the sacramental fornication of the orgies of Baal and Ashtaroth worship. And yet, out of the experience, Hosea could feel the heart of God for His people who had been faithless in blending their worship of Him with other gods. The prophet saw that what Gomer had done to him, the people of Israel had done to the Lord. Hosea could not give her up even when she descended into sensual slavery as a participant in the fertility orgies of Baal worship.

And then he discovered something far greater than his pain: he encountered the grace of God. As He loved His rebellious people in spite of their sin and willful rebellion, so too Hosea must love Gomer. She must be extricated from her slavery and reestablished as his wife. He must love her as if she had not sinned! Hosea's love could not let Gomer go. He redeemed her from the Baal slavery for 15 silverlings and a homer-and-a-half of barley. But the price was nothing in comparison to the cost of forgiveness and restitution in his heart.

In this poignant life story we are ushered into the cross-shaped love of the heart of God. Eventually, long after Hosea's discovery, God would pay the price of ransoming His people. Calvary was the place. His own Son was the cost. And now, in spite of anything we do or say, His love is offered to you and me.

His love hath no limits, His grace hath no measure,
His power no boundary known unto men.
For out of His infinite riches in Jesus
He giveth, and giveth, and giveth again.
—Annie Johnson Flint

November 15

A Gifted Life

1 Corinthians 12:1-31

Now there are diversities of gifts, but the same Spirit (1 Corinthians 12:4).

IN 1 CORINTHIANS 12, PAUL tells the Christians at Corinth that the qualities of life for which they long most are not humanly produced but divinely imputed. He lists the gifts of the Spirit as wisdom, knowledge, faith, power to heal, power to work miracles, prophecy, discernment, speaking in tongues, and interpreting tongues. These were sought-after qualities in the church. Paul simply says that these gifts are the operation of the Holy Spirit, who distributes them to people in His church in order that the ministry may be done by all the people.

The greatest gift of all seems to be missing. This is held for chapter 13. Here Paul clarifies what is meant by love. Most important of all is the fact that it is a gift. We can receive it and be a communicator of it, but we cannot produce it. We cannot love in a giving, forgiving, free, unmotivated, unchanging, uncalculating way until the gift is given to us. All our efforts to love apart from God's power will be self-centered and selective. It will be reciprocal, a love with demands, always concerned for our rights.

The Spirit is love. When He lives in us, we are able to love because He loves through us. Have you received the Holy Spirit? This week we will consider the nature of the love-gift of the Spirit. Make a list of the relationships and responsibilities in which you desperately need this quality of love. Ask for the gift. The Lord will be faithful!

The need before us calls forth the gift God puts within us. I will live a gifted life.

November 16

The Gift of Love

1 Corinthians 13:1-3

Though I speak with the tongues of men and of angels, but have not love, I have become as sounding brass or a clanging cymbal (1 Corinthians 13:1).

PAUL TAKES ALL THE HONORED human qualities and exposes them one by one as inadequate unless we have received the gift of love. He sets them up and makes them march before our mind's eye as a cadre of devaluated causes. Make no mistake about it, Paul has disinherited some of our most cherished values and tells us that they are nothing if the gift of love is lacking.

Eloquence, humanly motivated or divinely inspired, is nothing without love. What priority we put on clarity and beauty of speech! But does it communicate love? Unless it does, it is no more than the noise of blaring brass or crashing cymbal, like an orchestra which only tunes up but can never play the melody of the score.

Prophecy was a cherished gift. To tell the truth about contemporary situations and to foretell God's truth about the future were considered great. Paul says that insight into life and discernment of the future mean absolutely nothing if we have not the gift of love.

Absolute faith cannot compare with love. The power to do miraculous things is nothing if we lack the power to love another person as God loves us. Even if this faith becomes sacrificial, and gives itself in radical acts of obedience, but does not communicate the imputed gift of love, the Christian has lost his purpose.

Paul has exposed all the things for which we live. They are empty and meaningless without the power of love.

We are nothing and we have nothing if we are not able to love.

November 17

The Gift of Gratitude

1 Corinthians 13:4; Ecclesiastes 4:4; 1 Timothy 6:1-21

Love does not envy; love does not parade itself, is not puffed up (1 Corinthians 13:4).

JEALOUSY AND ITS BEDFELLOW, boastfulness, are manifestations of separation from God. If we have either one, it is a danger signal that we have not been adequately filled with the Holy Spirit of love.

Jealousy grows out of the distance between what we are and what others have become, between what we have and others have, between our inadequacies and others' achievements. It breaks down relationships, destroys families, splits churches, and hinders the growth of the kingdom. What jealousy cannot have, it belittles with boasting. A snob is a person who has an exaggerated respect for social position and wealth because something else is lacking. A boaster is one who is unsure of his status before God and must overextend his self-advertisement.

When we receive God's love for us, we have a profound experience of self-acceptance and appreciation. We no longer need to compare jealously or blow our own horn boastfully. We accept ourselves as accepted and loved by God. Our concern is to use what gifts we have, not in competitive comparison, but in thankful enthusiasm. Jealousy and boasting melt before the truth of God's generosity. We become able to praise God for our own and others' gifts. Dante's Virgil was right: "Envy bloweth up men's sighs. No fear of that might touch ye if love of higher sphere exalted your desires."

The love of the higher sphere has been given us in the gift of love through the Holy Spirit. Have you received Him?

Love is not jealous or boastful.

November 18

Patient Love

1 Corinthians 13:4

Love suffers long (1 Corinthians 13:4).

HOW DO WE KNOW THAT we have received the Holy Spirit of love? How can you be sure? Paul gives us several tests. Today we consider that love is patient. If we have received the Holy Spirit, there will be a new capacity for patient endurance with other people. J.B. Phillips translates, "Love looks for a way to be constructive."

Love is patient because God is patient. An essential quality of His nature is given to our character. If we substitute the name of Christ for each time the word "love" is used in this passage, we get close to its meaning. In Christ, God's patience with man is exposed. He is not limited by man's standards of time and emergency. Above time He sees the eternal, big picture. Love will always issue in a patience with people's slowness to learn, respond, or grow. Patience can be real only if we see things from God's point of view and live on His timing. We live only for the fulfillment of His purposes in people and programs. If He can wait, why can't we?

This patience issues in kindness. This is an active expression of love. The self-restraint of patience prepares for the self-expression of kindness. Involvement with people in their needs and frustrations is an expression of kindness. It is love getting its hands dirty. Because we are freed by God's patience, we can love without plans and demands that people become something for our satisfaction. We are to help relate them to God and seek His purpose for them. A patient Christian is also kind to himself and his own failures. When he is, he inadvertently finds that he is much more understanding of others.

Love is patient and kind.

November 19

Love with Sensitivity

1 Corinthians 13:5; Luke 18:9-17

Love does not behave rudely (1 Corinthians 13:5).

MODERN TRANSLATORS OF the words "Love is not arrogant or rude" suggest that this means "Love does not have inflated ideas of its own importance" and therefore "has good manners." Our attitude toward ourselves radically affects our attitude toward others.

What's really important? What makes a person important? Who are God's VIPs? The greatest danger is that we will strive to become important for the wrong purpose. We all love recognition and the rewards of position and power. What goes wrong is that importance becomes a detriment instead of a gift.

No one can determine himself important. This is for others to do. We are to do our work as well as we can and leave the results to God. Self-appointed importance is the root of arrogance. At the heart of it is the desire to "play God" over others and our realm of life. In subtle ways we say with Napoleon, "I am not like other men. The laws of mortality do not apply to me."

The result of this is lack of consideration and rudeness with others. We run roughshod over others and their rights because we believe we are in control. Love liberates us from arrogance because it heals our need to be important. It gives us new energies to care infinitely for people and to work diligently. The outcome is that without seeking it, God uses us in His strategy of the kingdom. A person who has been made important no longer has to convince other people of his importance. He no longer has to push other people around to be sure they know that he is important. They will know by our life and the power of our love!

Love is sensitive to the needs of others.

November 20

Christian Maturity

1 Corinthians 13:6-7

Bears all things, believes all things, hopes all things, endures all things (1 Corinthians 13:7).

AN AUTHENTIC MARK OF a mature Christian is a graciousness which is free and flexible. J.B. Phillips translates our Scripture as suggesting that love is not touchy or quick to accuse or make judgments. When our own ideas or rights are so crucial to us that we cannot listen and adjust to others, we are not living by the power of God's love. Yet how many of us are like a powder keg, ready to explode when things don't go our way. We are edgy and quick to be offended.

A man in whom Jesus Christ's love has penetrated is slow to judge and accuse. He waits with caution and concern. Knowing how fallible and vacillating he is himself, he can understand the weakness and frailty of others. There is a loving acceptance about him. Judgments are irrelevant because even after our haughty judgment is made, we still must love and forgive. There is nothing we can learn about each other which gives us a right to exclude or reject. The person we condemn still needs our love. We cannot escape the responsibility.

Our insight into each other is the fuel for the machinery of deeper involvement and loving care. Yet how easy it is to keep mental accounts of the failures and faults of others and hold them over them by reserved relationships. Only when people meet our standards do we give ourselves. Love is not like that. God's Spirit of love enables us to give of ourselves without judgment or calculated standards.

Love is not touchy and does not gloat over the weakness of others.

November 21

Love Does Not Give Up

1 Corinthians 13:8-13

Love never fails. But whether there are prophecies, they will fail; whether there are tongues, they will cease; whether there is knowledge, it will vanish away (1 Corinthians 13:8).

THE INDEFATIGABLE QUALITY of God's love is amazing. Wave upon wave, in spite of our resistance or indifference, God loves. His love is not dependent upon our response or acknowledgment. He loves us in spite of everything. And that's the kind of love He can give us through His own indwelling spirit! Everything we think is important will pass away; love alone persists.

That love never ends is the theme of the whole New Testament. God has come in Jesus in spite of man's sin and because of it. With mature forgiveness, He offers Himself and meets man "eyeball to eyeball." Nothing that men can do stops His love. Even the final rejection of the cross becomes the ultimate triumph of God. He came back and picked up with man where they had left off at Calvary. He could not be dismissed or diminished. The love which had guided His people, sent the prophets, dwelt in Jesus, and brought Him from the dead was the same love which returned in the resurrected Lord. And He is loving still, utterly available to those who will believe and receive.

What is it that makes you say, "That's enough! I've gone far enough, suffered enough, given enough! That's all I can take!" Where is your breaking point? With people and with situations? We want to be right, and nothing debilitates love more than being right. Our distorted sense of justice justifies our terminated love. But God has allowed His love to outdistance His justice.

As God vindicated Jesus through the resurrection and spoke a final word of love, He will vindicate us and give us power to love even after all else seems lost. Love is the final word.

Love never ends.

November 22

When the Bind Is Broken

Romans 6:20-22

But now having been set free from sin, and having become servants to God, you have your fruit to holiness, and the end, everlasting life (Romans 6:22).

THEY HAD COME TO AN impasse. Their marriage was in deep trouble. Each had dearly delineated what the other would have to do to make things right to fulfill the other's need. There was now no question of what would be the cost to save their marriage. Yet neither could begin until the other proved that he or she would also begin. The multiplied rejection of the years immobilized both of them. They were stuck on dead center, immovable because of pride and the need to be sure the other would follow through.

Sound familiar? Of course it does, because it describes an experience which most of us have had in marriage, in the family, or with some other person. We desire things to be different, and we even know what will make them different, but we are stuck. We have lived under reciprocal love, give-and-take barter, so long that to give and forgive initiatively is almost impossible. We need to be able to say: "Resolved first: I will give myself in costly love and do the thing I know will communicate love in the language which will be understood. Resolved second: I will, even if the other person never does."

That's the essence of God's love, the Incarnation, the cross, and the way God invades our lives today. What if He waited to have us meet His standard, and do what He required? We would be exactly where most of us have relegated the people in our lives: immobilized, unable to change.

God has broken the bind in Christ. He loves whether we return love or not. What does that mean? Will you go first, today? For Christ's sake?

To love means to will someone's ultimate good and to put yourself on the line to make it possible.

November 23

Take No One for Granted

Matthew 25:31-46

Then He will answer them, saying, "Assuredly, I say to you, inasmuch as you did not do it to one of the least of these, you did not do it to Me" (Matthew 25:45).

TODAY'S SCRIPTURE BECOMES particularly challenging when we consider that Christ will meet us today in someone who is "the least of these." Christ has promised, "I will be with you always." We often think of this in terms of His coming to visit us at the point of our need to give *us* comfort and strength. That is often true. But don't miss the startling thing He has said to us today in this disturbing passage. Where will we find Him? Often in the most unlikely, "the least." Who is that? A person in need.

How do we describe a response to Christ? We use words like commitment, surrender, and dedication. Then are we not to respond to Him in the "least of these" in the same way? We are to be as committed to help, as surrendered to serve, and as dedicated to follow as if Christ appeared Himself.

We all have people in our lives who are the "least." They are the emotionally, spiritually, physically needy people in our families, among our friends, in our places of work, as well as in the more obviously indigent pockets of poverty in our communities. Be careful of the either/or. We can miss the needy in the community by preoccupation with our immediate circle; but we can also miss the needs closest to us by over-involvement in the more obvious needs in the community.

The danger is if we miss one or the other by lack of balance. The "least" often changes for us. It may be a spouse, a child, or a close friend; at another time it may be someone who is segregated or debilitated socially; or again, it may be someone who is lonely or hung up by life. How shall we know who it is for each of us? Ask Christ who the particular "least" is for you. The wonder of prayer is that He will show us.

We are to be as committed to serve the "least" as we are to serve Christ Himself.

November 24

Good Comfort

Philippians 2:19-24; 1 Thessalonians 3:1-13

For I have no one likeminded, who will sincerely care for your state (Philippians 2:20).

HAVE YOU EVER NOTICED HOW we subtly shift the values of the world around us into what we suppose is important to God? We baptize position, power, and prestige with spiritualizing and rationalization and are sure that God wills for us what we want to achieve. Yet the frenzied scramble for these very things often clogs our effectiveness for Him.

What Paul had to say about Timothy becomes a personal challenge to us."He really cares about you. Everyone else is concerned only about his own affairs, not about the cause of Jesus Christ." Timothy had been to Philippi with Paul on his first visit and had gone ahead for a second visit. Now he was to be sent back again to give comfort. Timothy means "good comfort," and he had lived out his name. He was the only one left with Paul who was free enough of concern about his own affairs to give himself to the cause of Christ, spelled out in the Philippians' needs. Others were too busy, but Timothy knew that there was enough time in any day to do the things God wanted him to do. Note the same emphasis about Timothy's visit to Thessalonica and Paul's love for his friends.

Most of us are overly concerned about our own affairs. Our time fills up with a daily round of demands and responsibilities. How do we know what's important? For Timothy it was the cause of Christ. Is what we are doing advancing the cause of Christ, or have we asked Christ to bless our causes? There were some great men around Paul at this time—Mark, Luke, Silas—surely they were busy for Christ. Yes, but perhaps too busy to hear the cry of human need. Timothy,"good comfort," had time and went to comfort people who needed him.

Who needs you to be a Timothy in his or her life today?

November 25

A Friend Who Won't Go Away

Ruth 1:1–4:22

And now, my daughter, do not fear. I will do for you whatever you ask, for all my people in the city know that you are a woman of excellence (Ruth 3:11).

THE LITTLE BOOK OF RUTH communicates a great truth. Ruth was a Moabitess. She married one of the sons of Naomi, a Hebrew who sojourned in Moab with her husband, Elimelech. When both her husband and father-in-law died, Ruth was indefatigably loyal to Naomi. She journeyed with her to Bethlehem of Judea. Even when Naomi gave Ruth freedom to leave her, she responded with the now-famous and oft-quoted words of fidelity, "Where you go I will go, and where you lodge I will lodge. Your people shall be my people, and your God my God. Where you die I will die, and there I will be buried. Thus may the LORD do to me, and worse, if anything but death parts you and me" (Ruth 1:16-17).

The author of the Book of Ruth stresses the commitment of Ruth to the Lord. Though she is a convert to the Hebrew faith, she expresses the faithfulness he longs for his readers to have to their God and to one another. Ruth's integrity and consistency of friendship to Naomi is rewarded by her courtship and marriage to Boaz. This is one of the most tender love stories of the Bible. It boldly contradicts the exclusivism which denigrated association with non-Hebrews and shows how a person can be converted from pagan gods to the Lord God.

Ruth calls us to question our constancy in allegiance to God and those He has given us to be our friends. A commitment to friendship with the Lord spells commitment to be a true friend to others. Are we dependable? Do people know that we love them with an unchanging faithfulness?

Christ is a Friend who will not go away. Once we are sure of that, we can be that kind of friend to others.

November 26

Happy Thanksliving!

Psalm 18:1-50

Thou hast also given me the shield of Thy salvation, and Thy right hand upholds me, and Thy gentleness makes me great (Psalm 18:35).

A LITTLE BOY OF A Vietnamese refugee family was having a difficult time learning English. He had a particular problem with "g's" and "l's." On Thanksgiving Day he attended church services with his family. After the service he tried hard to join in the Thanksgiving greeting. He shook my hand and said, "Happy Thanksliving!" Not a bad description of real thanksgiving. When we are truly thankful, it radically affects our living—our relationships, attitudes, moods, actions, and reaction.

In today's Scripture David acknowledges that the gentleness of the Lord had made him great. The original Hebrew word translated here as "gentleness" is variously rendered in other versions as help, goodness, and humility. The word actually means "condescension." That sparks profound thought. God has condescended to create us, to offer us a relationship with Him, and to care for us so graciously. David had discovered a liberating truth: all that he was, had, and did was because God condescended to bless him. No wonder this psalm ends with a crescendo of thanksgiving!

God's grace, plus our gratitude, equals greatness. When we give God the glory, greatness grows in our character. We become affirmers of others. When is the last time you told the people in your life that you are thankful for them?

I will give thanks for what I have received and be prepared for all that the Lord will give this day.

November 27

Before We Can Love Others

Mark 12:28-34

"You shall love the LORD your God with all your heart, with all your soul, with all your mind, and with all your strength." This is the first commandment. And the second, like it, is this: "You shall love your neighbor as yourself." There is no other commandment greater than these (Mark 12:30-31).

JESUS' SECOND GREAT commandment, to love our neighbors as ourselves, is not easy to fulfill. Why is it so difficult to love people without any demands, standards, and images of what we want them to be? The reason is given in the commandment itself: we are to love others as ourselves. But that's the difficulty. Often we do not love ourselves.

Pagan Friedrich Nietzsche came uncomfortably close to the truth: "Your neighbor love is your bad love for yourselves. Ye feel unto your neighbor from yourselves, and fain would make a virtue thereof! But I fathom your 'unselfishness.' You cannot stand yourselves and you do not love yourselves sufficiently."

I fear he's right. We lack self-acceptance and healthy self-love. The mark of Christian maturity is when a person can say, "All right, this is who I am; these are my talents; these are my liabilities, my quirks and my gifts." Each of us is uniquely gifted by God, and each of us has talents to be used for His glory.

A little girl received a new dress. She danced joyously about the room singing, "I'm glad I am me!" What a simple, untarnished, unblemished, and healthy self-appreciation! How many of us could say this? How many of us are glad we are who we are and where we are? Here's a sample prayer for Christ-centered self-esteem: Lord God, give me the healthy self-appreciation to say, "I am glad I'm me!" Help me to see all You have given me and how You have blessed and guided me through the years. And then, with real freedom, help me to enjoy the life You have given me. Amen.

Love for others flows from healthy self-love rooted in God's love.

November 28

The Other Half of Grace

Amos 7:1-9

This He showed me, and behold, the Lord was standing by a vertical wall, with a plumb line in His hand. And the LORD said to me, "What do you see, Amos?" And I said, "A plumb line." Then the Lord said, "Behold, I am about to put a plumb line in the midst of my people Israel" (Amos 7:7-8).

AMOS WAS A PROPHET OF righteousness and justice. In the midst of religious apostasy and neglect of human suffering, his theme was, "Let justice roll like waters, and righteousness like an overflowing stream." The Lord told him that righteousness and justice were His plumb line which measured and exposed the crooked structures of religious institutionalism. The issue was that belief in God had to be expressed in personal righteousness and social justice. Amos' cutting message slices through any religion which does not result in discovering and doing the Lord's will in our relationships and responsibilities.

The Lord's plumb line is lowered on each of us and our churches. Our bland toleration of anything which contradicts God's love is exposed. Judgment is a part of grace. The Lord does not pat us on the head with a solicitous, "Now, now—whatever you do is all right." He is profoundly concerned about our total life. There is no division of the sacred and the secular, the inner life and outward expression.

But God is no cranky, negative judge who is against us. He loves us so much that He does not want us to miss the abundant life and be co-adventurers with Him in bringing His peace and power in our homes, where we work, in our churches, and in our society. When the plumb line is lowered we can see what is out of line. Then we can ask Him to help us put the crooked straight. Judgment is an expression of grace. What does the plumb line tell you is wrong that He is ready to help you make right? List the people and situations.

Judgment leads to grace, and grace enables us to do something about what's wrong.

November 29

"You Are Mine"

Isaiah 5:1-7; Mark 12:1-9

Therefore what will the owner of the vineyard do? He will come and destroy the vinedressers, and give the vineyard to others (Mark 12:9).

ADVENT IS THE PERIOD OF weeks set aside before Christmas to prepare our minds and hearts for the awesome truth of the Incarnation. It is the time we prayerfully meditate on God's sovereign power over creation in spite of man's evil. Jesus' final parable in Mark's Gospel proclaims this truth with striking clarity. The parable of the vineyard tells us that God will have the final word, and that word is "love."

There is the picture of rejected trust. The Lord had entrusted Israel with the gift of life. They had rejected the overtures of God's loving judgment in prophet and priest. As we read the parable, Amos, Jeremiah, and Isaiah march before our mind's eye. The history of God's people is red with the blood of rejected prophets. But God was not done in by man's rejection. He sent His own son. In allegorical language Jesus clearly predicts His own suffering and death. Do you sense the persistence of God in the parable? He will not take "No" for an answer.

The parable is a word of truth and hope for us today. We now are the stewards of the vineyard. We are responsible to God for what we do with the gift of life. We belong to Him. He will not let us go. Think of the many ways we reject His claim upon us. We take things into our own hands, we run others' lives, we misuse our gifts. But still He comes. In experiences, in other people, in the quiet of our own soul, we hear Him say, "You're mine!"

God's final word is "love."

November 30

20/20 Hindsight

Mark 12:10-12

And you have not read this Scripture: "The stone which the builders rejected has become the chief cornerstone" (Mark 12:10).

WHAT MEN REJECTED, GOD elevated. Just to be sure that the leaders of Israel did not miss the point, Jesus quoted a familiar messianic text to clearly identify the Son of the parable as the Messiah and Himself as that long-anticipated Messiah. The rejected Jesus would be elevated to the keystone of the arch of God's revelation.

This was the confidence with which Jesus faced His death—that God would use the cross as the focal point of history. He trusted His Father to bring good out of evil.

Most of us have 20/20 hindsight. We can see how God has worked in the past, but it is difficult to see how He can use for any good the raw material of present crisis, of dreaded, future uncertainty. Yet Christians are given the vision which can sing, "Oh God, our help in ages past, our hope for years to come."

Do you have this kind of confidence? Can you say, "Whatever comes, God will bring final victory"? Any relationship with God which does not give confidence of forgiveness of the past, power for the present, and hope for the future is inadequate. Worry about what is to come robs us of joy in the present. Jesus Christ, who was, is now...will be forever. Give Him your concerns about the future, and God will give you 20/20 foresight of trust.

His purposes will ripen fast,
Unfolding every hour;
The bud may have a bitter taste,
But sweet will be the flower.
...God is His own Interpreter,
And He will make it plain.

—William Cowper

December 1

A Realistic Reason for Hope

Lamentations 3:1-66

This I recall to mind; therefore I have hope: the Lord's lovingkindnesses indeed never cease (Lamentations 3:21-22).

REALISM AND HOPE. They are difficult to keep together at times. For some people, realism about life and people leads to hopelessness. For others, hopefulness is almost totally unrealistic.

Jeremiah is both honestly realistic and authentically hopeful. His appraisal of conditions in Jerusalem under the rule of the Babylonians was filled with anguish. The ruin of the city and the Temple as well as the deportation of the best citizens to Babylonia broke the prophet's heart. Most of all, the people failed to connect what had happened and the judgment of God on their apostasy. Chapters 1, 2, and 3 through verse 20 express hopelessness. "So say I, 'My strength has perished, and so has my hope from the LORD'" (3:18).

Then note in verse 21 a shift in mood and spirit. Jeremiah not only remembers all the tragedy but now remembers the Lord's lovingkindness. His spirits begin to rise and then soar in exuberant joy. The Lord is not finished with the prophet or with His beloved people. But Jeremiah bases his hope on the Lord, not on any inherent goodness in people. "'The LORD is my portion,' says my soul; 'therefore I have hope in Him'" (verse 24). Jeremiah recaptures a basic thought which infuses his emotions with excitement. It is that God is good to those who wait for Him, seek Him, and completely trust in Him. When we do that, we will be able realistically to see things as they are but also hope for what God will do.

Realism gives us an honest appraisal of what we need to surrender to God and wait hopeful for.

December 2

Stand Up, Stand Tall, Stand Ready!

Ezekiel 2:1–3:27

Son of man, stand on your feet that I may speak with you! (Ezekiel 2:1).

THERE ARE THREE THINGS the Lord did for Ezekiel which He wants to do for us today. He got him on his feet, filled him with His Spirit, and fed him with His Word.

Ezekiel was called to be a prophet at a time of a great need in Israel. He was among the exiles carried off in the Babylonian exile. There he became God's spokesman and watchman to the exiles. The Lord first told Ezekiel to stand on his feet so that He could speak with him. The image is vivid. The Lord wanted Ezekiel at full attention, ready to hear what the Lord had to say. That's what He does for us right now. He gets us on our feet, ready to listen and then move on in obedience. God abhors fearful inactivity as nature abhors a vacuum. When we settle comfortably on the plateau of the status quo, He says, "Stand up! I'm going to get you moving again!"

But note the second gift. The Lord entered into Ezekiel and enabled His own command. The greatest need in Israel was for God's people to receive and live by the power of the Lord's Spirit. What He wanted to do *through* the prophet, He first did *in* him. The Lord provides for what He guides. Once He gets us on our feet, He gives us power to get moving.

The third command may seem strange to us. "Eat the scroll, and go speak to the house of Israel." The scroll was the sacred Scripture. The Word of the Lord had to be thoroughly digested so that Ezekiel could speak with the authority of God's Word. After we are on our feet and receive God's Spirit, we need to feed on His word. The Bible needs to be read and studied, and crucial verses memorized. In times of need and challenge, they will be a part of us. We will have comfort in trial as well as authority in our witness to others.

Get on your feet, get power, get food, get going!

December 3

Before You Give Up

Ezekiel 37:1-28

"Son of man, can these bones live?" And I answered, "O Lord GOD, Thou knowest" (Ezekiel 37:3).

THERE ARE TIMES WHEN we are tempted to give up—on some person, group, situation, ourselves. "It's no use," we say; "I've tried, done my best, and nothing has changed!" Ever feel that way?

This was the mood of God's people in the Babylonian exile. But God gave them a prophet who could see the worst and the best. Ezekiel revealed the judgment of God upon the people for what they had been, but he also communicated hope for the future. Ezekiel means "God strengthens." While the people were in exile, the tragic news of the fall of Jerusalem (586 B.C.) reached them. "What hope is there now?" they asked.

Ezekiel had a vision of the dry bones in the Valley Jezreel, symbolic of the dried-up vision and hope of the people. The prophet forces the people to realize that they had brought their plight on themselves by turning from the glory and holiness of God. "Our bones are dried up, and our hope is lost; we are clean cut off." When the true cause of the condition is acknowledged, the promise is given. The bones were going to come together and live!

The message of this for us has two parts. Before we give up, we need to confess what brought us to the time of discouragement. Instead of asking, "Why did this happen to me?" we must ask, "What did I do to cause this to happen to me?" Then we are ready for the most crucial question: "What is the Lord saying to me in what has happened to me?" That leads to a surrender of what is tempting us to give up. In response, the Lord gives us a new heart. This is what happens when Christ takes up residence within us. We are filled with His heart. And He never gives up!

Today I will own the bones and ask for a new heart. He has not given up on me or others. Nor will I!

December 4

Twice Born

John 3:1-8

That which is born of the flesh is flesh, and that which is born of the Spirit is spirit. Do not marvel that I said to you, "You must be born again" (John 3:6-7).

JESUS PUT HIS FINGER ON Nicodemus' deepest need. He was deeply impressed by His mighty works, but Jesus swept aside his compliments and got down to the Pharisee's real problem. He needed to be born again, to start all over, by a quickening to a new life by the Spirit of God.

Note that Jesus told the scholar that he must be born again to see the kingdom of God. This suggests that the real question he had on his mind was about when the kingdom would be restored to Israel, when Israel would be free again. Jesus shifted from the material realm to the spiritual. Only by rebirth could Nicodemus experience the kingdom—God's reign and rule in his heart. In response to the "How can this be?" Jesus told the spiritually impoverished leader who He really was and what he must do. Belief in Christ and an unreserved surrender to Him is the only way to be born again.

It happened! What Jesus explained to Nicodemus that night actually took place later. The leading Pharisee became a secret follower, then an open defender of Jesus. He risked status and position to help bury Jesus, and according to historical tradition became a leader in the church after Pentecost. The crucifixion must have had a profound impact on him. But it surely was the experience of the resurrected Lord that brought back the full meaning of what He had told him about being born again.

Put yourself in Nicodemus' skin. Experience what he experienced when the risen Lord fulfilled His own prediction. "Listen for the wind, Nicodemus!"

Without a new birth there is no beginning;
without going after the new birth there was no beginning.

December 5

Born Again to Hope

1 Peter 1:3-4; Romans 6:3-23

Now if we died with Christ, we believe that we shall also live with Him (Romans 6:8).

PAUL PRESSES US ON IN OUR understanding and experience of the new birth. He vividly pictures the before-and-after condition of our lives. Prior to being born again, we are dead in an old nature. The key to the whole passage is in the powerful verse we have selected as our key verse for today. We are born again when we die with Christ and are resurrected to new life in Him.

Throughout his epistles Paul tells us about the new birth as a death-and-resurrection experience. We die to our self, our plan, our purposes, our presuppositions. By the power of God we are raised up to a new life. How is your life radically different because of this experience?

A sure sign of our rebirth is lively hope. That's the triumphant note of Peter about the born-again experience. Our own present resurrection from death of self to a deathless life gives us courage to face life's problems and disappointments with the sure conviction that our Lord will intervene and infuse His power in our times of need. We can face anything with that assurance. Hope provides patience. We are able to take the long view of things. The shortness of time and the length of eternity give us patience with the trifles of life. A born-again person knows he belongs to Christ. His nature is being reproduced in him. Would the people around you say that your rebirth had made you a contagiously hopeful person?

Since we believe that Christ died for all of us, we should also believe that we have died to the old life we used to live. He died for all so that all who live—having received eternal life from Him—might no longer live for themselves...but to spend their lives pleasing Christ, who died and rose again for them.

2 Corinthians 5:14-15 TLB

December 6

New Wine in Old Bags

Mark 2:20-22

No one sews a piece of unshrunk cloth on an old garment; or else the new piece pulls away from the old, and the tear is made worse (Mark 2:21).

JESUS CAME NOT TO PATCH, but to transform; not to correct, but to convert. Those who had spiritual eyes with which to see could have understood that day that He subtly suggested a new and vital way.

Jesus wanted to indicate that He could never be an addendum to an already-complete life, but the answer and basis of a person's life and direction. The idea was that new wine expanded and pushed out the wine bag. The bags were made of the sheep's skin and were flexible for expansion as the wine expanded. Old bags would crack and split open and would not be able to contain the new wine.

Our Lord warned His followers that the new teaching which He proclaimed could not be contained in the old customs and practices. The security of the Jews was in their customs and practices and not in God. The people of God have always faced the problem of caring too much for rite and ritual. When those were threatened, they reacted with hostility and fear.

The message of the new wine in old bags is applicable to us as individuals and to our churches. Jesus Christ must be the basis of our life, not an addition. Most of us want all this world offers and heaven too. We want the security of our background, education, financial position, talent, ability, friends, and future plans. But we want Jesus also. The difficulty is that Jesus Christ is not satisfied with this. Conversion means a break with the old and a fresh start with Christ.

The new wine of Christ's message and His indwelling power is like new wine. It requires a new bag of fresh commitment to Him each day. Old ways, customs, and habits will burst with the pressure of His tumultuous reformation of our lives.

New wine cannot be contained in old bags.

December 7

An Authentic Encounter

Romans 10:5-13

If you confess with your mouth the Lord Jesus and believe in your heart that God has raised Him from the dead, you will be saved (Romans 10:9).

THE TEENAGER HAD BEEN to camp. The challenge of the lordship of Jesus Christ over all of life had been presented. At the close of the camp, an opportunity to let Christ run her life was given in a very simple but direct way. The young woman had given as much as she then knew of herself to as much as she then knew of Jesus Christ and was determined to trust Him to guide her in the midst of the ambiguities and complexities of living as a teenager in today's world.

"Well, what did you do at camp?" was the traditional question almost thoughtlessly asked by the girl's father at the dinner table after she returned home.

"I have decided to let Jesus Christ run my life!" was the direct answer, followed closely by a gentle but powerful question: "Have you ever done that, Daddy?"

The father was angered and challenged. He passed it off, but could not get it off his mind. Had he ever let Christ run his life, really? He had been a church officer, church-school teacher, community leader, and admired executive in his firm, but he had never discovered or experienced Christ's lordship over his life. That would mean praying about decisions, expenditures, investments! It would mean getting His help for relationships, plans, and programs! No, he had never done that. Christ was not very real.

His daughter's newly found joy in Christ forced him to realize that he was a religious man who needed Christ. Some time later he discovered the difference between knowing about Christ and actually knowing Him as personal Savior and Lord.

It is never too late to move from religion to life!

December 8

Through It All

Daniel 3:1-30

If it be so, our God whom we serve is able to deliver us from the furnace of blazing fire; and He will deliver us out of your hand, O king. But even if He does not, let it be known to you, O king, that we are not going to serve your gods or worship the golden image that you have set up (Daniel 3:17-18).

FOUR WORDS GIVE US FAITH for the fires of life: "If He does not." The faith of Shadrach, Meshach, and Abednego was firmly rooted in God's sovereignty over all creation and His righteous care for His people in Babylonia. But if He did not choose to extricate them from the fire, they would not worship the golden calf of Nebuchadnezzar. The story of what happened to Daniel's friends is a source of courage and confidence for us today. We are never left alone in our fires. The Lord is with us when we feel the blasts of difficulty and testing. He is ready to join us in the heat of life if we can say, "He can and will help me in this situation, but even if He chooses not to intervene in the way I want, I will not give up, for I am alive forever. Nothing in this life can separate me from His love."

That kind of surrender of life's pain and problems fastens the belief that we are never alone. The four words that brought the Fourth Man will release His power today. There is a wonderful breakthrough to power and peace whenever we know with assurance that no fire will have to be endured without the Lord and nothing can destroy our relationship with Him. We can have the joy of the Lord if we have an "in spite of everything" quality of faith. Our hope is not based on getting God to do what we want but in wanting Him regardless of how events work out.

Through it all, through it all,
I've learned to trust in God.
—Andraé Crouch

December 9

No Longer Part of the Problem

Psalm 24:1-10

The earth is the Lord's, and all it contains; the world, and those who dwell in it (Psalm 24:1).

WHO IS THERE WHO HAS not at some time felt the icy-cold sword of doubt about the ultimate purpose of the universe cut into his very soul? Each of us has at some time in his life faced situations for which he could find no logical explanation or solution. We have questioned, "What did I do to deserve this?" "Why did this happen to me?" "If there is a God behind this universe, why does He allow things like this to happen?" Often this tangled world makes no sense, and doubts "rap and knock and enter into the soul," as Browning put it. And by far the most devastating is the question of the ultimate purpose of God. In the deep recesses of the soul, "the deep heart's abode," we want to know.

Can we go with Bertrand Russell in saying that "history is only the outcome of accidental collocations of atoms?" Or with David Hume, who said, "Were a stranger to drop suddenly into the world, I would show him as a specimen a hospital filled with disabled people, a prison crowded with malefactors and debtors, a battlefield strewn with carcasses, a fleet floundering in the ocean, a nation languishing under tyranny, famine and pestilence." But is this all we can see?

No, there is much more! David saw something more: "The earth is the Lord's and the fullness thereof, and all they who dwell therein." History is an account of man's inhumanity to man. But God has given us freedom to accept Him or reject Him. What we have done to ourselves and each other breaks His heart of love. In Jesus Christ He came and comes today. The only answer to the riddle of life is in Him. Through His power we can be what we were created to be and live a part of His solution, rather than as part of the world's problem. God is not finished with our world. Those who trust Him can change history.

God has given us freedom to shape the course of history.

December 10

The Final Assurance

Psalm 56:1-13

Thou hast taken account of my wanderings; put my tears in Thy bottle; are they not in Thy book? (Psalm 56:8).

"HOW CAN GOD KNOW and care about me with all the billions of people?" The question carried a sense of uncertainty, a bit of pathetic loneliness in the immensity of the universe. But we've all wondered about that at times...on a crowded street or when reading the population-explosion statistics. We must dare to think magnificently of God. If He could create the universe out of nothing and make mankind, if He could reveal His light and love for us to see and experience in Jesus Christ the Mediator, we can dare to assume that He knows and cares about us individually. But the gospel goes way beyond that! It tells us that God not only knows and cares, but that He has chosen us to be His beloved. That's the one final assurance!

Jesus tells us what He told the disciples: "You have not chosen Me, but I have chosen you." By the mystery of election we are called, appointed, chosen people of the Lord. The undisputed origin of an authentic conversion is in that choice. It is not based on our achievement, adequacy, excellence, or exemplary life. The Lord constantly calls impossible people to do the impossible.

A sure sign of our election is our amazement that He should choose us. If we think we have been chosen as the best of men and women because of our stellar character or impeccable performance, we have missed the divine origin of our election. Paul constantly was astounded that the Lord had elected him. After all that he had done and been, the Lord's call was a source of humbling delight. We know how he felt!

Aim at heaven, and you will get earth thrown in.
Aim at earth, and you will get neither.
—C.S. Lewis

December 11

Old Measurements for a New Life

Zechariah 2:1-13

So I said, "Where are you going?" And he said to me, "To measure Jerusalem to see how wide it is and how long it is." And…the angel…said "Run, speak to that young man, saying, 'Jerusalem will be inhabited without walls…For I,' declares the LORD, 'will be a wall of fire around her, and I will be the glory in her midst' " (Zechariah 2:2-5).

AN ALARMING PICTURE INVADED Zechariah's vision. He saw a young man measuring Jerusalem so that it could be rebuilt according to the old measurements of the Holy City before it was destroyed in 586 B.C. There were two things wrong with that: the old measurements were too small, and no wall could ever be a defense. Only the Lord was a sure defense and His presence the source of lasting glory. The people should have learned that no wall was a sure defense and that there was no lasting glory in buildings built by man.

Zechariah had the rebuilding of Jerusalem in his heart. He was a prophet to the returned exiles who wanted to return the city to its original grandeur. History repeats itself because the only thing we learn from history is that we do not learn from it. The people had not trusted the Lord before. Destruction of the city and exile had resulted. Now they were about to make the same mistake.

It is our problem also. So seldom do we learn from past mistakes. We fail to trust God, we get into trouble, and we miss what the mistake has to teach us. We all have compulsive, repetitive patterns which get us into the same old problems again and again. The Lord wants to get to the reason for that. Becoming a new creation in Christ means that the old can pass away. But we all do what we do because of unmet inner needs. It is that raw nerve deep inside us which the Lord wants to heal.

The future is a friend. The Lord can help me overcome the past and not repeat its mistakes.

December 12

Heresickness

Job 36:1-33

Then Elihu continued and said, "Wait for me a little and I will show you that there is yet more to be said in God's behalf" (Job 36:1-2).

THERE'S A POINTED STORY of a young man who was sent away to boarding school. He was lonely, he found it difficult to make new friends, and he was challenged by his studies. A teacher sensed that he was having a difficult time. "What's the matter, John?" the teacher asked with empathy. "Have you got a bit of homesickness?" The boy thought a moment and then answered, "No Sir, I don't have homesickness; I have heresickness!"

"Heresickness" is a malady we all face at times—more often than we want to admit. The here and now of our present situation can be frustrating and unpleasant. The people and problems at this stage of life, the difficulties of the situation in which we must work, the demands of family—all make us wonder what God is trying to teach us at the present time.

For "heresickness" God offers "now-help." He comes to us to help us learn, grow, and mature. Often He sends a person into our lives to help us ask the right questions and deal with reality. When there is no place to go, the Lord intervenes to help us maximize where we are.

Elihu was that kind of friend to Job. All his other friends intensified the problem of his suffering with very poor theology and lack of empathy. Elihu forced Job to discover God's presence in the present. He enabled him to love God for God and to know that his Redeemer lived.

After we have experienced the incisiveness of an Elihu sent from God, we are ready to go to someone we know is suffering from a bad case of "heresickness." Who is it for you?

Once it was the blessing, now it is the Lord.
Once it was the feeling, now it is His Word.
Once His gifts I wanted, now the Giver own.
Once I sought for healing, now Himself alone.

—A.B. Simpson

December 13

The Boast That Banishes Burdens

Psalm 44:1-26

In God we have boasted all day long, and we will give thanks to Thy name forever (Psalm 44:8).

ONE OF THE GREAT WOMEN of our time was Corrie ten Boom. I noticed that she was able to praise God for the way He used her. Some years ago I asked her how she handled compliments and adulation from people.

"Oh, Lloyd," she responded, "that is no problem. Every time a person praises me for something I've said or done, I just accept it as a flower. Then at the end of the day I put all the flowers together into a lovely bouquet, get on my knees, and say, 'Here, Father, this bouquet belongs to you! The lovely things people have said about me, they were really saying about You. Thank You, Father, for using me.' "

Now there's a way to keep perspective when people give us adulation for what we've done or said! I used to find it difficult to take affirmation. I am so very aware of my need to grow in Christ that I realize that if anyone has been helped by a sermon or a time of counseling, it has been the Lord who has done it. Corrie helped me to enjoy being used, knowing that the power or wisdom has been a gift from the Lord.

I complimented a friend of mine for a message he had given at a conference. "Isn't that wonderful!" he responded. He knew that the Lord had blessed, and he gave Him the credit. He did not say, "Oh, it was nothing," when he knew that it had been a very special time of God's Spirit meeting the needs of people through him.

Today is a day to boast in the Lord. There will be no problem of false pride when we boast in Him and what He's doing. Each time something good happens and you're tempted to take the credit, add a flower to the bouquet to give to God at the end of the day.

All of life is a lovely bouquet to present to the Lord in gratitude.

December 14

With the Help of Our God

Nehemiah 1:1–6:19

So the wall was completed on the twenty-fifth of the month Elul, in fifty-two days. And it came about when all our enemies heard of it, and all the nations surrounding us saw it, they lost their confidence; for they recognized that this work had been accomplished with the help of our God (Nehemiah 6:15-16).

NEHEMIAH RETURNED FROM the exile in Persia in 445 B.C. with determination. He had two goals: to call the people back to faithfulness to the law and to rebuild the wall around Jerusalem. Nehemiah is an example of courageous leadership. He clarified goals, demanded accountability, engendered enthusiasm in people, and got in and worked with them.

But, like any outstanding leader, Nehemiah had his enemies. There were local leaders who did not want the returning exiles to rise to strength and industrious patriotism. The rebuilding of the wall was a sign of Nehemiah's growing power. Therefore, work on the wall had to be done under hazardous threats of attack, and the progress was slow. Nehemiah's life was in danger. Friends begged him to come down off the wall and enter the protection of the precincts of the Temple at night for safety. His response was, "Should a man like I flee? And could one such as I go into the Temple to save his life? I will not go in."

Courage is as contagious as fear. Nehemiah had charisma rooted in a firm trust in God's faithfulness. He was sure of His guidance and His strength for the task. The work on the wall was finished with half of the people building and the other half holding spears night and day against the evening attackers. When the work was finished, Nehemiah's enemies were dismayed. He said, "For they recognized that this work had been accomplished with the help of God." God gives us impossible tasks so that we can show others that with Him nothing is impossible

We all have some realm of leadership. We cannot flee from responsibility. The Lord will help us.

December 15

Ready for Christmas

Isaiah 40:1-31

A voice is calling, "Clear the way for the LORD in the wilderness; make smooth in the desert a highway for our God" (Isaiah 40:3).

IT HAPPENED AGAIN. I had promised myself that it would not happen again last year, but it did. I'm a last-minute, day-before-Christmas shopper. The department stores which had stayed open for me and my fellow procrastinators looked like a Sherman tank had been driven through them. The tired clerks looked as picked over and worn out as the merchandise.

In one store, a long line of exhausted people stood waiting at the cash register checkout with arms filled with frantically selected gifts. A woman in front of me had a frazzled, "if I can only hold out until after the holidays" look on her face. The public-address system played a worn-out record of "God Rest You Merry, Gentlemen" that must have been replayed thousands of times since Thanksgiving.

When she reached the man at the register, he asked her that thoughtless, innocuous question we hear repeated ad nauseam during the days before Christmas: "Well, lady, are you ready for Christmas? Her tired reply was, "As ready as I'll ever be!" How would you have responded?

Ready for Christmas! We ask and answer that question without reflecting on its profound meaning. What would it mean to be ready for Christmas? But there's a deeper question: Are you ready to live Christmas all through the year?

A man who had finished all his shopping and preparation said, "Now at last I am free to enjoy Christmas!" But he found that it took more than trimming the tree to get free to enjoy the real meaning of Christmas. How free are you to let it happen to you this Christmas? How do you think Christ would like you to celebrate His birth?

I will prepare a way for the Lord by planning my holiday schedule to be ready to be free to enjoy the real meaning of Christmas.

December 16

Open Before Christmas!

John 1:1-18

He came to His own, and His own did not receive Him (John 1:11).

MANY PEOPLE SPEND THE month of December buying, wrapping, decorating, and preparing for the festivities of the holidays but are not ready for a transforming Christmas, nor free to experience its real impact for all of life.

My greatest concern is that it won't make any difference, that we will go back to the same old life the same people as we were when it all began. It's possible to celebrate Christmas and miss Christmas!

Imagine a time around the Christmas tree in which you opened all your presents except those from one particular person. Feel the hurt of that rejection. Look at it from God's point of view. What do you think He wants to give you? Picture Him waiting for you to open and enjoy His gift.

I can remember when I was a boy how my mounting excitement in the days before Christmas was heightened by any present marked "Do not open until Christmas!" When I thought no one was watching, I would crawl under the Christmas tree, squeeze and shake the carefully wrapped presents, and imagine that what was inside was my heart's desire. Then, on Christmas Eve, I would go to bed to dream with excitement about what I was sure I would find the next morning when I opened my presents.

The gift I want to share with you during the days leading up to Christmas is marked a bit differently. The tag has your name on it. It says, "To be opened in preparation for Christmas and enjoyed all through the year!" The heart of Christmas is the heart. God's heart in Christ offered to you and me. The most tragic thing which could happen is to go through the Christmas season and never open and accept the gifts of love, joy, hope, and peace which flow from His heart to ours!

I plan to have a heart-to-heart Christmas this year!

December 17

The Crèche and the Cross

1 Timothy 1:12-17

This is a faithful saying and worthy of all acceptance, that Christ Jesus came into the world to save sinners, of whom I am chief (1 Timothy 1:15).

CHRISTMAS IS THE EXPERIENCE of unqualified love. We all need that quality of love more than breathing, eating, or sleeping. There's a love-shaped emptiness in all of us. Our deepest need is to be loved, to love ourselves, and to be free to love others. That's rooted in feeling special. The shepherds felt very special on that first Christmas. The good news of Christmas is that you and I are special to God!

The words of the angelic chorus really should be translated "Glory to God in the highest, and on earth peace among men with whom He is pleased." Let that soak into the love-parched place in your heart. In spite of all that we have done or been, God is pleased with us. We are His beloved; we belong to Him; nothing we can do or say will make Him stop loving us.

Christmas is your special time. God has something to say. Listen! Put the personal pronoun in the familiar words, "God so loved me that He gave His only begotten Son, that believing in Him, I should not perish but have everlasting life. For God did not send His Son into the world to condemn me, but that I, through Him, might be saved." Our hearts leap. God is for us and not against us. His love is unconditional. The deepest, most exciting discovery I've ever made is that life really begins when we let God love us!

But we are not only loved just as we are; we're forgiven for all that we've done, said, and been. To let God love you is to let Him forgive you.

Are you willing to believe that love is the strongest thing in the world—stronger than hate, stronger than evil, stronger than death—and that the blessed life which began in Bethlehem two thousand years ago is the image and brightness of the Eternal Love? Then you can keep Christmas.

—Henry van Dyke

December 18

The Gift of Self-Esteem

Romans 8:1-11

There is therefore now no condemnation to those who are in Christ Jesus (Romans 8:1).

CHRIST CAME INTO THE WORLD when we least deserved Him or wanted Him. And He keeps coming. There's nothing we can do to earn His loving forgiveness or make Him stop loving us. From the crèche to the cross, an open tomb to His impelling presence with each of us, we hear His imploring love: "You belong to Me. You are My loved and forgiven person. I came for you, lived for you, died for you, defeated death for you, and am here now for you."

That's God's Christmas gift to us. Don't leave it unwrapped! Open it and enjoy the healing, liberating, motivating power. There is no problem, perplexity, or potential facing you and me which cannot be conquered if we accept the gift. Love plus forgiveness equals freedom!

We will be free to love and forgive ourselves. Christ came so that we can get up when we are down on ourselves. What is it for you? What memory of failure haunts you and makes you negative and hostile to the most important person in your life—the inner you? Be gracious to yourself this Christmas. Give yourself a gift. Forgive yourself.

A new healthy self-esteem flows from that. So few people who celebrate Christmas feel really good about themselves. Is that why we become so busy in the rush of the season? Could it be that we are running away from the person who lives inside us? God loves that person very much. He knows us better than we know ourselves. Christmas is a time to say, "I'm glad I'm me!" Listen to the Apostle John: "See what love the Father has given us, that we should be called children of God...Beloved, we are God's children now" (1 John 3:1-2 RSV). Let that balance the scale of self-condemnation as you allow Christmas to happen to you.

Have you ever thought that in every action of grace in your heart you have the whole omnipotence of God engaged to bless you?

—Andrew Murray

December 19

A Christmas List of What to Forget

Ephesians 4:25-32

And be kind to one another, tender-hearted, forgiving one another, just as God in Christ also has forgiven you (Ephesians 4:32 NASB).

THE LITMUS TEST THAT WE have accepted God's gift of love and forgiveness is that we will be free to be initiative communicators of what we have received. Paul warns against grieving the Holy Spirit. That is to deny the reason God came in Christ: to love us and make us lovers. Billy Graham said, "God has given us two hands—one for receiving and the other for giving." We need to celebrate Christmas with both hands!

Who in your life is suffering from emotional malnutrition because you are holding back approval, acceptance, and affirmation? Whom do you need to forgive? Whose forgiveness do you need to seek? Imagine what Christmas could be now if all the hurts could be expressed and real reconciliation experienced! Many of us are burdened by the inner tension of the "if only's" and the "what might have been's" of life. I am convinced that the frustration which many people feel at Christmas is because of lovely things we do and give which contradict how we really feel. Perhaps we need two kinds of Christmas lists: one list of the gifts we want to give and the other of people whom we need to forgive or from whom we need to seek forgiveness.

Christmas is a time to remember to forget! Our problem is that most of us have a better memory than God has. We remember and nurse the hurts done to us. Then we spend our energies retaliating, withdrawing, and keeping people at arm's length. One of the greatest gifts we could give ourselves at Christmastime is a commitment to remember to forget all through the year. Forgiveness is love in action! Henry Ward Beecher once said, "To say 'I can forgive but I cannot forget' is another way of saying 'I will not forgive.'" Christmas is a time to look into the Father's face and tell Him you have accepted His gift of forgiveness and then to rewrap the gift and give it away.

"To err is human, to forgive divine."

December 20

Tidings of Great Joy

John 15:9-17

These things I have spoken to you that my joy may remain in you and that your joy may be full (John 15:11).

THE RECURRING NOTE OF THE Christmas message is joy. Joy is the outer expression of the inner experience of being loved. Robert Louis Stevenson was right: "To miss the joy is to miss all." I have a friend who has a favorite saying each time he closes a conversation and says goodbye. He takes hold of a person's hand and says, "Don't miss the joy!" A sure sign that we have allowed Christmas to happen to us is an artesian joy which lasts all through the year.

Joy is not gush or ho-ho jolliness. Joy grows in the assurance that God will use everything that happens to or around us for our ultimate good and for His glory. True joy is what Paul calls a fruit of the Spirit—a result of the Lord living in us. We sing the familiar carol's words, "O come to us, be born in us, O Christ Immanuel." Christmas is not only accepting the love of Christ's birth in Bethlehem, but opening our hearts for Him to be born in us today.

It's one thing to believe in Christ and quite another to receive His indwelling presence. The Lord Himself made the promise, "I will make My home in you." "Abide in Me and I in you." Life in Christ is claiming Him as Lord and Savior; life with Christ in us is the source of joy! Jesus said, "I came that you may have life and have it more abundantly." The abundant life is life with Christ abiding in us.

The authentic mark of a Christian is joy. More than circumstantial or dependent on people's attitude or words, joy is constant and consistent in life's changing problems. It is unassailable and vibrant. "Joy to the world, the Lord is come." Don't miss the joy!

Joy is the standard that flies on the battlements of the heart when the King is in residence.
—R. Leonard Small

December 21

The Hope of the World

Lamentations 3:21-26

Therefore I have hope (Lamentations 3:21).

CHRISTMAS IS A FESTIVAL OF hope. And there is nothing our world needs more desperately than authentic hope. We have placed our hope in all the wrong things. The false gods of human progress, inventive genius, the future, armed power, financial security, governmental effectiveness, movements, great leaders, political parties, negotiation—all have fallen from their thrones. They have been exposed as unreliable sources of hope. We have discovered that to hope in any of them is to know eventual disappointment and to ultimately experience despair.

But hopelessness is also profoundly personal. People disappoint us when we place our hope in them. It's heartbreaking when they fail us or are unable to be our source of happiness. We place hope in our careers, our financial planning, and our abilities. Life's reversals shock us with the realization that our hope has been misplaced. Our plans for the future may pull us on to tomorrow with the longing that things will happen as we've dreamed. But things seldom work out as we've planned. Circumstances, people, ourselves, and our talents are not reliable sources of hope.

What we need is a hope that's more than wishful thinking or blind expectation that everything will work out smoothly. We need a hope that is vibrant in pain, consistent in grief, indefatigable when people break our hearts, unassailable in disappointment, and unflagging in life's pressure. Do you have a hope like that? Is your hope ultimately reliable?

True hope is inadvertent. It does not come from searching for hope. It grows out of two basic convictions: that God is in charge and that He intervenes. This is why a true experience of Christmas give us lasting hope.

The ground of our hope is Christ in the world,
but the evidence of our hope is Christ in the heart.
—Matthew Henry

December 22

An Anchor of the Soul

Hebrews 6:9-20

This hope we have as an anchor of the soul, both sure and steadfast (Hebrews 6:19).

THE LORD IS FAITHFUL. His promises are sure. The promises made through the prophets concerning the Messiah all came true. Now we have the promises of Christ to anchor us. This Hebrew passage assures us that through Christ we have access into the very heart of God and we can never drift off the solid anchor of His care. We are never alone. There is no situation, circumstance, or problem which is too big for our Lord. That's the tonic we need to fire our blood and give us courage. The Christmas present to be opened every day of the year is written in the Lord's own hand: "Lo, I will be with you always." We have great uncertainties, but we have a great Christ for our uncertainties.

After Christmas we can stride into a new year knowing that problems are but the prelude to a fresh intervention by the invading Lord. There will be that decisive moment when He will come. He will give us what we need to do more than cope. He has unlimited resources of people, unexpected surprises, wisdom, and spiritual power to release at just the right moment. The deep conviction of my life is that the Lord is always on time—never early, never late. We can let go of our worried grip on life. If we hang on to yesterday's troubles, tomorrow's fears, and today's anxieties, we will overload and blow the circuits.

But now, because of Christmas, we can identify our deepest needs and surrender them to our Lord. Don't let Christmas come and go without an experience of release from tension. Our hope is built on our Lord's faithfulness. He's there with you now. Trust Him. And then expectantly anticipate that at the right time and in the way that's most creative to you and all concerned, He will intervene and infuse you with exactly what you need. What an exciting way to live!

The celebration of Christmas is setting an anchor in the faithfulness of the Lord. He came, comes, and is coming!

December 23

Peace for Broken Pieces

Isaiah 9:1-7

And His name will be called...Prince of Peace (Isaiah 9:6).

WE'VE HEARD AND SEEN a lot about peace during the preparation for Christmas. The word has been artistically embossed on cards we've sent and received. Banners on street lights, placards on store windows, and advertisements in newspapers expose our longing for peace. We ache for peace on earth, in our relationships, and in our hearts. International crises force us to feel the pulsebeat of the heart of God when He grieved over Israel long before He came Himself in Immanuel. "They have healed the wound of my people lightly, saying, 'Peace, peace,' when there is no peace" (Jeremiah 8:11). When we get in touch with the turbulence in our world and the anguish in people, or identify our own conflicts, we realize how much we need Christ's peace.

The very conditions in the world today heighten our longing for peace. What men and women cannot produce, only Christ can give. To be a responsible person in a time like this is to discover lasting peace for ourselves, between us and others, and then seek to introduce people to the Prince of Peace. He came to establish the peace for forgiveness and reconciliation. Peace of soul comes only through accepting His love and forgiveness through Calvary. Then we can know the peace of trusting Him with our daily needs.

Peace is righteousness—right relationships with Him, ourselves, and others. It is a cleansed conscience and a future surrendered to Him. Why is there so little peace? To reword a great saying, "It is not that the world has tried the peace of Christ and found it didn't work; the world has never tried the peace of Christ!" How would you like to give up the broken pieces of your life and allow the Christmas Christ to give you an unbreakable peace?

Christ does not give peace; He is our peace.
When He lives in us as Lord of all, there is peace.

December 24

Christmas Peacemakers

John 14:25-31

Peace I leave with you, My peace I give to you (John 14:27).

TRUE PEACE IS AVAILABLE ONLY in knowing Christ intimately. All that He said, did, and does is to bring peace in our hearts. He was born to bring it; He taught to explain it; His life modeled it; He died on the cross to establish it; He rose from the dead to defeat all the enemies that rob us of it; and He is with each of us now to give the gift. It pervades our hearts when we put Him first in our lives. Second place is the one place He will not accept. His presence is our secret source of peace. When we are lonely, frightened, or insecure, He comes as He came to the disciples when they were gripped with fear in an angry storm on the Sea of Galilee. What He said and did for them He offers us now as a special "Christmas-for-all-the-year gift." He calms the tumultuous sea of life and says, "It is I; do not be afraid."

Then we can be peacemakers, combating negativism, criticism, gossip, and innuendos which destroy relationships. We will become active in working for peace between us and others, between people who need to understand, forgive, and accept one another, and in our society. Think of what the future could be if your sole purpose was to bring reconciliation among your family, friends, and people in your community. Picture what you would be like as a peace-possessed person. Then use your imagination to focus what you will be like as you communicate Christ's peace in active peacemaking. Thank the Lord that it shall be so by His power in you.

Peace is ours only if we give it away.

December 25

Christmas Day

The Experience Which Changes Everything

Luke 2:1-20

Let us now go to Bethlehem and see this thing that has come to pass, which the Lord has made known to us (Luke 2:15).

THE ACCOUNT OF WHAT happened to those lonely shepherds is a before-and-after story. We can identify with the before; we need to become involved in the after; and in between is the experience which changes everything!

The "before" is a tableau of life as we know it. It's your portrait and mine. Picture the scene; put yourself in it. As we try to get into the skin of those shepherds, we suddenly realize that we are in our own skin.

Like the shepherds, we live in two worlds now at Christmas: the outer world filled with hatred, conflict, and international tension, and the inner world of personal struggles. Get in touch with your feelings. We all suffer from future jitters over our war-weary world gripped in soul-sized issues. None of us is free of difficult situations and impossible people. And inside are the hopes and hurts, disappointments and discouragements, fears and frustrations we all feel.

Most of all, we feel a horizontal flatness about both worlds: if anything is to be done, we must try alone, and most of what needs to be done may never change. The hopes and fears of all the years are ours as we join those shepherds out under the stars. Silence. Sleeping sheep. A banked fire. We are about to have an experience which changes everything!

Suddenly, piercing the silence is a magnificent sound, and dispelling the darkness is a glorious splendor that makes the night as day. No wonder the shepherds crouch in fear, clutching one another, looking and listening with astonishment. Hear the angel's words as if for the first time: "Don't be afraid—I bring exciting news for you and everyone. A Savior, Christ the Lord, has been born in Bethlehem! This is the sign: you will find a Babe wrapped in swaddling clothes, lying in a manger."

December 25

Fall on the knees of your heart as the heavenly host joins the angel to sing the most love-drenched, hope-infusing words ever sung: "Glory to God in the highest, and on earth peace, good will to men."

Everything within us wants to shout, "Let's go!" We can't wait to see for ourselves! Our feet cannot carry us fast enough as we run with breathless expectation. Thoughts of what we have heard tumble about in our minds. "The Savior. The Messiah. Born this night! Why were we, of all people, told the good news? A manger? That must mean the cattle cave near the inn in Bethlehem. What a place for the Messiah! Why not the Temple, a palace, at least a room in the inn?"

We stop dead in our tracks when we reach the roughly carved-out cave on the hillside. A profound reverence grips our hearts as we enter. The love-filled eyes of Mary beckon us to come closely to the manger. With inexpressible delight she draws back the coarsely knit blanket. Can it be? The Son of God asleep in a feeding trough for cattle? Immanuel, God with us! Our hearts begin to sing; nothing is impossible now. God is down to earth!

The "after" picture of the shepherds is bold in contrast. They could not contain themselves. Everyone had to know!

A paraphrase of Luke 2:20 catches the triumphant transition: "The shepherds went back to work different people because of what they had seen and heard." They glorified and praised God. That was the difference. Glory means manifestation—praise and unfettered adoration. Now the shepherds manifested God in the way they lived, and all of life was freshly alive with gratitude for His presence in their world.

It's what happens after Christmas that makes all the difference. In a few hours we too will go back to work—back to old relationships and pressing responsibilities, back to our troubled world as it is, back to the frustration of all-too-familiar problems. But if we are daring enough to accept the gift which changes everything—Christ's love, joy, hope, and peace—we can go back to work different people because of what we have seen and heard, accepted and experienced.

Because of Christmas Day, nothing can ever be the same again.

December 26

The Heart of God

Luke 4:31-32; Mark 1:22

And they were astonished at His teaching, for His word was with authority (Luke 4:32).

EMERSON SAID OF SENECA, "His thoughts are excellent, if only he had the right to utter them." Jesus had not only the right but the power. He could illuminate, reveal, and communicate God because He was God Incarnate. Today let's claim what we know of God because of His own Word about Himself and Jesus Christ. Christ illuminated God:

- as a loving Father who is vitally interested in all His children's needs, and knows and cares for each individual soul.
- as a God who is in constant search for His children.
- as a God who does not wait for His children to be ready or adequate.
- as a God who forgives before man confesses—not because he confesses, but so that he may.
- as a God who, because of His love, has allowed His children to be free and who stands with them even when they fail and cause themselves or others pain.
- as a God who exercises His sovereignty over the universe and shows His power in suffering love of the cross to heal hatred, sickness, and pain.
- as a God who is constantly bringing His children of all races and creeds together to be brothers because He is Father.
- as a God who is utterly available to His people through the creative conversation of prayer as a lifeline for guidance, power, and peace.
- as a God who has created man for an eternal relationship which death cannot end.
- as a God who is ultimate and final as Lord of history...the One who was, is, and ever shall be!

Jesus has authority because He is the Author of life.

December 27

Therefore!

Romans 5:1; 12:1; 1 Corinthians 15:58; 2 Corinthians 5:17; 1 Thessalonians 5:11; Ephesians 5:1

I beseech you therefore, brethren, by the mercies of God, that you present your bodies a living sacrifice, holy, acceptable to God, which is your reasonable service (Romans 12:1).

WE HAVE JUST READ A group of passages in which the traditional word "therefore" appears. I had us do that for a very crucial reason. Each time Paul uses this word "therefore," it is after he has said something great about what God has done in Christ. He then goes on to spell out what that should mean for our character and daily life. A friend of mine said he never asked God for anything; his prayers were always of thanksgiving. I asked him, "Does your thanksgiving spur you on to live differently in grateful praise?" That's the issue: hearing the gospel and being thankful is one thing; doing it in adoration is another.

Take time right now to review the difference Christ has made in your life. Draw a line down the middle of a page. List the things for which you are most grateful on one side. Across from each of these write what you have done in each area to express your gratitude. At the top of one side put "God's Grace and Mercy," and on the top of the other side put the word "therefore." Chances are the "Grace" side will overbalance the "Therefores." That should fire us with creative motivation to live and love today in response to God's amazing grace. How would your life be different today if responsibilities were responses to God's love?

To those who fall, how kind Thou art;
How good to those who seek;
But what to those who find? Ah, this
Nor tongue nor pen can show
The love of Jesus, what it is,
None but His loved ones know.

—Bernard of Clairvaux

December 28

Old Attitudes in a New Life

Romans 6:12-14

And do not present your members as instruments of unrighteousness to sin, but present yourselves to God as being alive from the dead, and your members as instruments of righteousness to God (Romans 6:13).

THEREFORE! YESTERDAY WE began our thinking about this stirring word of transition and implication. Today's Scripture again spells out a joyful truth which is possible because of what has gone before. Paul has carefully delineated what God has done in Jesus Christ to liberate man from the power of sin. The power of evil has been defeated, and now man is able to live a new and exciting life in fellowship with God.

"Therefore! If this is true, why do you live as if it were not true?" Why go on living with old attitudes, behavior, and problems if God has truly forgiven, truly accepted, and truly empowered you for a different kind of life?

In the light of all that we believe, why are we living the way we do in frustration, anxiety, and fear? How easy it is to acknowledge the fantastic truth of the gospel and go on living the way we did before we believed it was true for us! We are like prisoners who find it difficult to believe that we have been pardoned and are free to live as released men and women.

We have the choice. We become what we concentrate on; we become the kind of person we envision. Our picture of our life will be fulfilled in action and deed. What if we accepted the true picture of our life as under God's control and as an extension of His love? How would we act if we truly believed we were no longer instruments of sin but instruments of God's righteousness? Hold that picture, and that's exactly what you will find you are able to do.

Mahalia Jackson said, "God can make you anything you want to be, but you have to put everything in His hands." When we put everything in His hands, we want to be what He wants us to be.

December 29

Spread It Out Before the Lord

2 Kings 19:14-19

Then Hezekiah took the letter from the hand of the messengers and read it, and he went up to the house of the LORD and spread it out before the LORD (2 Kings 19:14).

RECENTLY A FRIEND SAID to me, "My biggest problem is being too busy to listen carefully to the Lord. How can I want to listen and act on what He wishes?" The only way to know God's will for our lives is to listen.

Note how Hezekiah spread his dilemma before the Lord. There are three steps to discerning the will of God. First, tell Him your need. Ask Him to give you the wisdom to know what He wants and the courage to do it. Second, wait! Silence is crucial. Give God a chance to impute insight and direction. Read the Bible quietly. It is His Word, and He uses it to instruct His people in His will. Then third, act on what you've discovered, knowing that He can use even our mistakes for His glory.

"How can I be sure a direction is God's will for me?" This question forces us to consider some of the basic tests of any action or venture. Here are the ones that have helped me through the years. By doing it, will I grow closer to the Lord? Is it in keeping with the message of Jesus Christ? Is it in keeping with the Ten Commandments? Will the kingdom of God, His reign and rule, be extended? Will it bring the ultimate good of all involved? Is it an expression of love? Can I do it feeling comfortable with the Lord's presence in it? Will it be for the Lord's glory or just my own? I find that when I ask these questions long in advance of a decision and give the Lord time to work in my mind and feelings, the rightness or wrongness becomes very clear.

Love is the greatest thing that God can give us, for He is love; and it is the greatest thing we can give to God.
—Jeremy Taylor

December 30

The Lord's Prescription

Isaiah 43:14-21

Behold, I will do something new, now it will spring forth; will you not be aware of it? (Isaiah 43:19).

ONE TIME IN A BIBLE STUDY group in which my wife and I were participants, each of us was challenged to write out a prescription that he or she felt the Lord would write. It was enlightening to hear what each person wrote. Though many in the group are seasoned saints who have lived the Christian life for years, all of us knew that we had barely begun. The Lord is up to magnificent things in all of us. We all needed affirmation of the progress He has made with us, and a clear delineation of the next steps in being distinctly different people.

We all bring an old nature into the Christian life. The new creation in Christ is both immediate and gradual. When we surrender our lives to Christ, accepting Him as our Savior and Lord, we are ushered into a dynamic relationship. The moment we say "Yes!" to Him, we are assured of eternal life, His presence, *and* a never-ending growth in His likeness. The reason for this is that becoming a new creation in Christ is a thorough, ongoing character reorientation. We have been conditioned by the religious, cultural, and social values of our time. Attitudes, reactions, goals, and thought patterns have been inadvertently ingrained into the fiber of our natures. When we become Christians, everything is suddenly exposed to Christ's scrutinizing renovation.

Focus on the areas where you need to grow in the new life in Christ. If He were to diagnose your next steps, what would He prescribe?

Identify the evidence of the new creation in you.

December 31

Remembrance and Resolve

Psalm 116:1-19

Return to your rest, O my soul, for the LORD has dealt bountifully with you (Psalm 116:7).

THE PSALMIST HAS GIVEN himself an admonition we all need on the last day of the year: rest and be thankful. Verse 7 is the fulcrum of the psalm. Before, it is the reason for thanksgiving; after, it is what the Psalmist wants to do in praise to God. In the secret place with God he remembers what the Lord has done, and it changes his attitude about the future. That's how it works: remembrance leads to new resolve. For what are you most thankful? What does that inspire you to do and be? The backward look, the inward look and outward look, and the forward look are all part of a vital encounter with the Lord. Reflection reminds us of what He has done; introspection exposes our need; awareness reveals what we are to do; and vision charts the future. Then we can say, "I love the Lord, because He has heard my voice and my supplications."

What supplications has He heard and answered for you? Allow your mind to drift back over your life. Consider all the times you prayed and the Lord stepped in to give you what was best for your life. Remember? Now rest and be thankful. A new year, a new beginning, is before us!

Courage grows out of that reflection. Karle Wilson Baker once said, "Courage is fear that has said its prayers." We can say with Paul, "If God is on our side, who can ever be against us?" (Romans 8:31 TLB). The backward look and the inward look has led us to a courageous forward look for today and all our tomorrows. Blessed New Year!

Where there is faith, there is love;
Where there is love, there is peace;
Where there is peace; there is God;
And where there is God, there is no need.

—Leo Tolstoy

Topical Index

Scripture Index

107:2	7/5
116:1–19	12/31
118	3/27
118:1–29	9/18
139:1–24	1/17
143:1–12	9/7
146	1/5
146:1–10	1/5
150:1–6	6/28

Proverbs	*Month/Day*
12:1–28	2/11
16:1–9	10/24

Ecclesiastes	*Month/Day*
2:12–17	2/15
3:1–8	2/3
3:7	8/23
3:10–15	2/4
4:4	11/17
9:10	3/19

Song of Solomon	*Month/Day*
8:6–7	11/3

Isaiah	*Month/Day*
5:1-7	11/29
9:1–7	12/23
29:17–24	3/7
33:5–6	2/24
40:1–31	12/15
40:31	5/24
43:14–21	12/30
45:9–10	6/16
61:1–2	6/15
65:24	7/21
65:24–25	1/8

Jeremiah	*Month/Day*
8:11	12/23
29:11–13	1/1

Lamentations	*Month/Day*
1	12/1
2	12/1
3:1–20	12/1
3:1–66	12/1
3:18	12/1
3:19–26	6/22
3:21–26	12/21
3:24	12/1

Ezekiel	*Month/Day*
2:1–3:27	12/2
37:1–28	12/3

Daniel	*Month/Day*
3:1–30	12/8
3:17–18	12/8

Hosea	*Month/Day*
1:1–14:9	11/14

Amos	*Month/Day*
7:1–9	11/28

Jonah	*Month/Day*
1:1–4:11	11/13

Zechariah	*Month/Day*
2:1–13	12/11
9:1–10	3/29
12:1–10	3/29
12:10	3/29

NEW TESTAMENT

Matthew	*Month/Day*
3:11–12	5/27
5:3	6/10
5:4	6/12
5:5	6/14
5:6	6/18
5:7	6/22
5:8	6/23
5:13	6/27
5:14–16	6/29
5:16	7/19
5:21–26	7/7
5:33–37	7/8
5:38–40	7/13
5:41–42	7/14
5:43–48	7/15
6:1–4	7/17
6:2	7/18
6:3	7/19
6:5–6	7/20
6:5–8	7/21
6:9	7/23
6:9–15	7/22
6:9–15	7/29
6:10	7/24
6:11	7/25
6:12–15	7/26
6:13	7/27
6:13	7/28
6:16–18	7/30
6:18	7/31
6:19–21	8/4
6:22–23	8/8
6:24	8/9
6:25–29	8/12
6:30–33	8/13
6:31–34	8/12
6:34	8/19
7:1	8/20
7:2	8/22
7:3–5	8/21
7:6	9/1
7:7–12	7/29
7:7–12	9/2
7:13–14	3/15
7:15–20	9/3
7:21–23	9/4
7:24–25	9/9
7:26–27	9/10
7:28–29	9/11
9:2	10/17
10:1–42	8/15
10:38–40	3/20
11:28–29	1/27
11:30	1/9
12:31–32	6/6
13:53–58	4/23
16:13–20	7/3
17:14–21	3/10
17:20	6/9
19:16–21	11/10
20:29–34	3/17
21:28–32	2/13
21:28–32	6/23
21:28–32	7/8
25:14–30	7/11
25:31–46	11/23

Books Authored by Lloyd John Ogilvie

Asking God Your Hardest Questions	*Harold Shaw Publishers*
Autobiography of God	*Gospel Light*
Climbing the Rainbow	*W Publishing*
Facing the Future Without Fear	*Gale Group*
God's Best for My Life	*Harvest House*
God's Strength for This Day	*Harvest House*
Praying Through the Tough Times	*Harvest House*
Quiet Moments with God	*Harvest House*
Quiet Moments in Prayer	*Harvest House*
When You Need a Miracle	*Harvest House*
You Are Loved and Forgiven	*Regal Books*

Other Harvest House Books by Lloyd John Ogilvie

GOD'S STRENGTH FOR THIS DAY

These 365 profoundly personal devotions offer you gladness, refreshment, encouragement, and renewal...the rewards of spending time alone with God and His Word. Getting to know Him and His power, you will find yourself ready to meet the challenges of the day with a strength that is beyond your own—a strength that comes from Him only.

PRAYING THROUGH THE TOUGH TIMES

The author gently guides you to pray for God's desires: confidence in His nearness; His grace to love others; and ability to see with His vision, grasping what the future can be when you put it in His hands.

QUIET MOMENTS WITH GOD

These daily, heartfelt prayers will help you nurture a special intimacy with God. You will experience God's blessed assurance as you are comforted by His boundless love and His promises to provide guidance and give strength.

WHEN YOU NEED A MIRACLE

Are your greatest needs—with family, work, relationships—going unmet? Are you limiting your life to only what is possible in your own strength and talents? From his longtime pastoral experience, Dr. Ogilvie points the way to the God who can meet your *every* need because He is Lord of the *im*possible—the One who can bring about miracles of healing, reconciliation, and growth!

HARVEST HOUSE
PUBLISHERS

Other Harvest House Books by Lloyd John Ogilvie

GOD'S STRENGTH FOR THIS DAY

These 365 profoundly personal devotions offer you gladness, refreshment, encouragement, and renewal...the rewards of spending time alone with God and His Word. Getting to know Him and His power, you will find yourself ready to meet the challenges of the day with a strength that is beyond your own—a strength that comes from Him only.

PRAYING THROUGH THE TOUGH TIMES

The author gently guides you to pray for God's desires: confidence in His nearness; His grace to love others; and ability to see with His vision, grasping what the future can be when you put it in His hands.

QUIET MOMENTS WITH GOD

These daily, heartfelt prayers will help you nurture a special intimacy with God. You will experience God's blessed assurance as you are comforted by His boundless love and His promises to provide guidance and give strength.

WHEN YOU NEED A MIRACLE

Are your greatest needs—with family, work, relationships—going unmet? Are you limiting your life to only what is possible in your own strength and talents? From his longtime pastoral experience, Dr. Ogilvie points the way to the God who can meet your *every* need because He is Lord of the *im*possible—the One who can bring about miracles of healing, reconciliation, and growth!

HARVEST HOUSE
PUBLISHERS

Books Authored by Lloyd John Ogilvie

Asking God Your Hardest Questions	*Harold Shaw Publishers*
Autobiography of God	*Gospel Light*
Climbing the Rainbow	*W Publishing*
Facing the Future Without Fear	*Gale Group*
God's Best for My Life	*Harvest House*
God's Strength for This Day	*Harvest House*
Praying Through the Tough Times	*Harvest House*
Quiet Moments with God	*Harvest House*
Quiet Moments in Prayer	*Harvest House*
When You Need a Miracle	*Harvest House*
You Are Loved and Forgiven	*Regal Books*